THE EDUCATION OF FANNY LEWALD

D1260347

MAR 13 1997

SUNY Series
WOMEN WRITERS IN TRANSLATION
Marilyn Gaddis Rose, editor

ʿ88ʿ 8 I

The Education of
Fanny Lewald

AN AUTOBIOGRAPHY

Translated, edited,
and annotated by

HANNA BALLIN LEWIS

STATE UNIVERSITY OF NEW YORK PRESS

Published by
State University of New York Press, Albany

© 1992   State University of New York

All rights reserved

Printed in the United States of America

No part of this book may be used or reproduced
in any manner whatsoever without written permission
except in the case of brief quotations embodied in
critical articles and reviews.

For information, address State University of New York
Press, State University Plaza, Albany, NY 12246

Production by Bernadine Dawes
Marketing by Lynne Lekakis

Library of Congress Cataloging-in-Publication Data

Lewald, Fanny. 1811–1889.
    [Meine Lebensgeschichte. English]
    The education of Fanny Lewald : an autobiography / translated,
edited, and annotated by Hanna Ballin Lewis.
        p.   cm. — (SUNY series, women writers in translation)
    Translation of : Meine Lebensgeschichte.
    Includes bibliographical references.
    ISBN 0–7914–1147–8 (acid-free) : $57.50. — ISBN 0–7914–1148–6
(pbk. : acid-free) : $18.95
        1. Lewald, Fanny, 1811–1889—Biography. 2. Authors, German—19th
century—Biography.   I. Lewis, Hanna Ballin, 1931– . II. Title.
III. Series.
PT2423.L3Z4513   1992
833;.7—dc20
[B]   91–35930
CIP

10 9 8 7 6 5 4 3 2 1

*T*o my son and editor,
PAUL BALLIN LEWIS

Contents

Fanny Lewald (1861) at the time of the publication of the first edition of the autobiography. Aquarelle by Michel Stohl, 1861. Landesbibliothek Weimar.

Acknowledgments

For its support in the research and time required for this book, I am indebted to Sam Houston State University for two Summer Research Grants.

I am also indebted to Gisela Brinker-Gabler for bringing this book to the attention of the contemporary reader with her abridged German version; Regula Venske for giving me a completely new and delightful view of Fanny Lewald; Kay Goodman for her astute analysis of the autobiography; Marilyn Gaddis Rose for initiating the present project; Margaret Ward, Irene di Maio, Tamara Felden, Linda Siegel, and Helga Watt for sharing difficult-to-obtain material and information with me; and Carola Sautter for assisting in its publication.

Translator's Note

This translation includes less than fifty percent of the original text of the three volumes of the 1871 edition of *Meine Lebens-geschichte*. I have retained the separate chapters, but elisions have not been indicated except where they interfered with the continuity of the text. In those cases, I have included parenthetical explanations of omitted material. German titles as part of a person's name (e.g., Frau Hofrat Schmidt), especially in the case of wives, have been ignored if they are irrelevant to the text (e.g., translated as "Mrs." Schmidt), since these titles are very awkward in English. I hope that an unabridged translation will be feasible in the future.

Introduction

Fanny Lewald-Stahr is one of the foremost German woman writers of the nineteenth century. During her lifetime (1811–1889), she was ranked by the critic and scholar Karl Frenzel with George Sand and George Eliot as one of the leading women writers of the nineteenth century (148). Marieluise Steinhauer's 1937 dissertation calls her the German George Sand. In the introduction to her translation of *Prinz Louis Ferdinand*, Linda Siegel remarks on the similarities between Lewald's and Eliot's lives and works, and on their friendship and the influence they had on each other (79–82). For several generations after Lewald's death, she fell into relative obscurity, an obscurity exacerbated by her sex and during the Nazi regime by her Judaism. Since 1967, she has been rediscovered and several of her works have received new editions. She has been taken up by feminists, historians, and sociologists, praised for her ideas about the emancipation of women and her successful struggle to become a self-supporting woman, one able to chose her own mate; yet she depended heavily on male role models, particularly her father, older brother, and husband, especially early in her career. Her first three novels have received special attention because they deal with issues of controversy in the nineteenth century—among others, forced marriages, the German-Jewish princess and the emancipation of the Jews in Germany, and the dissolution of a failed marriage by divorce. Her essays on the necessity of educating women more adequately for their roles in life, whether they are to be working women or housewives, her perceptive travel memoirs, and her political writings also continue to be of interest to the modern reader. In the later novels, male heroes predominate, but there is certainly no lack of intelligent, strong, and believable women characters.

The apparent contradictions in Lewald's life and works have been the subject of considerable comment by Gisela Brinker-Gabler, Renate Möhrmann, Regula Venske, and other scholars. Lewald believed in educating women for careers, but considered the role of wife and mother the ideal for most women. She was submissive to her father and used male advice for her early and most of her subsequent writings. She married a man who was better educated but far more narrow-minded than she and let his opinions influence hers. She did not believe in universal suffrage for women unless they were ready to learn about political candidates and vote independently of the views of their husbands—but then she stated in the essays "Die Frauen und das allgemeine Wahlrecht" (Women and Universal Suffrage) (1870) and "Und was nun?" (And What Now?) (1871) that no one should have the franchise who was not politically knowledegable. These are still dichotomies that exist for many contemporary women, who feel it would be "the best of all possible worlds" to have a happy marriage, healthy children, and a brilliant career, but realize that compromises must be made. In an article in *Die Zeit*, which appeared on the occasion of the hundredth anniversary of Lewald's death in 1989, Doris Maurer reprises these problems succinctly:

Just because of her contradictions, her efforts to relax the dogmatic bourgeois rules for the behavior of women and in her own insecurity— "because I constantly listened for someone else's judgment, because I lacked that self-confidence which let men, who were far less significant than I, pursue their goals with calm unconcern"—Fanny Lewald is typical for the feminine dilemma and not only of her day. Limited by herself, by the considerations and concepts of a woman's role which were part of her upbringing, she nevertheless brought about significant changes. Her contradictions do not diminish her achievements, to which later generations of proponents for women's rights keep referring again and again. (19)

This is what makes Lewald's autobiography so pertinent today. One does not find the glamorous existence of a George Sand here, but a well-bred, middle-class Jewish girl, from a normal family, growing up in a provincial capital and becoming a famous writer because of her own intelligence and persistence and a modicum of happenstance, as the text shows. Lewald titled her autobiography "The Story of My Life," but it is really only the story of her childhood, young womanhood, and the beginning of her writing career. It ends when she is thirty-four and has published only a small part of her tremendous oeuvre—twenty-seven novels, many of them in multiple volumes, more than thirty novellas, short stories, or collections of them, at least fourteen travel descriptions or memoirs, more than thirty essays or collections of them for journals and newspapers, and countless letters to relatives, friends, and acquaintances. She has yet to meet her future husband and has barely started on her extensive travels. The three books (in six volumes) of the original work are only the description of how she came to be the woman she was when she wrote them sixteen years later and revised them slightly twenty-six years later. They delineate the education of Fanny Lewald.

It would be unfair to the author to anticipate her by writing too much about her early life, but a summary of it and her later career would be helpful to the contemporary reader. Fanny Lewald was born as the eldest of eight living children to the merchant and banker David Markus (later changed to Lewald) in the city of Königsberg (at present, Kaliningrad) in East Prussia. Both her parents came from old established Jewish families, her mother's less assimilated than her father's humanistically inclined one. Fanny was a much loved and wanted child and received the full attention of her parents until the next child, her brother Otto, was born. A few months after her birth, a massive fire destroyed her father's business and the family was in financial straits for a considerable time, since the insurance of her father and his partner and older brother had just lapsed the previous day. It was a long time before her father's new wine business restored the family to prosperity.

Whether in good times or bad, the Markus-Lewald household was strictly regulated and well-run. Her father expected absolute obedience, and her mother, a loving and submissive wife, was happy to obey. David Markus was a despot, but a benevolent one, totally devoted to his family and only wanting what was best for them. The contemporary reader will find some of his measures in dealing with his children unnecessarily harsh, but for a father of his generation and society, he was unusual in the personal attention he gave his children, who loved and respected him deeply. He obtained for Fanny the best possible schooling in East Prussia at the time and supervised her further education at home as best he could. A Victorian British middle-class father and mother would have turned the education of their children over to others—not so, the Markuses. They (especially he) supervised the upbringing of their children at all times and spent as much time as possible with them. Although he did not encourage Lewald's writing career at first, David certainly accepted her decision to pursue it when she showed her determination. There is no doubt that there was tremendous love between her and her father, and there was something special between David and his oldest child, although he tried to treat all his children with impartiality. This special relationship also caused a rift between her and her mother, who, according to Lewald, envied her daughter for the education she herself had never had. The children born immediately after Fanny were her brothers Otto and Moritz, and they were her closest playmates. The world of her childhood was one where her male relationships were the truly important ones. It is no wonder that she relied on them for advice and support.

At the age of six Fanny was enrolled in the Ulrich School, which seems to have provided an unusually good education for a girl of her generation. The school was co-educational, but most classes were not. It had a strong Pietistic strain, since many of the teachers were involved with a Pietist-related denomination, the "Muckers."[1] Unfortunately, the school closed when Fanny was fifteen and there were no secondary educational institutions for women in Königsberg. Fanny was forced to stay at home and perform household chores, although her father did set up a rigid schedule for her that included education in the home, as well as the hated piano lessons, which were her albatross almost till his death. There were expeditions to parks and parties given by family friends. At one of these, she met a young theological student,

Leopold Bock, and they planned to get married. Her father, who first supported the match, turned against it suddenly, forbidding Fanny and Leopold to see one another again. Leopold died not long afterwards of what we may assume was tuberculosis or cholera.

Although Fanny's parents never converted to Christianity—her father was not very religious, and conversion would have damaged his business relationships with Polish Jews—her brothers were encouraged to convert to expedite their careers. David Markus did not consider conversion necessary for women—if they married Jewish men, it would be a hindrance, and if they married a Christian, they could convert later. But Fanny was finally allowed to convert after the death of Leopold, perhaps as compensation for her loss. At first she was very enthusiastic, but her essentially pragmatic nature would not let her accept any religion wholeheartedly, particularly one that relied more on faith than reason. Her beliefs were, in essence, a type of Spinozaism or deism, accepting the existence of God but denying the preeminence or superiority of any organized religion.

Seeing her discontent at home, her father took her with him on an extended trip through Germany: Berlin and Baden-Baden, where, in the circle of her uncle, Friedrich Jacob Lewald, she met important political figures like Ludwig Robert (Rahel Varnhagen von Ense's brother) and Ludwig Börne.[2] She was in the vicinity of the Hambach Festival,[3] which her father attended. Her father returned alone to Königsberg, but she was allowed to accompany her uncle and his family back to Breslau, where she met his many interesting and intellectual friends. Far more significant was her meeting with her cousin Heinrich Simon and his mother, Minna, her father's eldest sister. Minna became her favorite female relative, the "mother" she wanted her own to be. Her unrequited love for Heinrich lasted many years, and his involvement in German and Jewish political affairs gave her an added knowledge of them, long after any hope of a marriage had been destroyed and their relationship had become that of close friendship.

Returning to Königsberg after a year, she found her mother in very poor health. Instead of turning the management of the household completely over to Fanny, her father decided that it would be fair for all the sisters to take turns in managing. This gave Fanny insufficient outlet for her energy. Her father would not let her take a paid position as a governess or companion, since this would have reflected badly on his ability to provide for his family. After turning down a marriage of convenience to a provincial lawyer and magistrate, she retreated to the hypochondriacal condition so typical of underoccupied and intelligent nineteenth-century women. She did continue an extensive correspondence, and her cousin, August Lewald,[4] editor of the Stuttgart periodical *Europa*, published one of her letters about the Mucker trial as an essay. Fanny's career as a writer had begun.

In 1839, Fanny traveled to Berlin again and lived for a longer period of time with relatives. She was there when Frederick William III died and returned to Königsberg in time to witness the ceremonies accompanying the assumption of the throne by his son, Frederick William IV. Now August Lewald asked Fanny for a special report on these events and of the new monarch's speech for *Europa*. Lewald printed it and sent Fanny a check and a letter praising her talent and encouraging her to use it. Her first stories and novels (*Clementine* and *Jenny*) were published anonymously because of her father's wishes, but he relented and allowed her to begin publishing under her own name. Her younger sisters were still not happy about the notoriety of having a professional writer as a relative.

Released from her household duties by the death of her mother and her ability to earn her own living (even if very modestly at the beginning), she moved to her first apartment alone in Berlin near her brother Otto. In 1845, she made her first major trip abroad to Italy without an accompanying family member. In Rome she became acquainted with a group of expatriate German intellectual women, including Adele Schopenhauer (the philosopher Arthur's sister) and Ottilie von Goethe (Goethe's daughter-in-law), both already well established writers. She also met and fell in love with Adolf Stahr, a cultural and art historian from Oldenburg, an unhappily married man with five children. It was not until his divorce in 1855 that they were able to get married.

After she began to be recognized as an interesting and readable writer and was able to afford the costs, Lewald (who used the surname of Lewald-Stahr after 1855) traveled extensively in France, the British Isles, Switzerland, and Italy and wrote numerous perspicacious travel memoirs of the political and cultural conditions in those countries. In Berlin, where she and Stahr made their home, she had a small salon frequented by many of the intellectuals of the day. Adolf Stahr died in 1876, and Lewald mourned him until her death in 1889.

Like many of her nineteenth-century fellow writers, Lewald, as previously stated, produced a massive oeuvre of novels, novellas, short stories, travel memoirs, essays, and letters. They vary in literary quality. Lewald wrote as a professional, to provide for herself (and eventually her husband and the children of his first marriage). As her fame grew, she insisted on being paid the highest rate per page offered by her publishers. She admitted she would have probably made as good a physician as a writer, if a university education had been available. Both her strength and her weakness as a writer lie in her objectivity; many of her characters do not come to life, but their situations are well and clearly defined. She is at her best in nonfictional works, describing political and social events and problems and suggesting answers. The rationalism imbued in her from early childhood by her father stands her in good stead when writing about the 1848 revolutions in Europe, the national differences between countries, the education of working and middle-class women so that they can earn their own living, the establishment of satisfactory boarding and eating establishments for single women, even the running of a well-managed household. Her friendships with the leading liberal and Jewish intellectuals and writers—Heinrich Heine, Ludwig Börne, Heinrich Simon, Eduard von Simson, Johann Jacoby, Berthold Auerbach, Luise Mühlbach, Willibald Alexis, Hermann Hettner, Arnold Ruge, Johanna Kinkel, Franz Liszt, Georg Herwegh, Hermann Althof, among others—gave her a particularly good insight into the political problems of her own country, even though her eventual pragmatic acceptance and even enthusiasm about Bismarck caused some differences with Johann Jacoby.

Her own influence on other writers was not inconsiderable, including that on Theodor Fontane, Marie von Ebner-Eschenbach, and Paul Heyse.[5] Because of the emancipatory essays and her own literary success, she received much fan mail from young women who felt that they could also earn their living in a career so suitable to a woman. Her comment on this idea is probably best expressed in the somewhat cynical portrait of the young woman writer of *Adele* (1855), the eponymous heroine of which becomes a somewhat successful writer because she has no other skills for earning a living. Lewald herself admitted no actual influence but that of Goethe. There were writers she admired—among others, Heine and Börne, of course—Auerbach, Sir Walter Scott, Bulwer Lytton, Honoré de Balzac, Gottfried Keller, Gustav Freytag, Paul Heyse, and the young Theodor Fontane. Her youthful pleasure in George Sand had diminished by the time she herself began to write; for other women writers of her day she had a certain respect, e.g., Therese von Bacheracht, or severe criticism, e.g., Countess Ida von Hahn-Hahn, whose works she mercilessly and hilariously parodied in *Diogena* (1847). In general, however, Lewald eschewed literary judgments because, as she wrote in a letter to Stahr in 1846, she considered "criticism the destroyer of productivity" (Steinhauer 20).

In 1899, the *Deutsche Rundschau* cited her autobiography as her best "novel" (462). Modeled to a large extent on Goethe's *Dichtung und Wahrheit*, Lewald's book is influenced by the fact that a bourgeois Jewish woman in the nineteenth century did not have the same access to events and persons outside the home that a man from the upper strata, the "establishment" of Frankfurt, did.[6] Just before the publication of the second edition of the autobiography in 1871, she wrote in her diary, *Gefühltes und Gedachtes* (Emotions and Thoughts)—not published until after her death:

My autobiography is just as much "fiction and truth" as that of Goethe. I have left the fiction and its explanatory representation to others, however, and told the complete truth about myself to the best of my ability. (148)

BOOK ONE

At Home

1

I was born on May 24, 1811, in Königsberg, Prussia, and am Jewish on both sides of my family. My parents were also born in Königsberg. My mother, from a wealthy family, was the youngest of twelve children. Her father had come from Posnania, her mother from Courland, to Prussia. They held firmly to the faith and the tenets of Judaism. They were uneducated people, but placed great value on a decent outer appearance, while being extremely frugal in the running of their household, using and displaying their wealth only under special circumstances.

When we were adults, my mother liked to tell us of the large salon in her parents' house, a room filled with yellow damask furniture and mirrors that was opened on holidays for the free reception of all strangers, masked or unmasked, who happened to be in her house for the Jewish carnival, Purim. She would recall as well the solemn observance of the High Holidays, Passover, the Festival of Booths, and the Day of Atonement. It always made an unfamiliar, solemn impression on us when we heard how our grandparents had summoned all their children on the eve of Yom Kippur and blessed them, how Grandmother, in a white dress edged with exquisite lace, would accompany Grandfather to the synagogue, how they would not return until late in the evening, how a servant would quietly divest Grandmother of her stylish capelet of yellow-lined black taffeta, how they would fast on the following day, and not break the fast until the stars appeared that night. Then life had resumed its normal course.

Good miniature portraits of these grandparents hung in our living room. Grandmother's was of a pale woman with a quiet clever gaze, dressed all in white, a lace kerchief covering her throat and breast, and a white lace headdress that fit closely to her forehead and temples and let not a single strand of hair show.[7] She wore beautiful large pearl earrings and a matching necklace. Grandfather had a refined face with light blue eyes, a small powdered wig, a blue coat with large buttons; they were both the very picture of cozy cleanliness and peace. There was something solemn about their physiognomies; this aspect impressed me deeply whenever I looked at these pictures.

I do not know what type of business my grandfather might have conducted in his early years. According to my mother, he had retired early and lived on his investments. My grandparents' residence for thirty-six years was the house at the corner of the Kneiphof Langgasse and Magisterstrasse, across from the Royal Bank near the Green City Gate. My mother emphasized that the president of the bank and many other important people treated my grandfather with special respect. Even Professor Kant[8] always greeted him in a friendly fashion during his daily promenade, when he saw Grandfather sitting in his customary place by the window or on the bench in front of his house. At that time, it was still a distinct honor for a Jew to be treated with respect by Christians.

The intellectual level in these grandparents' house must have been rather low, although the five sons received a good education. Two studied medicine; the older was a greatly respected physician in Königsberg. The youngest, Doctor David Assing, later converted to Christianity and married Rosa Maria von Varnhagen.[9]

The older daughters were taught French, music, dancing, and other superficial skills. They even had a tutor in "charm," who instructed them in what to say in society and to young men and how to say it. But all that ceased with my grandmother's death, and almost nothing was done for the younger daughters because my grandfather considered the education of women superfluous. My mother, the youngest child, bemoaned this misfortune her whole life. She had a great desire for knowledge but lacked the fundamental skills to acquire it later in life. She could barely write or do basic sums and had no scientific training at all.

Neither of my grandparents ever left Königsberg after they settled there. Life in their house seems to have been carefree and content, but not very lively and very limited intellectually.

A completely different atmosphere prevailed in the house of my paternal grandparents. The Markuses had lived in Königsberg for four generations, and this grandfather had already traveled around Germany as part of his education and later married a woman from cosmopolitan Berlin.

He was a handsome and witty man. He and his wife had reached the intellectual level of the Jews of Berlin, and were not too happy living in Königsberg. Grandmother did not like life in the provinces. She never felt at home there, and Grandfather would also have preferred living in Berlin or Hamburg. But he had lost the fortune he had inherited a few years after his marriage because of unfortunate speculations; although his colleagues considered him a shrewd businessman, he did not succeed in acquiring another fortune. He led a life filled with worries—a life that in later years was even wretched—and that was the reason people all the more resented a certain reserve and self-containment in his attitude. He and his wife were considered haughty. He did not have much to do with others but had a great predeliction for studies of all kinds, especially mathematics, with which he busied himself continually. He spent all his leisure hours reading and writing, and he was said to have expressed himself excellently in speaking and writing. When he died, a number of logarithmic tables that he had calculated and prepared for publication were found. His favorite readings were the works of the French encyclopedists; he and his wife were completely enlightened people. Therefore they observed the Jewish ritual laws only enough to avoid offending the Jewish community, which then was still very close-knit. Their sons received Hebrew lessons, and my grandfather visited the synagogue because social conventions dictated he must. In this couple's domestic life, though, there were no religious observances of any kind, and the greatest liberalness reigned in all religious matters.

At that time the family name was Markus. There were seven children: four sons and three daughters. They were not sent to Christian or public schools, but were instead required to teach themselves. This type of education imbued them with a tendency toward intellectual interests, a desire for universal knowledge, and a leaning toward a firm and serious self-determination. My grandfather hated for us to speak about trivia or to use superfluous words in expressing ourselves. His maxim, "Express it in depth and not in breadth," has remained with us. Thoughtless uttering or listening to a stupidity was an anathema to him, and he punished his children severely for it.

Once an old servant of his returned after an absence of several months. One of my uncles, still only eight or nine years old, made an inane remark, "Skatt has grown a lot," and my grandfather, without uttering a word, boxed his ears. Likewise, if one of the children said something clever or witty that found applause, he ordered them to be quiet, so that they, flushed with success, would not be tempted to add something stupid.

My grandfather's family was somehow related to the Itzig and Ephraim families in Berlin, whom Frederick the Great used for his financial operations. When the economic situation in my grandfather's house was particularly bad, there was always a hope that these Berlin relatives would one day help him out by letting him participate in some sort of financial undertaking. However when this opportunity finally arrived, it resulted in a terrible misfortune.

Frederick the Great had used the Jewish bankers, including the Ephraims, to convert subsidy moneys from England into base coinage (two-groschen pieces) and distribute them. My grandfather was one of the agents for the Königsberg coins in this royally authorized business. At his own cost, he had built a silver smelter, which my father later inherited and which I saw many times. When accusations of counterfeiting became stronger and stronger under Frederick William II, the government used the expedient of blaming the Jews, who had been acting under government mandate, for the counterfeiting. To assuage the indignation of the populace, or at least offer them a concession, some Jews were imprisoned in various places. Among these was my grandfather. Like many others of his faith who had experienced this unfair treatment, he demanded a complete investigation, but the government would not permit it. After a lengthy detainment the accused were released as they had been imprisoned, without indictment or trial. The purpose was achieved of besmirching the reputation of these men and shifting the complaints against the government onto the shoulders of the Jews.

This captivity, aside from making his profession as money-hanger for Christians difficult for the rest of his life, also resulted in completely ruining his already fragile health. He was in his late forties when arrested, and he suffered from an illness of the eyes, caused by severe stomach problems. He was dependent on the care of his family. The authorities would not release him from prison, but they allowed his oldest daughter, Minna, then fifteen, to attend him there. With deep emotion, I often heard her, a woman whom I regarded as one of the most significant I have ever known, recount how quietly and nobly our grandfather bore his misfortune. She remembered how he would always dress himself impeccably each day and how he would ask that a small mirror be brought—so he would not neglect his outer appearance—how he had occupied himself for several hours daily by reading and writing French and perusing serious books, so that this unfortunate time would at least have some good results. This aunt respected her father deeply, and indeed, all the children almost idolized him. Even when they were old, they never thought of him without sadness and tears.

My father was the third son. He was just eight years old when his father was incarcerated. The oldest son was sickly and had to be protected, because he suffered from severe stomach cramps in his youth. The second son was rather lazy; and since my grandfather's health deteriorated steadily in prison, this son used my father, his brother, as much as possible in his exchange business, which barely supported the family. I have heard my father tell with what bitter keenness he felt the pressure of these circumstances. Once, at the age of fifteen when he had to return home without having completed a transaction, which would have relieved the financial pressure on the family, he felt such sadness and despair, that he was tempted to throw himself off the bridge—so terrible it was to him to have to give his very sick and worried father such awful news!

I do not know exactly when my grandfather died. It must

have been about 1800, seven or eight years after his incarcera-
tion. After his premature death at the age of fifty-one, the fortunes of the family took a more positive turn. The eldest daughter, who had been sent to relatives on her mother's side in Berlin,
married a well-educated and prosperous merchant in Breslau.
She became the mother of Heinrich Simon of Breslau, who is
well-known because of his role in our political history.[10] In conse-
quence, my grandmother and her youngest son also moved to
Breslau, and her second son then followed her; he joined an
uncle's mercantile business. Only the eldest brother, Beer
Markus, and my father stayed in Königsberg. They established
the business firm of Beer Markus and Company, and the two
younger sisters, Johanna and Rebekka, ran the household for
their brothers. Completely reliant upon themselves, the four
remaining siblings, the oldest of whom was scarcely twenty-two,
never abandoned the tendencies of their father's house. None of
them, as far as I can ascertain, had a regular school education,
but they were all intellectually gifted, very ambitious, persever-
ing, and not easily discouraged. Their characters were such that I
have always felt it an advantage to belong to such a family.

Of course my parents knew each other by sight from childhood on, since the Jewish community was very small at the time.
My mother told of sitting at the window one day with her father,
when she was twelve and seeing my father, three years older,
passing by her house. She had heard only good things about him;
whenever the unending misfortunes of the Markus family were
discussed, people always praised the wonderful children, and
especially the zeal and faithfulness of young David who worked
day and night for the good of his parents. This so touched my
mother (along with my father's great handsomeness) that on that
day, in childish enthusiasm, she suddenly cried out, "Oh, Papa! I
want to marry that David Markus!"—which naturally aroused a
wave of laughter from her siblings. But there was no real social
contact between the two families; my parents only met personally
when my mother was seventeen and my father twenty.

By that time, both were orphaned. My mother lived with a
sister, and my father was already prepared to support a wife,

even if she had not had a substantial dowry, as my mother did. But it was not easy for Prussian Jews to get married at that time; each Jewish family was allowed a permanent-residence permit in Prussian territory that could only be given to one child.[11] In my mother's family, the permit had been used for the benefit of the eldest (and very homely) daughter, so that she could find a husband; my father's eldest sister had married a Jew with a permit, so my uncle Beer Markus owned the permit for the Markus family. He was disinclined to pass it down to my father, since Beer himself was in love with, and in fact courting, my mother!

All my mother's siblings favored his suit. My mother was the only daughter still unmarried and at home. From her family's point of view, it was most convenient for the youngest sister to marry in Königsberg without further ado or special requests to the government; furthermore, my uncle Beer was a hard-working and cultivated man. But he was very sickly, and, although my much-wooed mother at first accepted and encouraged Beer's courtship, she soon turned her affections toward the younger and more handsome brother. This inclination became a matter of vital concern for both families, because the young couple encountered so many obstacles.

My mother's relatives resented my father making their sister's comfortable marriage difficult. Conversely, my father's sisters were very unhappy that he was causing such misery for his older and ailing brother. So the two unfortunate young people found themselves in somewhat isolated and hostile positions. Only one of my mother's sisters and Dr. David Assing, her favorite brother, her confidant, and a friend of my father's, were loyal to them, and my mother was grateful to them for the rest of her life.

If my mother had been in control of her fate (had she been of age), the young pair would have used the expedient of converting to Christianity. The idea held a strong appeal for my mother, and my father was completely indifferent to any religious dogma. But all my mother's family, particularly the brother and brother-in-law, who were her guardians, would not hear of such a step. They did not spare the customary threats of cursing and banning. My mother could not handle such dissension, and there was no solution for the betrothed couple but to go to the authorities with petitions, with bribes, and with personal pleas to get permission to live in Prussia. These permits were becoming increasingly difficult to obtain as the Jewish community became more prosperous and eager to marry. This years-long struggle produced in my mother, who was basically a very mild and gentle soul, a strong antipathy against Judaism and everything connected to it. She considered it a misfortune to be Jewish. As for my father, whose strong intellect clearly perceived the irrationality of the contemporary Prussian laws concerning the Jews, the obstacles he personally encountered only strengthened his antipathy against all irrationality and tyranny.

At that time, the issuance of a residence permit for a Jew in Prussia depended upon Chancellor von Schrötter.[12] He was well-regarded in the province; his wife, born Countess Dohna, was said to be an excellent noblewoman, and a son or younger brother of the chancellor had been a childhood and university friend of my uncle David Assing. On his advice, my mother, for whom such a step must have been very difficult because of her shyness and youth, finally decided to ask for a personal audience with the chancellor's wife, to request her help in obtaining a permit.

Happily, this personal appeal was successful; after a long courtship, my parents were finally joined in a marriage, which was an example, indeed a model, of domestic harmony for the thirty years of its existence.

2

My father was in very good financial shape when he married. He and his brother had a considerable banking and shipping business; and the additional capital my mother brought him, at a time when money was worth almost double its present value, made it possible to expand the business.

Beer and the unmarried sisters took a separate apartment; my parents moved into a house in the suburbs. To my mother's delight, it had a small garden tucked away behind a large courtyard. She settled in snugly; and this is the house where I was born on a Sunday morning. My father was twenty-four and my mother twenty-one when I arrived.

I have always considered it an advantage to be the oldest child. After all, the first-born is always a special good fortune to its parents. But it was also a good fortune for all us siblings that our parents married so young. As much as I have always been happy that I was the one who first acquainted my parents with the joys of parenthood, who first called them father and mother, we all benefited, the more the family size increased, from our parents' youth. They felt the effort and inconvenience we caused less than older people would have; they had an understanding of our wishes and faults because the memory of their own childhood was still so close. The main thing was that we ourselves, as we grew up, felt closer to them than we would have to older parents. To have young parents is an inestimable advantage for children.

When they showed me to my father, I was very tiny, but already had a head covered with curly black locks. "I was very happy with you," he told me later, when I was a young girl and the conversation turned in my presence to my birth. Even much later, he would occasionally take my face between his hands, and as he kissed me, tenderly add, "My oldest child!" We loved each other very much.

My mother could not nurse me herself. A wet nurse was hired, a pretty, good-natured blonde. She stayed with us for many years and lives in my home town today, still robust in good health. My parents were as happy in the first months after my birth as only a beautiful young carefree couple can be, two people who love each other tenderly and have just had their first child. But that suddenly changed in the summer of 1811.

My father was going to the stock exchange as usual at noon. My mother, with me on her arm, accompanied him to the door, from which she watched him as long as she could. Then she went back into the house, laid me down, and was sitting quietly at the side of my cradle, when she heard a fire alarm from the street a half hour later. Immediately thereafter, my father, pale and shouting, "The warehouses are on fire!" burst into the room.

[Lewald's father's warehouses and his prosperity vanish in the wake of a disastrous fire that destroys much of the commercial section part of Königsberg. Unfortunately, he and Beer had not renewed their insurance because they had planned to change certain provisions of the policy. Lewald's parents are forced to move to a few rented rooms, furnished with hand-me-downs. Her mother's dowry is spent to rebuild the business, and her father works hard to regain his fortune.]

Königsberg had scarcely recovered from this disastrous fire when yet another major event occurred for the merchants of Prussia: the march of Napoleon's troops through the region on their way to Prussia. From the spring of 1812 on, the whole province of East Prussia was like a giant military camp. At one point, 300,000 infantrymen and more than 40,000 calvarymen were gathered there for several weeks. The country was exhausted and oppressed by this burden. The poverty, the disease, the inflation in the cities were tremendous—but whoever still had something to sell could get the highest price for it. In the enormous provisions necessary for the maintenance of these masses of soldiers, money itself was one of the most important items of trade. The bankers and money changers did good business and gained considerable profit.

As soon as possible, my father moved out of the cramped apartment and leased a three-story, two-window-wide house. His affairs were flourishing again; in addition to the shipping business, he and Beer had begun to have a considerable financial trade. Beer and the youngest brother, Friedrich Jakob, his cousin, the well-known writer August Lewald,[13] who still lives in Stuttgart, and some clerks all worked together in the business; and since Beer was scarcely thirty, my father twenty-five, Friedrich Jakob eighteen, and August Lewald twenty, they formed a jolly group that lost no chance to make life agreeable for themselves and others, despite the hardships of wartime, which spared no family entirely. Friedrich Jakob and August Lewald lived at my father's house. They were two very good-looking men; my father's sisters, one of whom, Johanna, was a ravishing beauty, were often there. Conditions were terribly crowded in this house, especially since French officers were frequently quartered there. Yet these unwelcomed guests also included many cultured and considerate men who provided good company. They tried to alleviate the inconvenience and extra work they caused by being especially helpful and gracious. Many a Frenchman, who had reluctantly left wife and children at home, was happy to recall life with his loved ones for a few days in his stay with a foreign family. So, almost everywhere, including at my parents' home, a camaraderie developed between the hosts and the officers quartered there, to the point in some cases that farewells were said with regrets that an enmity had to exist.

The usual Königsberg habit of an early breakfast at seven or eight o'clock, a second at eleven, dinner at one, and then two or three additional meals of coffee, snacks, and supper, had to be changed because of the occupation. In the houses of merchants, this was also necessary because of the press of work. There was a proper breakfast and supper, but one did not eat dinner till after the theater, and might stay up until late into the night. When they were there, the French officers participated in this changed lifestyle; this hurried existence. Hardened warriors told of their campaigns throughout Europe, their victory at the Pyramids, the glamor of life in Paris, and of the wonders accomplished by their emperor. Young soldiers spoke of honor, fame, and the distinctions they were sure they would win. Their tales had something mesmerizing, something that roused the imagination and tended to carry even normally calm individuals away. They had seen the son of a pastry baker become King of Naples, the son of a lawyer the conqueror of the world, boys who had risen from the lower classes become generals and marshals through the world, for which their master wrote the laws. In later years, when I heard Prussian families tell of the French occupation and the war years, it was always with an excited wonder not really driven by anger against the enemies of the fatherland. It seemed to me, moreover, that these stories expressed an especially vivid memory, as if people had a realization, or at least sensed, that they had led a more interesting life in that time—truly a time for the young, for the young ruled everywhere—than was ever their lot before or since in the tranquillity of our remote province. Even if they complained about the French, about their measures that had aroused considerable resistance, the Prussians realized that they themselves had become more aware of their own nationality and nascent power. As much of a burden as the war years had been, their memory still warmed and lifted the spirits of almost everyone in some way, especially when compared with the dull peacefulness characterizing the following period.

In the Jewish families, there was a decided ambivalence with regard to the French invasion. The French Revolution had guaranteed equality under the law to all religions. Although Napoleon had made his peace with the Catholic Church, he did not dare to touch the religious freedom and civil rights of the different religious denominations. In France and the areas under French rule the Jews were emancipated; in Prussia, lack of freedom and ridicule still burdened them. It was natural, therefore, that among many Jews the question arose whether freedom under a foreign ruler was not preferable to serfdom under a native royal family. I feel the great self-denial and patriotism of some Jews have never been sufficiently acknowledged—of those who joined the fighters against France as volunteers in 1813 to help a country regain its freedom, only to be rewarded with renewed humiliations and limitations of all kinds instead of their own emancipation. The behavior of the modern state, the behavior of our century against the Jews, will one day form a particular chapter in cultural history, a chapter made extraordinary by injustices perpetrated and logic ignored. That adherents of one sect condemn the members of another sect, that one race has an aversion to another, is very unreasonable but not unusual. The history of the ancient Jews is a good example. They could hardly have complained if the Germanic race, for example, had stated firmly that it required its rulers to shun all Jews and let no Jews reside in their territory— presupposing that the Germanic race could say and had said this two thousand years ago or at least in pre-Christian times. But Jews were admitted into the German states, allowed to assume the burdens and responsibilities of citizenship, and finally permitted to work—but they have been barred from full civil rights.[14]

This is the behavior the annals of cultural history will one day have to record in all its tragic and ridiculous details.

My father knew the value of the French Revolutionary reforms quite well as they concerned the Jews. He appreciated the liveliness of the French, could speak the language well, and felt a sympathy for Napoleon (whom he resembled to a remarkable degree) that was based strictly on the Emperor as a person. The tenacity, the self-confidence, the reserve, and even the violence in the Emperor's character found a kindred element in my father's nature; the wonderful career traced by Napoleon had the charm for my father that a recognition of an extraordinary will and ability and its concomitant achievement have for another person of strong character. He was not a blind adherent of the Emperor's; on the other hand, I cannot believe he was an ardent Prussian patriot at that time. To cherish a country, simply for having been born there, or to love a dynasty only because it happened to rule, was not his way. He venerated Frederick the Great, as he respected Napoleon, as a significant man. But the situation in Prussia since the beginning of the reign of Frederick William II[15] was not calculated to arouse much enthusiasm, least of all in the mind of a man whose father had been thrown into prison through governmental caprice and who had himself suffered from Prussian restrictive laws.

But there was another element which made the continuing foreign occupation unacceptable to him. My father's cultural background was completely German. He loved the German spirit, and he loved and admired German literature and its classics with a deep understanding. Since each person is the product of his time and its spirit, a streak of German romanticism had found a place next to my father's sharp reason. This alone would have been enough to make him hate a foreign domination of his country, even if the arbitrariness of the conquerors in general and the lack of consideration and arrogance of individual Frenchmen in his house had not been unbearable to this autocratic young man. My mother later often told me how worried my father was any time he refused an unwanted quartering or protested against one of the measures of the occupation. If he could not protect his rights himself, he demanded redress and satisfaction from the French authorities, although the Prussians warned most strenuously against a hostile appearance before the French and even the magistrates in special decrees urged the citizens to endure all sorts of injustice patiently.

Once, when an older French officer made some sort of exaggerated demand, my father protested and asked the officer to leave the house, without success. The officer received a reprimand, but remained in the house. Although he restrained himself, he threatened revenge. My father paid no attention; the officer was now served his meals, formerly eaten with the family, in his room, and my poor mother, who did not understand one syllable of French, worried three times as much about what he would do to my father. She could not rest day or night; she believed the family was concealing the officer's threats from her. When his corps received its orders, she counted the hours till his departure. The days passed quietly; the final day came; it seemed nothing would happen. My mother was sitting in the nursery with me after dark, when suddenly she heard terrible screaming, a rattling, cursing, and a fall on the stairs. She rushed out and in the dim light saw the Frenchman with a riding crop in his hand, gesturing furiously toward the lower floor and shouting at someone, while below, the residents of the house hurried to the scene. She was convinced my father was being abused by the Frenchman, so she flew down the stairs, but the intended victim of the officer's cowardly revenge was not there—one of the shop clerks had received the blows intended for my father. The officer had noticed that my father usually came to my nursery at dusk to see me before I went to sleep. He had thus concealed himself in a corner of the hall to launch his attack from there. Since my father was delayed at the office, an unfortunate employee had suffered instead. He himself had luckily been spared, and to boot he finally achieved the arrest of the officer. But generally, the complaints about the crude behavior of the German troops, especially the Hessians, Bavarians, and Würtembergers, were much stronger than the complaints about the French, and people credited the latter with great consideration for the sick and with friendliness toward children.

I remained my parents' only child for two and a half years. My mother therefore had a lot of time to spend with me. She was very friendly and sweet, and my nurse was young, merry, and talkative, and so it was no wonder that I learned to speak early and very clearly. They told me I always had a good memory and was able to recite verses I had picked up somehow, before I was even two. I must have understood them, too, to a certain degree, because I knew just when to come out with them. A certain occasion that was supposed to have demonstrated my precocity occurred just before my second birthday, in 1813, after the French retreat from Russia.

Many French songs were popular just then, including some that rendered current conditions in broken German. My mother had a lovely voice and must have often sung the song of "Jean Grillon," which was on everyone's lips. I remembered parts of it, and still know it by heart, since my mother also sang it for us often in later years. It went:

> I am a Frenchman, *mes dames*,
> *Comme ça* with the wooden leg.
> Jean Grillon is my name;
> My pride is my wooden leg.
> I joke, I kiss, I caress
> *Comme ça* with the wooden leg.
> In my heart I remain a Frenchman,
> Even if I were made of stone.

One day a troop of retreating French soldiers came through, and one of them, who had lost his leg to frostbite in Russia, was quartered with us. When they carried the severely wounded man from the wagon, I happened to be in the room to which they brought him. I looked at the officer with amazement, and seeing he had a wooden leg, ran to him and cried out in a friendly fashion, "*Comme ça* with the wooden leg!" The young man broke into tears. "I have a child like that, a little girl, at home," he told my father, and reaching out his hand to him, added, "For this child's sake, have mercy on me. I am suffering terribly!" That was a cry that could not be ignored, even if the misery of the young Frenchman had not spoken for itself. He remained at our house for some time, was carefully nursed, and did not leave Königsberg until the beginning of the fighting in the spring of 1813. He gave me a string of malachite beads, which I lost at a children's party when I was seven or eight years old. He had probably seized (i.e., stolen) them in Russia, but I bewailed their loss nonetheless.

During the final retreat, Russian booty played a considerable role in Königsberg trade, and therefore in my father's exchange and banking business. As miserable and suffering as the retreating French army (or its remnants) was, it nevertheless dragged back with it a tremendous amount of loot, and was trying to exchange it hurriedly for French or German money. The soldiers had plundered indiscriminately and passionately from whatever fell into their hands—churches, convents, palaces, families—and often had come out with cheap finery, which they believed to be gold and jewels. By this time, so many unusual treasures were available in Königsberg in such great quantities that it was easy to acquire magnificent silverware and princely jewelry for very low prices. Truly great values went through my father's hands in this manner, and my grandfather's old silver smelter, which had fallen into disuse, was reactivated. Altar vessels, silver apostles and saints, candelabra, and ornaments from Christian and Jewish churches[16] ended up in the smelting pot; the jewelry was broken up, the stones sold, the setting smelted, and the gold and silver bullion sent to Russia and to Berlin, where money had to be coined for the coming war.

Profit from such business was considerable, but so were the work and problems associated with it. My mother said the carts of the fleeing wounded were lined up day and night on the narrow street in front of our house. Cripples and sick men of all sorts crowded the office; the front hall of the house was full of them, and the way they pleaded and begged us to take their plunder and give them money, so they could move on, was heartrending.

Since 1807, we in East Prussia had become very accustomed to great suffering and misery, to wounded men and epidemics. After the battles of Eilau and Friedland,[17] Königsberg had thousands of wounded and the most terrible hospital fever within its walls. The corpses from the churches and city halls, which had been converted into hospitals, were piled by dozens into the already-prepared lime pits in front of the Friedland Gate. But the suffering and distress of the now-retreating soldiers was even worse, and the contrast between this flight and the proud confident advance toward Russia was terrible.

All the government buildings were once again full of wounded. Typhus and hospital fever raged in the city; the doctors died with their patients. From the homes of the aristocrats, again turned into hospitals, the dead were thrown down directly into the wagons on the street; typhus also struck private homes. In my father's house, inhalations of vinegar and cloves were poured over heated stones every two hours to protect against infection from the foreigners coming into the office. The famine, the daily threats and dangers, the demands made of every individual, men as well as women, were tremendous. But people finally became accustomed to doing the extraordinary; there was an excitement that helped in coping with the moment. In 1813, when General Count Wittgenstein,[18] following closely on the heels of the French with his Russian troops, occupied Königsberg, hopes for the fall of French domination rose again all the more strongly in the secret thoughts of people now used to action.

For the moment, we had exchanged one foreign occupation for another, the French regiment for the Russian one, the French billeting for the Russian—and the latter, because of its lack of culture, was generally even more unwelcome than the uncouth Hessians and Bavarians, or even than the French. But just as the first ray of sunshine suddenly brightens and illuminates everything, the determined action of Count Yorck[19] brought the realization to all hearts, that there were no chains that could not be broken, and that you could become free, if you wanted to be free, if you were ready to wager everything.

Of course, I, in my nursery, was not concerned with all that. I was only delighted to hear the sounds of the shots fired during a skirmish between a troop of fleeing Frenchmen and the Russians pursuing them in front of the gates of Königsberg, and was as happy with the dog belonging to one of the Russians billeted with us as I had been with the sugar candy of the poor wooden-legged Frenchman. But the great events of the times and the habit of experiencing large changes in their own fates and those of others steeled my parents' characters. It gave them an equanimity that protected them in good times and bad. Their calmness and diligence set for us a good example, without their actually instructing us in those virtues.

3

My earliest memories are of the time between the ages of four and five. In the spring of 1814 we had moved from the two-windowed house occupied by my parents during the occupation into the three-windowed house across the street. We lived there until 1820 so I spent my whole happy childhood there.

[Lewald describes her home in great detail.]

The living room, with its commodious furniture covered with black horsehair, with its yellow chintz curtains printed with pagodas and Chinamen, was as liveable as possible, and there was nothing there we could hurt. The pictures of our grandparents on both sides hung on the wall, and over them, a large life-size portrait in pastels of me in a white dress with blue shoes. In front of me sat my older brother in his little shirt on a pillow on the ground; he reached for a grape I was holding in my raised right hand, while I carried a little basket of fruit on my left arm. It was one of the usual motifs of the day. A girl born then to a fairly affluent family had probably been depicted this way with her little basket of apples—or, if a boy, the child would be on a rocking horse or driving a hoop before him. Our portrait had the poor delineation of hands and feet typical of these paintings, but the facial likeness was so striking that even as an adult I was amazed at the similarity of the painted brows and eyes to our own.

As far back as I can remember, I had two brothers. The one closer to me in age was born on May 2, 1813, on the day of the battle of Lützen, and the younger on May 31, 1815, on the day the Allies marched into Paris. My father impressed such facts on us in this manner; and so I too could have a remembrance, he told me, that on the evening of my birth, the news of the birth of the Duke of Reichstadt[20] had been announced in Königsberg. My two brothers were my real companions all through my youth. I played with them, learned with them, and had the first experiences of my life with them. We shared all our joys and sorrows; a step forward for one of us was always progress for all three, and writing my memoirs brings back constant reminders of them.

4

If you want to understand what has shaped a person's character, you should not inquire about his place of birth, but rather what kind of household he was born into and how he spent his early years. I am firmly convinced that a large portion of our talents are developed into certain characteristics during the first years of our lives.

We were extremely prosperous at this time. My parents were very well-off; you might even say rich. They were happy together, had no worries, loved us very much; we saw only happy faces around us. Love of pomp or extravagance was alien to my parents' nature, but the style of the household was lavish and expansive.

We had three maidservants, and also a nanny who was certainly under thirty but seemed very old to us; we called her "Old Anne." My earlier wet nurse had remained in the house as a cook. Another maid, Regine, was not very young and always rather cross. A big, fat man with a very handsome face named Mankatz served as both porter and office messenger. All these people served my parents for a long time: the nanny for thirteen years, Regine for seven years, my nurse until her marriage, and likewise the two office messengers, Mankatz and Hermann Kirschnik, and my father's clerks.

That gave our lives a firm foundation. We did not have to accustom ourselves to new impressions constantly; we were not confused by many changes. These people were ours, at one with us, and just as the people around us remained the same, so our outside environment only changed once until I was eleven, when my father took us all on a trip to Memel. It was not considered a necessity in those days to have a summer residence every year; my mother or one of us children would have been very ill indeed, for my parents to have considered such a separation from each other. They had married for love and lived in the belief that that is why people married—to be with each other as much as possible.

The constancy of this situation had the great advantage for us, for me particularly, of making us feel totally at home in our little world. I do not believe that the children of today, accustomed to the fashionable gypsy life of families constantly traveling and changing residences for the summer, have the slightest compensation for the loss of that feeling of being at home. As quiet as our lives were, we still had many diversions that seemed wonderful to us. My father's banking business put him in touch with Russian and Polish houses. My oldest uncle was in St. Petersburg often, my cousin August Lewald in Warsaw; many Polish and Russian businessmen recommended by them came to visit us. Sometimes they had their wives with them, and a few even brought their children. The parlor was opened for these foreign guests; a hired waiter came to set the table with silver not usually in service. He folded the napkins into fancy patterns, put fruit bowls on the table, and filled our best blue vases with flowers. Although the room was still ice-cold, and the busy waiter was constantly shooing us out, "because we were always under his feet," it was a great treat to have a big towel tied around us as an apron and stand with red freezing hands, to look at the servants dressed in their best or to marvel at the table, on which lay the silver serving spoons and the glass bowls of fresh and preserved fruits promising the pleasure dessert would bring.

When everything was ready in the parlor and the doors were closed until the meal, we went down to the ground-floor kitchen. As in all Königsberg houses, it was small, cold, and dark. But on such days, the fire on the stove burned three times as brightly as usual, because a roast was on the spit. Over and under the great copper cake pans, the coals glowed, and the assistant cook, who usually shrank completely into a shadow next to our despotic cook, reached everywhere with her arms and eyes. The main pleasure in these visits, since we were even more under foot and pushed out of the way than in the parlor, was that great determination was required to invade the kitchen or even stay in it a short time.

When it was finally time to eat and the guests had arrived, our nanny collected her frozen and unruly mob of children, cleaned us up, and dressed us in our best clothes. We had to sit obediently waiting for a long time, so as not to ruin our appearance; when we were finally summoned and brought into the parlor (always both festive and strange to us with its lights), our pleasure was immense. We were admired, caressed, and fed, got to see the pretty people, and then were removed again to talk and dream about the events of the day in our quiet nursery.

There were other days, when our parents went to parties — then we could watch Mother get dressed! She was a delicate woman of average height, very slender, and so graceful that even at the age of fifty, she would still appear youthful in her step and posture. Her beautiful complexion was enhanced by thick black hair and light blue eyes as well as fine facial features and an extremely sweet expression. Her whole being was one of grace and good taste, and these two qualities, combined with a very good mind and great kindness, compensated for the lack of education and knowledge in her running of the household or her relationship with the guests. She was too intelligent to try to pass for something she was not, and while her education scarcely went beyond the basics, she knew how to make her house pleasant for important men and how to earn their admiration and friendship.

To look into her little jewel case, from which a small bottle of attar of roses spread its scent, to admire her, as she drove off to the ball in a black velvet dress with a little diamond comb and a red rose in her hair, pearls around her neck, beautiful lace around her nape and bosom, was as entertaining for us as only the entrance of a princess would be to more spoiled children.

But we did not need such great events, which were an exception, to have fun. There were the chickens in the narrow courtyard and five geese in their shed. A pair of turkeys was always being fed in the courtyard. Pigeons kept secretly by one of our clerks, Mr. Rubinson (who considered himself a great violinist and sometimes played his old fiddle for hours with a terrible whining sound) were our special joy. The "secrecy" of this pigeon-keeping was part of the pleasure because everyone in the house knew about it and about the corner on the grounds where five or six pairs of pigeons lived; everyone had seen the roost set into a few raised roof tiles. My father, who had forbidden pigeon-keeping because of police regulations, knew it; my mother, who loathed the droppings on the ground, knew it; and our fat cousin Zacharias, who also worked for and lived with us, knew it, too. And when the latter mentioned certain pigeons casually at the dinner table, and Mr. Rubinson turned red, thinking an interdict would now surely follow, we children looked at our father anxiously—but the interdiction was never spoken. My father had been an enthusiastic pigeon breeder himself at one time, and my mother ignored the droppings because she knew how much we children enjoyed the pigeons. So they were and remained an open secret until a few years later, when Mr. Rubinson, trying to lure outside pigeons to his roost, climbed out the attic window and suffered a bad fall onto a neighboring roof. This brought him to a long convalescence and the pigeons out of the house.

We were with my mother only during certain hours of the day. It helped her in managing the children that we lived on different floors. Each floor had a small wooden gate on the stairs to safeguard the children; if this was closed, we were forced to stay on our own terrain. If we did not want to play with each other, there was nothing to do but look out the window. Just as I never tired of examining every corner and drawer of the house, so I could kneel for hours on a chair by the window and look at the houses and the neighborhood.

No one, at least in our house, knew anything about the current method of entertaining children, of meaningful play, of Frö-bel's theory.[21] Instead, we had all kinds of toys, doll houses, dolls, and play forts. Some of these were very beautiful and costly, given to us mainly by our oldest uncle when he returned from St.

Petersburg or elsewhere. But you cannot play long with store-bought toys, and until I was old enough to sew and tailor for the dolls myself, all our toys, even my most expensive dolls, were only objects of curiosity for me. I wanted to know how they were made, what they looked like inside; to find out, I worked on them until they were broken.

My parents, who only gave us simpler things, scolded me. They did me an injustice, although they did not know it. My nanny, who was not particularly fond of me, supported them in this. She assured them that I did not care about beautiful things, that threats were of no avail, and that I was not satisfied until everything was broken and ruined. They completely overlooked the child's inborn drive toward activity and investigation—in fact, they did not even understand it. They did not consider what an impression it would make on a child, with its scanty knowledge of death, to hear a wooden bird or dog make sounds and mysterious movements. "Why doesn't the dog in my picture book bark?" asks the child. "It's only painted," is the answer. "But why does this wooden dog bark?" it questions further, without realizing that by drawing these comparisons among a painted, wooden, and living dog, it is analyzing the difference between animate and inanimate objects. "It's made like that inside," is the answer, one that really forces the child to investigate further.

Even today, I remember how scared I was, standing in front of a small, broken barrel-organ, on which a small bird cage with a yellow bird circled, while a tinkling little tune played. I had really wanted to see the insides and had therefore loosened the white leather between the sides of the organ, but to no avail. I could not see anything; I had to tear it open some more. Now I had done it; I turned the handle again, but it did not sound right. The thought that I had broken something again overwhelmed me. Without knowing what I was doing, I tore all the leather away. There lay the two white sides and I now saw the five thin horsehair strings, stretched over a little bridge, and at the crank were two pieces of quill, which passed over the strings when the crank was turned. That was all! Now I knew it, and I really wanted to enjoy the toy. I turned and turned, the birdcage circled as much as I wanted, but the bird had forgotten how to sing. Having destroyed my own pleasure, I had yet another problem. Totally crushed, I had no excuse in the face of the reproaches heaped on me, save that I had not wanted to break the bird at all, and could not help the fact that my toy had fallen apart.

It was even worse with my dolls, when, wanting to know how they were made, I quietly dug into the back of their heads with a needle or scissors, first with one finger and then with two, very carefully, to feel inside. And then when the wax or papier-mâché suddenly began crumbling and falling at my feet, I was as appalled and downcast each time as if it had never happened before.

From these experiences I discovered that one should really differentiate between a bad, irrational, destructive drive in children, which must be quashed immediately, and natural curiosity, which is also often destructive, but unintentionally so, and to some extent with perfect justification. People have told me that that is why you should only give children basic toys, Fröbel cubes and blocks and sticks, to play with, to direct their play toward creativity and accustom them by progressive steps to various kinds of objects, so that they will not be surprised by the unusual and be driven by amazement to destruction. But I think such abstract development and instruction are not possible in our world; you should not prevent a child from thinking and progressing in its own way. I have usually seen only limited minds and pedantic souls result from such systematic education. The person who has not learned on his own by trial and error will also have problems coping with the thousands of unpredictable vicissitudes and events of later life. If you have a strong personality, you are already too much of an individual as a child to be educated according to general principles and theories. Whenever I see a child being sinned against by the use of half-understood systems, I thank the Fate that saved me from all experimental education. It does far less damage to a child to commit or suffer an occasional injustice, than to repress his natural talents and deprive him of the little bit of freedom he needs by imposing rules and maxims in the playroom.

5

[Lewald tells of the neighboring families.]

The family living on the middle and second floor of the tinsmith's shop fascinated me. They were what we called orthodox Jews, i.e., Jews who still lived totally according to Jewish laws and customs. They were poor, somehow related, and were very concerned with our welfare. The old, very tiny, very friendly, and extremely clean lady of the house had assisted my mother during childbirth, visited us when we were sick, and signaled with her head or hand (if she happened to be sitting at the front window) to my mother, when we children were doing something dangerous in the window of the nursery or down on the portico.

"How can you protect children?" my mother asked Madame Japha during one such occasion, when we had caused her considerable alarm.

"No one can protect children," answered the old lady, "if God does not keep watch over them with his angels."

That is, word for word, the touching and charming expression of hers that has remained in my memory all these years. I liked the fact that the angels were keeping watch over us!

Mr. Japha was at home frequently. He had a small gray beard and always wore a white, stiffly starched nightcap—the only nightcap I had ever seen at that time. Early in the morning he stood praying and swaying in the window, and I saw him inclining and making movements that I did not understand. Later in the day, he sat at the same place at the window, smoking a pipe and now and then taking a pinch of snuff. Friday evenings, candles were lit in the room, and I saw more activity than usual there. I knew that there was some kind of holiday going on, that a prayer was said over a large loaf of bread, covered with a white cloth, and a blessing was uttered, but I had never seen it myself; so I was very interested. They gave us Easter cakes and little sugar lumps at Easter, which were especially made for that holiday; at another time of the year, in the fall, during the Festival of Booths,[22] palm fronds and large citrons, a kind of lemon, lay in a certain corner of the window. The main festivity, however, occurred in the winter or in late fall, when there was already rain and snow in the streets, and the days, which are considerably shorter in East Prussia than in central Germany, seemed even shorter because of the fog and clouds. Then all at once, in the room across the street, one candle appeared on the window sill in the evening—and now the splendor, the "fireworks," of my childhood began. On the next day two candles burned, on the third, three, and so it went on, steadily becoming more brilliant and brighter, until perhaps seven or nine lights were burning[23] and the splendor was over all at once. That was the Jewish Christmas, they told us. We did not worry too much about the contradictions in this explanation, because when Mr. Japha was finished with his "Christmas" celebration, ours was imminent, and we forgot the Jewish Christmas so we could think about our own.

I often visited Madame Japha, or rather her daughter, who was unmarried, lived with her parents, and helped support the family with her handwork. She was considered one of the best seamstresses in town, and she had made part of my mother's trousseau, so my mother was glad to have me receive my first sewing lessons from this good lady. I liked being with her. First of all, she let me sit across from her on a chair at the window, and not on a child's chair or small bench as I had to at home, so I seemed far more grown-up to myself than at home. Second, I could see our house and the other side of the street from there, and third, she gave me answers to many questions for which I had received none at home.

I learned from her that we were Jews, and that they kept this from me at home, because other people could not stand Jews. From her I learned the names, the meaning, and the ceremonies of the Jewish holidays. She showed me a small tin capsule on her door frame. She said that it contained the Ten Commandments and it was attached there so that you would always have them in your eyes and in your heart.[24] Then she let me see a cloth of white and blue wool her father wore on his body and said it was also supposed to signify the Ten Commandments. She showed me a prayer shawl and a long white shirt, which she called a "Kittel."

She explained to me that her father donned it on the High Holiday, on the day of the long night in the synagogue, when God reconciled himself with mankind for another year. Her father would be buried in this shirt when he died.[25]

When I began to speak of these things at home, no one stopped me, but no one encouraged me either. And when I insisted on dwelling upon the subject, I was told that I could not understand things like that; I would learn all about it later. To my specific question, "Are we Jews, too?" my father's answer was, "You are our child and that's all you need to know."

That was supposed to take care of the problem, but I was all the more interested, and the Jews and their holidays and customs became uncanny and mysterious to me, attractive and repulsive at the same time. That we were Jews and that it was bad to be a Jew—those were facts of which I was fully aware when I was only five or six, before I even went to school. As nice as we looked in our silk and fur coats, despite the dignity of our nanny when taking us on walks, there were still times when ragged and dirty children yelled "Jew" at us derisively. Our nanny would always say that it was all my fault because of my black hair.

I never talked about such street incidents at home. I do not really know why. In children, consciousness is sometimes very hazy and incomplete, but somehow there is an awareness that makes them do (or prevents them from doing) many things far beyond their comprehension, so that they often act wiser than they actually are. You might say they are acting out of an instinct which abandons them, more or less, as their self-consciousness grows.

I liked going over to Madame Japha even more after those experiences. Everything the family owned—a Jewish prayer book, a small old balsam box—became significant and valuable objects for me. Just as our copper etchings at home represented all of art for me, the Japha family represented the religious and mystical element in my childhood. I could sit for hours, hemming a dust cloth next to Mademoiselle Japha, asking question after question. I loved her, because she was the first confidante of my life, the first person with whom I shared a secret. When she tired of my questions she sat silently, or even sang some songs (mostly sentimental) in her weak voice as she worked. One song, "Here you rest, Karl; here I'll rest with you in one grave," always moved me to tears—it was a popular song with the organ grinders at the time. At such times another pastime began, peculiarly pleasurable to me: I would stare at her. She was so homely, the good soul! Her face was scarred by smallpox, her nose broad, her mouth large; and somehow, during her siege of smallpox or some other time, her earlobe had split in two. I found this minor flaw horribly fascinating. I always thought I would be glad if only she just did not have this earlobe, but I could not tear my eyes away from it, and stared at her so stupidly that she finally pulled her long curls, fashionable at that time, down far enough so I could not see her ears.

This pleasure in something which disturbs you usually stays in your mind until old age. There is something unhealthy about it, though, and I am glad that I encountered it in such petty things as a child because I had a masochistic imagination. I think I was more unnecessarily afraid of everyday things than most children. The crowing of a cock, for example, or a loud trumpet blast would completely devastate me as a young child. My father dealt with these fears by deliberately keeping cocks in the courtyard and taking me to the changing of the guard himself. It was a homeopathic cure, perhaps not to be recommended for everyone, but it certainly worked with me.

These were minor fears, though, compared with those imposed on me by my imagination. I did not know about ghosts as a young child, but when I was put to bed, I always saw visions before my eyes: giants, cities, birds, dwarves, famous people, and pictures, constantly changing, flowing into one another, reforming, disappearing again, more and more rapidly, more and more frighteningly. I called my nanny, I cried, I held her hand, I asked her to tell me something; I did not want to see these things any more. But whatever she told me was immediately incorporated into my visions, and I did not stop crying and pleading till she had fetched my parents. They were always able to calm me. A trace of these involuntary visions before going to sleep have remained with me all my life. Now they are very rare and only appear when I am ill or have worked too hard, and I am usually able to control them by forcing myself to concentrate on one object. However, this "imaging" must happen to many people. The famous physiologist Johannes Müller[26] called it a "plasticity of fantasy in the light and dark field of vision;" he himself experienced and described his perception of it in great detail. I experienced it just as he described it. As a child, I could not produce the images at will, but was forced to endure their appearance helplessly. Even now, when something happens to make me see such an image before going to sleep, I still cannot control the following series of them by myself. They still have the haziness of "dissolving views," and I can only stop them completely.

The ideas of Frau von Krüdner[27] were very popular in Germany in 1816 and 1817. People talked a great deal about her prophecy of the impending end of the world, as they had a year earlier about the collision of the earth with the comet.[28] In addition, there was a serious outbreak of plague somewhere. I thereupon conceived the idea that we would all get the plague or else perish in the coming apocalypse, and I was terrified. Whenever I could catch the attention of anyone with the patience to talk to me, I would ask about the plague and the end of the world. No jealous lover would have been more eager to obtain evidence of his misfortune than was I to know as a certainty that we would all perish. One day I would cry because I had to die, the next day because my parents would die and leave me alone.

My parents were very patient. My mother sat for hours at my bedside; my father talked to me seriously, giving whatever reasons he thought I could understand at the age of six. If this did not comfort me, he scolded me and slapped me several times, not in anger, but deliberately, since this was supposed to be as effective with children as a draining blister plaster. I was so frightened that I stopped talking. That was, indeed, my father's main purpose—children often overexcite themselves with their own words. The reaction to the slaps was quite natural; I began to cry because of the pain and quietly cried myself to sleep.

If my parents were not available, matters were far worse. Our nanny, who was not overjoyed at having to care for a very precocious, serious child, whom she often did not understand, found it intolerable when my fantasies ruined the last quiet hour of the evening, to which she had been looking forward all day, or when I prevented her from going to bed, by holding her fast by the hand at my bedside. She would scold me severely, and would threaten, pointing to the house across the street: "Just you wait. Mr. Peppel is coming!" The terror that these words created in me, and later in my siblings, is as difficult to describe as for me to understand, even now, how and why poor Mr. Peppel aroused such fear. It is one of the mysteries of my childhood, for there was not the slightest reason to fear the man.

Mr. Peppel was probably between thirty and forty years old. A clerk in a mercantile company, he had a quiet, completely friendly face. He was not at home much during the week. In the morning he tied his white neckerchief at a mirror by the window and combed his hair. If he came home at noon, he read by the window. In the evenings, his blinds were down. No one at our house knew him personally; we children had never spoken to him or heard anything bad about him. I do not know how our nanny came upon the idea of making him our bogeyman, except that he was one of the few persons living near us who was a completely unknown quantity for us. The fact was that we had an overwhelming fear of Mr. Peppel; the mere mention of his name, the threat that he was coming, made me break out in a cold sweat—it was even more terrifying to me than my customary dread of plague, death, and the end of the world.

I have no doubt that there are many children whose imaginations create such bogeymen. It seemed as though I always had to have something to make me afraid, against which I felt powerless. I never derived my bogeymen from a supernatural world, but rather from everyday things I encountered. With the exception of the totally irrational terror created by mention of Mr. Peppel, my fears always focused on a matter that really was frightening and had a reasonable basis. Just as the small child longs for the moon because he has no concept of the distance involved, I could not measure how close or far away my demons were. My fearstruck imagination unfortunately destroyed all barriers of time and space.

I do not know if in such cases any good can be achieved with rational explanations. It does not help to tell the child that the country where the plague is, or where there was an earthquake, is far away. Far and near are not clear concepts for him. He immediately inquires, "Isn't the disaster coming here, too?" Any reassurances you give him derive from your own experience, and the conclusions drawn from this experience mean nothing to the child. They lose their efficacy as soon as he no longer sees his parents' faces backing them up. There are basically only two effective tools against childhood fears: occupying the imagination with happy pictures and with strange characters (i.e., literature, fairy tales in particular[29]) and disciplining the unreasoning speculative mind by education. And soon I was given these two diversions.

6

My first day in school was April 1, 1817. I had learned my ABCs and a few poems at home from my mother, but I do not remember looking forward to going to school. I had to get up earlier than usual. I was given a fairly large white basket, with two lids, packed with a writing slate, a primer by Lähr, a handkerchief, and a buttered roll wrapped in paper. My father himself took me by the hand to escort me to school. My mother accompanied us to the door, and the nanny (who usually favored my brothers, as she had raised them from birth) put a piece of candy in my hand. I had an uneasy feeling, as if I were going on a trip to a place where something unpleasant would happen to me.

The way was not long. We went through the town square, through Brodbänkenstrasse, across the small cathedral square to the large cathedral square, on which stood our schoolhouse. This was a quite ordinary city residence, because the Ulrich School I attended was a private institution. My father was very merry with me on the way. He let me clean the heels of my boots on the steps, reminded me to be sensible and obedient, and said someone would fetch me when school was over.

The wife of the principal, a still youthful, attractive woman with beautiful long blond curls on both sides of her face, greeted me downstairs in a small room. She kissed me, promised my father they would be considerate of me, then my father left. Madame Ulrich took me by the hand and led me to the large back room on the ground floor, where morning prayers were being said.

This room—large, dark, and cold, like all these Königsberg back rooms—was filled with benches, and what seemed to me an immeasurable quantity of people. Against the walls stood what to my eyes were grown-up and intimidatingly large young women. (They were probably fifteen or sixteen years old.) Further toward the front were the younger girls, and in the very front, children my age, among whom Mrs. Ulrich indicated my place. The girls all stood in rank and file, talked and laughed loudly with one another; the little ones next to me asked who I was. I felt overwhelmed and numbly gazed upward at the heavy stucco garlands of flowers and fruit on the ceiling, which were darkened by age.

In the meanwhile, several teachers had appeared and took their place with Madame Ulrich next to the piano. One teacher, Mademoiselle Anne, came and told me to set my basket down at my feet and to fold my hands when the morning anthem was sung. Then Mr. Ulrich entered. The talking suddenly stopped, all the faces became serious, and Mr. Ulrich scanned the room with his large, somewhat protruding eyes earnestly and severely. Then he sat down at the piano, opened a songbook, and named the song, "How lovely shines the morning star," and the whole group of young voices began to sing.

It was the first religious service I had ever attended, and it made a great impression on me. I really did not understand the words of the song, but the festive melody moved me. I did understand the words of the prayer Mr. Ulrich spoke spontaneously after the song. It had the same ideas as the evening prayer I always said before going to sleep, and I was happy to find it at school. Then an event disturbed the pleasure I was just experiencing.

Mr. Ulrich, who, although he was still a young and very handsome man, had a severe face, came over to me right after the prayer, to greet and encourage me. He said he had already seen that I was a very clever girl, so that I should be especially diligent and attentive; then everybody would all like me. "But if you don't work hard," he added, laughing, looking up at the ceiling, from which an empty chandelier hook hung down into the room, "if you don't work hard, Fanny, we'll pack you in your big book basket and hang you up there!" He laughed again, the other little girls laughed, too and I—I took his threat literally and began to cry. It seemed to me as if I had landed in the ogre's cave.

Madame Ulrich and Mademoiselle Anne quickly came to console me and one of the little girls said, good-naturedly, "Don't be so dumb; it's all a joke." A few of the adults picked me up as I passed by and kissed me and I calmed down. But I had become suspicious of the school, and I never liked the large back room again.

Luckily, we little ones had no lessons there. We were about eight or ten children, and we were kept busy the whole morning by Mademoiselle Anne, the daughter of a French immigrant family, and Madame Ulrich in a friendly second-floor room facing the street. After an hour I became so accustomed to the room and the other children that hunger (which I had lacked at breakfast at home) asserted itself. I pulled out my roll to eat it. I had scarcely done this when the whole class began to laugh and Mademoiselle took my roll away, with the remark that I could not eat it now. She set the bread on a cabinet, another hour passed quietly, and my head began to hurt because I was so hungry. When Mademoiselle Anne left the room at the end of the lesson, she forgot to give back my breakfast. I would not have dared to take it, even if I could have reached it. The others, occupied with enjoying their snacks during the recess, did not think about me. I was too embarrassed to ask them for help. The next teacher did not know what had happened. I sat there until twelve o'clock with a terrible headache, ravenously hungry and with the roll, rightfully belonging to me, always within sight. I decided firmly never to go to school again, because it was horrible.

The statement that I was not going back to school was the first thing I uttered when I came home. Luckily, my parents had agreed with Mr. Ulrich that I should only attend school in the morning throughout the summer and not participate in the needlework lessons. I was therefore able to forget my unhappiness while playing with my siblings. The next day, the encouragement of my parents and the realization that I had caused my own problems made me decide to try again. My father gave me a note which stated how innocently I had gone hungry, and, since the teachers now realized what kind of child they were dealing with, they treated me so kindly and considerately that I soon became reconciled to my fate and even began to love it.

I learned easily, my father helped me at home, and the praise I received both at school and at home gave me great satisfaction. We still learned spelling by the old tedious method, and learning to read was a difficult piece of work, compared with the ease with which children nowadays learn reading and writing almost simultaneously. But I believe that even if Mr. Ulrich had known about phonics and all the easier methods of today, he would have scorned them just because they were easier. For him, the primary purpose of learning (something I only understood much later) was to develop the strength and energy of the mind. He often failed to carry out this idea. However, when his opinions and personality combined with those elements that were congruent with his methods, he actually accomplished much in developing the character of his students. There are surely many of my fellow alumnae gratefully willing to acknowledge this as I am.

Our school did not have very much in common with today's institutions of learning, and it would be an impossibility in Prussia today, as the government does not permit such an institute. It would be difficult to find parents who would entrust their children to it. Mr. Ulrich had never passed an examination of any kind, but had started early to teach and educate. Then he married the daughter of a very prominent Königsberg lawyer and opened his own school, which was soon attended by the daughters of the best families. When I entered the school, only one generation of girls had been educated there, so it must have been founded in 1810 or 1811. Approximately one year after I arrived, a number of boys who had previously had special lectures were added. These boys also belonged to prosperous families. Boys and girls took their lessons together but sat at separate tables. Another difference was that boys were taught classical languages in the afternoon while we girls were instructed in needlework.

Not only was this arrangement somewhat peculiar, but so was the price of tuition. Mr. Ulrich determined this according to his own personal estimate of the student's family income. There were boys in the school whose parents paid ten or twelve thalers a month for regular tuition and two daily study periods supervised by a teaching assistant. Other boys and girls paid three, four, or six thalers per month. Later, when my father found himself in financial difficulties and four of his children were attending the school simultaneously, Mr. Ulrich offered voluntarily to teach us all for ten thalers a month. His theory was that such a school for the public benefit, while not scrimping in paying for good teachers, should be supported by the parents according to their means. He considered it justifiable to get as much for tuition as he could, but he occasionally hired an especially good teacher for one or two gifted students, to give them personal instruction, if they had outgrown the regular courses. I and another girl, who still lives in Berlin, benefited from this practice, as we received special lessons in French from a superb teacher for a long time.

This method of being occasionally instructed in different groups according to ability depended on the concept of individualizing students, an idea easier to carry out in a small private school than in a large public one. This created great problems for class schedules, and those who were in the average group could have several free hours, during which they had to be busied with dictations or listening to another class. But the system was generally successful and helped the students, because they discovered their ability in one special area and directed their energy and inclinations toward it.

We only had five classes, which were very small except for the one in needlework. Promotions to a higher grade level were very rare, because the whole course of study was nine years, from the age of six to fifteen. When I was attending, there were only two students who had started their education there. I was one, and the other was a pretty, sweet girl, Angelika Michalski, a few years older than I, the daughter of a rich ironmonger, whom I loved, because she was so beautiful and friendly.

Mr. Ulrich was partial to both of us. He liked to emphasize that we were his "special" students; luckily this meant we were among those who did not suffer much from the negative aspects of his character. He was capable of unrestrained violence, exercised with great roughness and hardheartedness. If he was annoyed by lack of attentiveness, a mistake, or a childish naughtiness, he rose like a madman; and if he found no relief in his own terrible profanities, he satisfied himself by boxing the pupil's ears, jerking him around the room by the arm, or throwing books at his head. Sometimes he struck a boy on the head with the stem of his long pipe—he always smoked during the first two morning lessons—which was really supposed to hurt. The regular punishments of his very Draconic system were nothing compared to these. It was better to be struck with a ruler on the hand regularly and intentionally than to be punished in a rage. The lazier students were used to staying after school or having to recopy a badly written exercise five or six times before the next day. They really did not mind that too much. Those who had lined their pages badly stayed behind and lined fifty pages as a penalty. If you forgot a book, you stood in the corner. I do not believe there was ever a school day when no one was punished.

Mr. Ulrich's moods were very changeable. We all believed—I cannot say why—that he played cards for high stakes, often staying awake most of the night, and that he was in a truly foul mood toward us when he had lost heavily. I can relate one incident from personal experience. He came into our room once during morning prayers, although we had been expecting him much earlier. He looked frowzy and had on a long gray coat reaching down to his feet, but we could tell he was not dressed suitably under it. All the teachers, even his wife, who brought him coffee during the first class, avoided him carefully all day. Anybody who did not have classes with him at such times considered himself lucky. He paced around gloomily, chewing his nails, in his hand the chalk from the blackboard. He bit into the chalk at times until his lips were covered with white dust, making him look even more ominous. However, his teaching remained excellent, and although we were all afraid of him, and had all experienced the most excessive injustices from him—had even resented, with our childish sense of fairness, his harshness toward his faultless wife and Mademoiselle Anne—there were only a few children in the school (except those untalented pupils toward whom his behavior was really inexcusable) who did not respect him in their heart of hearts and who do not remember him with gratitude.

It is not difficult to explain this. Even the most naive of us had to recognize that Mr. Ulrich was passionately trying to advance our knowledge; our welfare was important to him, and every step we took forward made him happy. Likewise he felt personally grieved by our mistakes. I remember him pulling a very lazy, indolent, adolescent girl from her seat violently, exclaiming, "I am not a teacher for dummies! I can only teach clever children!" He then set her back on her bench. Shortly thereafter, she left the school; she was really not suited to his style of teaching there. But that day made a deep impression on me. I was only ten or eleven, but I finally understood the character of our teacher, and I felt a distinct empathy with him.

Moreover his method of teaching was the most pleasant and stimulating I have ever encountered. He presented the facts by asking short, well-defined, and rapid questions, and this method enabled us to discover the cause of things, which had seemed strange and surprising to us at the beginning of the lesson. He also lectured very little, and we learned to speak easily and confidently and enjoy a sort of feeling of victory from the constant use of our minds. "Look, you figured that out all by yourselves; it's quite simple," he would say, after he had prepared the way to our new understanding so well that it would have been impossible for us to miss it.

Actually, we probably learned far fewer facts than children do today. We had lessons in reading, writing, arithmetic, religion, geography, history, German, and French, and very bad instruction in singing and drawing. The sciences and the history of literature were not taught at all. Nobody even considered the former much then; and as far as literature and its history were concerned, learning to recite a poem by Schiller,[30] or another classical writer, in the first grade sufficed. We could surely start to read Schiller's or someone else's works when we had the time. This was necessary for our education but we could do this outside of classes because it would be fun for us. Likewise, we were told to read the stories by Becker[31] and the necessary mythological explanations for our own pleasure after our schoolwork in ancient history. It was assumed we would help ourselves—and we did.

The most attention was given to the German language, history, and arithmetic; to be able to do quick calculations in your head was a matter of honor in the school. We did not have many books. Mr. Ulrich dictated German grammar to us in the simplest of sentences; we learned them by heart and then wrote our own examples. For each subject we would normally use only one book. These few volumes were the only ones I owned in the seven and a half years of my formal schooling.[32]

All the other educational aids now used (and probably available in other schools even in those days), such as globes or boards for the explanation of geography or mathematics, were not much in evidence. Mr. Ulrich's eccentricity or maybe his limited financial resources made him disdain such aids. Even now I laugh when I recall an experiment that was supposed to show us the movement of the earth on its axis and around the sun. The sponge from the blackboard represented the earth, two shoe horns from the next room were placed at the position of the poles, and, while one of the girls held a piece of chalk denoting the sun, Mr. Ulrich circled around her as the earth, holding his sponge and shoe horns. But the lesson and the whole attitude of the class were so serious that we never saw the humor of the situation then. The division by meridians and parallels was drawn out for us on the board, and we copied them at home; the same was true of maps and history charts. In effect, we actually created our own books. It was all calculated to lead us to independent thinking, to self-reliance.

Mr. Ulrich held his students to strict observation of structure and moderation, probably in compensation for his own lack of same. His sharp eye and keen ear caught the slightest bad habit of expression or speech in us. An immediate reproach followed a girl's temperamental expression or gesture. A scream of fright, which our sex is particularly prone to utter, was called "common," and it was an unalterable law to dress most carefully when leaving school and to have nothing disorderly about one's appearances. The little girls were dressed by the big ones, and I really believe that Mr. Ulrich would sometimes stand on a street corner, to see that we did not linger on the way, speak too loudly, or commit some other carelessness. One girl, who had casually sauntered along with her book bag thrown over her shoulder, was reproached about it for a long time; she was reminded time and again that a girl who could throw her book bag over her shoulder was capable of anything.

Strict adherence to order and self-control, firm submission to discipline, and the proper external education for inner freedom were the tasks Mr. Ulrich had set for his pupils. We had to write two long German essays every week, sometimes in the form of letters, which were then actually delivered in an envelope. We learned to make the envelopes ourselves and how to fold different types of letters and cards correctly in a two-hour special lesson. We had double essay notebooks, so that we could make our corrections very carefully.

Mr. Ulrich never permitted us to discuss anything that was not relevant to the lesson. Occasionally he threw in a generality or comment, only a brief remark, directed toward protecting us from being deluded by pretentions and pedantry. "You are supposed to learn something," he would say, "in order to amount to something. If you don't assimilate what you learn, it's only plunder. If it doesn't become part of your flesh and blood and make you strong, it does you no good. If you don't know it when you need it, you don't have it, so learn to collect your thoughts."

According to this axiom, it was necessary to answer loudly, quickly, and with certainty. We were required to do this from our first day in school. Undoubtedly it contributed greatly to the reputation of the pupils' excellence, so that the daughters of the most prominent merchant families continued to be sent to our school—although Mr. Ulrich's personal lack of moderation was common knowledge and was criticized, even condemned, by many people.

When I was a child, I received a light blow on my shoulder from him as punishment for not paying attention. My father, to whom I had complained, used this opportunity to have a serious conversation with Mr. Ulrich. This meeting between the two men not only preserved me from further harm, but also created a mutual sense of respect between my father and my teacher that was very much to my advantage. Mr. Ulrich would tease me at times because of my delicacy, but he always treated me with consideration—significant because even in this small world, the slaves could create or be given their own tyrant if, for example, the children did not complain or the parents were so weak that they let their children suffer injustice without any protest.

7

I have always felt sorry for girls who were educated at home. It is just the ones totally immersed in family life for whom school offers a preparation for life in the larger world of strangers. Even if they have many siblings, those girls are exposed to the same bad influences at home as are only children and the offspring of princes. They are spoiled; everything is there for their sake. The teacher comes only for them, is paid for them, has no purpose but them. Their playmates, their society, are chosen for them. They can be kept from injustice and rudeness and if they are, they will not recognize or judge these evils by themselves or learn to protect themselves against such problems. These girls are necessarily more restricted and less free than those educated in larger groups in schools with their peers. Whenever I have had the opportunity to observe the results of such an education closely, the so-called purity and delicacy that wealthy and aristocratic families think are fostered through tutoring at home proved to be only shy sensibility, which retreated into a complacent arrogance, because the girl feared the rough side of life. Those who are destined to stray much in life gain considerably, because they learn early from their situation and others' that mistakes carry their own punishment. They can sometimes learn such a lesson by observing their schoolmates.

Aside from this morally instructive element, school also offers the advantage of giving the process of learning a more important and serious meaning. Just as one cannot really do without the benefits of attendance at church service at certain periods of life to remove oneself from daily routine, the child experiences quite a different world in the schoolroom than at home. He does not hear his mother's voice, his siblings calling him to play, or the bustle of housework; there are no distractions or diversions.

We had no regular promotions, report cards, or examinations. But, since the school emphasized order in every facet of its operations, any lack of order in the outside world had little negative influence on us, and the evidence of our written assignments gave our parents the necessary benchmarks to measure our progress.

I finished the three primary grades more quickly than most. Thus, when I was nine, I found myself in a class with girls who were all two or three years older and who looked down at me disdainfully or treated me like a toy. I was too serious for the latter attitude and too proud for the former. I had a very good opinion of my own abilities and knowledge. Mr. Ulrich had only one way to curb this; he constantly held before me the example of a boy who had attended the school just recently and had progressed much more swiftly and accomplished more than I. This boy was Eduard Simson, who is now well-known in our political circles.[33]

Whatever I did, whatever I started, even when he praised me, Mr. Ulrich always added, "Eduard Simson was much further along at your age, Eduard Simson could do equations at your age, Eduard Simson could do this or that." In short, Eduard Simson, who had been a good playmate of mine from earliest childhood outside school, became for me simultaneously a bogeyman and a shining example.

Those were the days of child prodigies. The name of Karl Witte[34] was on everyone's tongue, and although Mr. Ulrich was far too sensible to want to make prodigies of his pupils, he was very proud that his student, Eduard, had gained very early admission to the upper level of the Gymnasium Fridericianum. He liked to show off my own rapid progress whenever strangers visited the school.

A nature less healthy than mine would have found a negative comparison to such a paragon discouraging, but in fact, it only increased my ambition and thirst for knowledge. I was so busy in those days that I had no necessity to brood or worry. Whole new worlds were opening for me. From the suspense with which I followed the deeds of Columbus and Cortez, from the empathy I felt for the suffering of Montezuma, my enthusiasm now turned to the Greek heroes. I remember how we sat there with flaming checks when Mr. Ulrich described for us the courage of a Leonidas or the greatness of a Themistocles, or when he spoke of Alcibiades' enchanting charm and his attachment to his teacher Socrates. People never realize fully that lively children experience the details of world history quite personally, that for them America was just discovered, that all great and heroic deeds are just happening for them, and that in only a few years they might just be called upon themselves to live up to all the surprises and delights of previous ages.

My passion for fairy tales and poetry began simultaneously with or perhaps even earlier than my interest in world history. This inclination was strengthened at home by the availability of as many books as I could wish for. My father chose them very carefully, and I never received a new book until I had read the previous one numerous times. Some of my parents' relatives and friends were concerned that so much learning and reading could damage my health, but my father and mother had seen the practicality of providing outside stimuli for me and luckily did not pay attention to such concerns. Since I had started school and had learned to read and entertain myself, I had become a healthy child. All the foolish, misunderstood concepts that had robbed me of peace and sleep, the fears about earthquakes, plagues and death, the wild images that had tortured me, suddenly disappeared. I now had a thousand things to think about, and if I wanted to use my imagination, Snow White and Tom Thumb, the horse Fallada,[35] and the magic cap of invisibility were there to soothe me, until the stories in *The Arabian Nights* drove all others from my mind.

I still have the relish for this Oriental fairy tale world; the broad, free realism with which the fantastic is depicted in it, the great style with which the story is handled, seem incomparable to me even now. The German fairy tale, even though it comes from the Orient, is somewhat limited and anecdotal. You tell it on cold winter evenings with limited detail; its adventures appeal to the poor and oppressed, its miracles are squeezed into a narrow house, and even its kings and princes somehow cower into themselves. In the Oriental story the treatment is broad and epic. When you listen to it, you think that the tale probably originated in the open shops of the bazaars, in the tents of the traveling caravan, that warm summer nights ripened it, that the murmur of the fountains accompanied the sound of its words, and that color and light, splendor and magnificence, could be found abundantly in the imagination of the authors. A great, one might say timeless, breeze blows through them. Life there is full of movement, the action is passionate, and the elements of tragedy and suffering are handled with such humor that they do not perturb the reader for long, because he recognizes the misfortune as something that will pass. Bagdad, the humane Caliph Harun Al Rashid, Sheherezade, Sindbad, and the talking fishes were a constant source of pleasure for me. My joy was increased by the fact that my father read all these stories with me, that he had the wonderful ability to enjoy them like a child. He never tired of having me read the same tale aloud to him again and again, or of reciting the verses of the red, yellow, and blue fishes to me as often as I wanted-ed and discussing the stories endlessly.

To my enthusiasm for the Greeks and Romans at school, and my fascination for the glories and miracles of the Orient in my leisure hours, life at home offered me a very healthy and practical contrast. The number of my siblings had rapidly increased. Before

I even started school, a sister, Clara, had joined the two brothers, and in 1819, a third brother. So there were many children's activities around me, and I joined in these with particular gusto, since, as the eldest, I always had to arrange and invent games.

We were in school for six hours every day and had about one hour of homework. I had begun music lessons early, so I also had to practice piano an hour daily. By the time I was seven or eight, I had a daily schedule of seven or eight hours of work except on Wednesdays, Saturdays, and Sundays. At an early age, I learned to work seriously and to enjoy the pleasure of a holiday.

[Lewald describes her afternoon excursions through various areas of Königsberg with her siblings and the people of different classes she meets and observes on these occasions.]

Wherever we were taken, we had fun and were safe, because my parents were very careful and would join us without notice, so that our nursemaids could not take the chance of not watching us at all times or doing something improper. I cannot remember ever being bored. No child is bored when it is given the chance to observe the world freely and to notice the different classes of people on its own. This freedom offered us in our childhood, not with a real purpose in mind, but because it was the most convenient thing to do, bore the best fruit for me my whole life long, because I have always felt at home among people and the working classes. Usually that is not the case with children, especially girls, from the so-called privileged classes. They are raised in formal isolation; their parents think they are giving them an advantage by instilling in them an aversion to a lack of culture or anything not like them. Later, when they are confronted with the task of providing for their less fortunate fellow human beings the best they can, they do not have the facility to cope with it. They must really overcome something in themselves, to make a sacrifice to enter the homes of the uneducated. From one point of view, such people are really making a much greater effort than I, but what they achieve as far as helping or comforting the poor is another question.

8

Children have no real sense of the separation of time into days, weeks, months, or years as adults do, and they are not able to count forward or backward according to the calendar. They go by seasons and holidays; if the adults can increase those special days, the child receives considerable benefits, because both the dim horizon of its memories and its future are illuminated with bright stars. Our family was rich with such special days.

In addition to our parents' birthdays and anniversary, for which we always had company in the house, and for which, from early on, we had to learn and do something, we had our own birthdays to celebrate. Besides the usual holidays, the first snowfall and the first Sunday of Advent were also landmarks of our childhood.

In Prussia, the first snowfall is often as early as the first half of October. Sometimes we were reluctant to stay away from the windows on foggy or rainy days, because we were hoping this would be the day when the first snow would fall and then we would get to look into the "big box" when Father came home. We only saw it once a year, on this very occasion.

I do not believe any Egyptian priest could have studied the rising of the Nile more carefully than we did the first snowfall. If the year was mild or dry, and the snow was delayed, the smallest flake in the air led to a combined rush into the living room with the cry: "It's snowing!" But that was of no avail; with the remark that such a dusting in the air did not count and it would have to be a proper snowfall before the box could appear, we were condemned to further waiting and new expectations. Our joy was therefore even greater when the big white flakes fell abundantly from the dark sky, when the roofs, the balconies, and the window sills were covered with thick snow, and its white gleam gave us the promise of the glories we longed for.

We children would ask all afternoon, "Will it be seven o'clock soon?" as apples were laid in the stove for baking, and their sizzling and aroma heralded the coming festivity. The time always seemed terribly long to us; each passing minute was a burden. At the stroke of seven we went down to where our parents had already taken out the "big box" and laid it on the table in front of the sofa.

What were the contents of this box, to which we had looked forward the whole year, which we so longed to see—even when I was already twelve or thirteen and quite mature—which, if I were to see some piece even today, would stir my heart deeply?

The box was nothing but a small old side drawer of my father's desk. All it contained were a few memorabilia he kept there. There was a red morocco book listing our birthdays, illnesses, and first day of school—in other words, the house chronicle. There were small gold frames containing wedding portraits of my parents, an epithelium for them, and a green silk drapery with an inscription, which had veiled the portrait of me and my brothers, when Mother gave it to Father for his birthday. The box contained one of those silver goblets made from rubles to commemorate the battle of Kunersdorf,[36] poems August Lewald had sent my parents on my first birthday, assorted wallets, coin purses, and watch bands crocheted or embroidered for my father by sisters and friends, which he had never worn—in short, all sorts of trifles such as any fairly prosperous family keeps. It was the kind of treasure trove each family can collect for its children to give them unforgettable pleasure in the simplest way.

By way of this box, our parents unintentionally recapitulated our whole limited past to us. We heard eagerly on which day and hour we had been born. We were amused at how badly we had composed our congratulatory poems for our parents' birthdays only a year ago; we learned from the little souvenirs about the friends of their youth and their acquaintances. Best of all, after we had devoured the first baked apple, we were aware of having celebrated an important event and began to anticipate the first snowfall of the next year eagerly.

Our delight at the first Sunday of Advent had an even slighter cause. It was a little toy, made of two gilded apples stuck on wooden skewers, and decorated with a few bunches of boxwood and several rough clay birds; only the imagination of a child could have found them lifelike. The whole pyramid probably cost six pennies, but—and that is what we loved about it—it could only be purchased Advent week. We were given it every year for the first night of Advent and we were sure this would always happen. For us it heralded the approaching Christmas season. It was a wonderful annunciation, and the angel with the lily who appeared to the Virgin Mary to announce the birth of the Saviour could hardly have made her happier than the sight of our parents coming home in the evening, bringing the first ginger cookies and the little apple tree, made us. A true golden glow of hope emanated from it; everything we wished for and expected to receive appeared on the horizon. From this day on, we began to count the days until the sun of happiness, whose beams were not to dim throughout the rest of the year, arose with Christmas Eve.

My father participated actively in our winter games. Despite his seriousness, he had a gift for being a child with his children. Tired and burdened with work as he was, with many worries, he participated in our games as fully and as long as we wanted. We never got the impression that he was condescending or only playing with us. No good intentions can replace this talent for the person lacking it; children always sense it.

What did we play? Mostly imitations of what we had seen. We played sawyer if we had been at a lumberyard. After we attended a circus, we played bareback rider all winter long. A hundred times, I ventured my "salto mortale" as Mademoiselle Rosalie from the threshold that led from the living room to the dressing room and received my father's "Bravo!"; a hundred times, my brothers made the trampoline leap over a footstool. We saw a menagerie with a trained elephant, and my father as the elephant lay on the floor every evening and let us climb on him and lifted us with loving arms over himself as we had seen the elephant do with his trunk to children. We visited a booth with so-called wild men, and every evening, for a long time, at a command from my father, we plunged, hair loosened and screaming wildly out of a hut we had built of sofa cushions under the piano, to begin our war dance. But all these games did not last long. They stopped on the first word from my father; their short duration increased our pleasure.

I do not believe my father ever read any books about raising children (except Jean Paul's *Levana*[37]) or had ever given a thought to what he should do to raise his children properly. It was clear to him that children must see, hear, and learn to obey; obviously we learned this.

My parents were both very orderly, especially my mother, so a sparkling cleanliness was evident in our house, and the smallest item out of place, the tiniest thing lying in the wrong spot was obvious and had to be removed. "Didn't you see that scarf lying there? Does that ribbon belong there?"—those were natural questions, and if you replied that you just had not seen it, the inevitable answer was, "You should have seen it. Why do I see everything?"

If we went for a walk and a wagon loaded with barrels or crates drove by, my father immediately asked, "What is packed in those barrels/crates/bales?" If we did not know, he would say, "You saw boxes like that at the spice shop. Those are boxes of raisins. Do you remember noticing bales like that at the scales? Those are bales of cotton. You've seen old barrels like that often; those are oil barrels. If you don't know, why don't you ask? You have to keep your eyes open and not look at anything without thinking and asking: what is it?"

In the same way, we became used to not letting an expression unfamiliar to us go by without asking its meaning. Since we had to pay strict attention, we learned many new things and concepts without realizing it, something other children had to acquire much more laboriously. It is bad not to accustom children at an early age to ask questions about what they do not understand. I saw this trait lacking in the grown children of an educated family, when we had to make elaborate efforts to explain foreign words that had become part of our language to them. They did not know how to use these words or used them in a completely opposite sense.

Learning to obey was as obvious for us as the exercise of our senses and attention. We never heard or saw disobedience at home, not even dissatisfaction or quarreling. In the thirty-one years of my parents' marriage, I and my siblings never heard my father utter a violent or unfriendly word to my mother nor any but those of love and respect from my mother to him. She was filled with untiring concern for him and he with the most considerate tenderness for her. We lived in an atmosphere of love and harmony, and only good things happened to us there, so we considered the subordination and harmony between my parents as something natural and practiced them ourselves.

But this love went hand in hand with a strict seriousness and a strong determination. We knew how much our parents wanted to make us happy, but we also knew there was no contradiction permitted to my father's commands; indeed, we had not the slightest idea that we did not have to obey unconditionally and without question. Everybody in the household obeyed Father to the letter; our mother, his co-workers in the business, his subordinates, and the servants. In speaking to the servants, Mother always referred to Father as "the Master";[38] "the Master wants it" and "Father said so" were expressions that had the weight of the judgment of God for the whole house.

My father's manner of speech was terse and very determined on the whole, and his communications with the employees, who all lived in our house, limited to the factual. And although this was no longer the usual custom in Prussia, he addressed our male and female servants as "Er" and "Sie."[39] But this brevity in precision of expression made it difficult to misunderstand him; he was mostly well served and seldom had to rebuke anyone or use strong language. I never saw him vehement in dealing with his wife or children, and all who served him considered him a strict but just and good master. After all, it is usually lack of culture and dignity on the part of those giving the orders which creates bad servants.

A man who has been able to have his wife and servants obey him trustfully does not need to educate his children to be obedient. We were inoculated with obedience along with the air we breathed. All virtue is the result of practice, however, and children especially need controls for their tantrums and moods. We were taught never to address our parents without adding the adjective "dear" to the words "Father" and "Mother." As insignificant as this rule seems, it was very significant, and I tested it myself when I was older. I find that when I address someone with a friendly word, I cannot say anything disrespectful or disdainful at that moment. The form of the conversation sets limits, which exclude any vehemence and rashness, aside from the fact that adhering to certain forms is beneficial for family life. For example, because it was our custom to kiss our parents' hands when greeting them in the morning, after meals, and before going to bed, one of our severest punishment was the denial of this pleasure. Even after my brothers were adults and lived, one as a lawyer and the other as a doctor, outside of Königsberg, each return home would bring the desire to kiss our parents' hands after they rose from a meal. If strangers were present, Father would wave away his sons, saying, "Aren't you embarrassed, you grown men!" but he smiled as he said it, and many a guest probably remembers the family feeling of our house fondly.

In the midst of all the love and peace, however, the development of each child took its own, not always good, course. I was very happy in school, learned easily, progressed rapidly, was praised much at school examinations, and was considered one of those children whom we called—schools for girls had their own jargon—"parade horses." The examination in front of our parents, which took place every year and a half, did not satisfy the individual ambition as much as the visits that Councillor Dinter,[40] famous in Prussian educational history, made to our institution now and then.

Every child in town knew Councillor Dinter by sight. They had all seen him, a man of average height with broad shoulders and a round, open face that, although Dinter walked with head somewhat bowed, peered out so amicably with its bright eyes under the long gray hair. Everyone recognized Dinter's broad-beamed Quakerlike black tailcoat and his black kneebreeches, which were never buckled firmly and had to be hitched up by the wearer at regular intervals; this looked very comical because this movement had become a mechanical habit for him. A small, completely squashed hat and sagging stockings completed the picture of an old-fashioned scholar. But anyone who had ever looked into

Dinter's eyes, or to whom he had spoken with his bright intelligent friendliness, forgot his odd appearance (or cherished it). Everything you heard about him was calculated to awaken liking in the children and young people for him. He was unmarried, but had a large household, because he had taken in twelve indigent boys, whom he considered his children and raised and one of whom he even adopted legally. He is still living in Königsberg, this Doctor Gustav Dinter, treasured by all as both physician and human being. We had all heard countless anecdotes about his home life, how the boys living with him had to busy themselves sharpening quills in the evenings during communal readings, while Doctor Dinter knitted. Some of these tales were true, some invented, but we all felt that he loved children and that attracted us to him.

His method of questioning was like that of our teacher, but always paired with cheerfulness. If Dinter had to praise or reprove someone, he always did it with an air of good humor, which we especially appreciated since we were unaccustomed to that at school. When he came to us the first time, I had probably been there for three years. I had to demonstrate my skills in arithmetic to him, which I did excellently, and was asked many questions about geography. Unfortunately I was having a stupid day in that field and was too stubborn to let Mr. Ulrich help me, so that part went badly; but I was able to redeem myself somewhat in Dinter's eyes by my proficiency in French and history. Mr. Ulrich was not satisfied with me, but Dinter patted me on the head and said, "Well, your head would be better on a boy." But then he added nicely, "But if you become a fine woman, that's all right, too."

I came home from school that day very excited, with flushed cheeks. I related everything that had happened, I reproached myself for not knowing anything—but I lingered far longer on the praise I had received. Without realizing it, that perspicacious man had touched one of my private sorrows; I had long envied all boys, because they were boys and could study at the university, while I had a rather low estimate of women. This may seem foolish in a nine-year-old child and unreasonable in my case, but the thought had not originated in me. For a long time, when strangers praised my abilities, they would add with an air of regret, "What a shame she isn't a boy!" I had gotten the idea that boys were something better than girls, and that I would have to be more and better than the other girls. The example constantly placed before me was a boy, Eduard Simson, and my mother, who later suffered from this false attitude of mine, had, with the best intentions, nurtured in me the thought that knowledge was the most important matter and everything else was secondary.

Full of love for all of us, she took great pleasure in my talent and progress. She was proud of having such a clever child, she loved to boast of my knowledge to my aunts and uncles, and, since she had had no education herself, she greatly overestimated the little I had learned so far. I, on the other hand, realized after a year and a half in school that my mother could not help me at all with my work, and when I was eight, I actually knew more than she. If I had had the mind of an adult then, I would have realized that my mother's other excellent qualities far outweighed her lack of formal education, but since she herself so deeply felt this lack and constantly emphasized the possession of knowledge and my good fortune in receiving what she had missed, I underestimated my mother as much as she overestimated me.

I loved my mother with all my heart, but I loved my father even more, because I could always get advice and help from him, even if they came with far more frequent and stricter reprimands than my mother gave. My father read with me and played with us, and although Mother would have given her life for us, she gave no outward signs of affection as Father did. He was careful with these and did not show them often, but they were something magic for me, because I needed a response to my own feelings.

If my mother praised my progress, I thought she really did not understand it. If she reproached me for a trend toward untidiness, or about my vehemence, I thought she was being unfair, and it did not matter if only I learned and knew a lot. Most of the women I knew then had little education, like my mother, so I began to think that women were inferior to men, and it was appropriate for them to keep order and tend to the household. I, however, wanted to learn like a man so I did not have to be neat. I had a vague recollection of a woman of whom I had heard, who was a professor in Bologna, and this added to my total confusion.

My father was completely aware of this false concept of mine and the more reason he had to love and respect my mother, the more he opposed this bent. I still have a letter he sent me before I was even eight from Warsaw, where he had gone on business. I am citing it here to show how my father dealt with me in regard to this situation.

Warsaw, October 11, 1818

My dear Fanny:

I enjoyed your nice little letter, which arrived eight days ago; it was quite well written and not as short as the earlier one. I will bring home the cards you wanted, and that you just lost a baby tooth is good, since you must get new ones.

Just as your teeth grow or change, so will everything else about you: your opinion about what happens around you, your thoughts about this, your range of knowledge, actually, everything! If you want to be a good girl, you must be very careful to ensure that this change is always for the better.

In your opinion about what happens around you, you must always notice who those persons acting are and never forget that older people usually understand everything better than you. If you realize that occasionally you know something better than an older person, it is surely because the latter has not had the opportunity to learn this; otherwise she would obviously know it better than you, and you must therefore always be very modest.

You must never brag about what your parents are letting you learn now and later. You would hardly know anything if you did not have teachers and sufficient time to learn, while other children of your age must already do something to be useful to their parents, tend to younger children, or something of the sort. Your situation is very fortunate; you can use all your time to become a good and loving child.

I love you very much, my dear child, as I do all my children, and just because I love you, I want you all to be very good children. You are the oldest, you must set the proper example, and the others will follow your lead. Play with them as much as you can, and, since you are still a child yourself, this play time is also very useful and appropriate for you. I would be so happy to find out, when I return home, that you have always been well-behaved.

Greet Mr. Ulrich and your music teacher from me and give Heinrich and Klärchen a big kiss from your and their father. I shall write your two other brothers separate letters.

The letter reflects the manner of friendly seriousness with which our father always dealt with us (when he was not playing with us). The tone of his voice, though, the look in his eyes and his expression were so benevolent, so full of life and spirit, that we always lived in sunshine.

We very seldom received praise, real praise from him. As hard as I would try, with the excellent report cards I always brought home, I seldom heard anything but "That's good; that's the way I like it." Once, when strangers congratulated him on our hard work and ability, he said quietly, "They are our children, after all." He thus took all the credit for our talents. Actually, we really had the feeling that we had him to thank for the fact that we were gifted and diligent.

My father was not at all the man to encourage me in my whim for higher education and against the usual pursuits for women, especially since my untidiness had become rather an article of faith for me. I thought it was attractive not to bother about trifles, and gave my mother ceaseless worry in this matter; I have to thank her for my whole training here. Year after year she never tired of making me straighten up my book and toy shelves every evening, of reminding me of personal hygiene, and, as much as possible, holding me to those household chores which were supposed to train me to be attentive and orderly. The strict discipline in our school helped her; but there were suddenly complaints about me even there, involving bad handwriting, missing blotters, ink spots, and other slovenly behavior. Only when some new thought had driven the memory of the woman professor from Padua out of my mind did I finally return to being neat. I had consciously and intentionally, really, arrogantly, become untidy.

9

[Lewald survives an attack of scarlet fever and tells of two other important incidents of her childhood.]

They relate to the murder of Kotzebue[41] in 1819 and the ensuing persecution of the Jews throughout Germany.

After he left Russia, Kotzebue lived for a while in Königsberg. My uncle, Doctor Assur, was his personal physician. Before I began school, Uncle Assur often took me along in his carriage when he visited patients; since he usually stayed at Kotzebue's house chatting for a while, he let me roam about, and I was welcomed and given the sweets that were always on a table. Once, my uncle happened to mention to Kotzebue that I had received a fairly serious injury (because of the negligence of one of our maids); the state councillor (as he was called) sent me a lovely doll, and when I was well, I went with my uncle to thank him.

All my memories of Kotzebue were therefore pleasant. The arrangement of his beautiful house on the grounds of the Royal Garden next to the theater had a certain formality that I liked, although I did not know why. I also liked Kotzebue very much as I recall him, a slight elegant man, with his black pumps and silk stockings, his jabot and cuffs. Now he had been murdered, and there were those who said he deserved it, that he had been a traitor, and that Sand was a hero, whose name would be mentioned in the future with those of other martyrs and heroes.

The most fervent defenders of Sand at our house were a poet and a musician, Raphael Bock[42] and Gustav Wilde. They were both good friends of my parents, and, as I now realize, real romantics, each in his own way. Bock had gone to the university and later received the post of curator in the Wallenrodt Library, which he held until his death. He was a tall, lean man with a stoop. His sunken dark eyes looked out gloomily from a face framed by long black hair. Bock belonged to that group of the friends of my father's youth with whom he had gone through the romanticism of that age. My father had outgrown this; his legacy from Bock was his predeliction for the works of Zacharias Werner.[43] Another friend of his youth, Ludwig Sachs,[44] had given him the writings of Jakob Böhme,[45] and Father's affinity for Bock and Professor Sachs was his only souvenir of his own romanticism. He never interrupted Bock when the latter was praising the convicted Sand as a hero and proclaiming his deed as the beginning of the rebirth of the German fatherland. Father let him continue, as you let a lunatic rave on; Bock really had the unbridled fanaticism of a madman. Only when my piano teacher, Mr. Wiebe, a young blond handsome man, joined in the enthusiasm for Sand, did my father say reprovingly, "Don't be a fool, Sand just lost his head, and he is going to do so literally, poor devil!" Such simple utterances create a lasting impression on children.

On the other hand, Father excused Sand and vilified Kotzebue when talking with my uncle Assur, who was filled with passionate bitterness toward the man who had murdered his friend. I stood there and did not know what to think. The concepts of an enthusiastic patriotism and a sacrificial death for your country were quite familiar to me, as the deeds of Mucius Scaevola, Horatius Cocles, of Harmodius and Aristogeiton,[46] had made a strong impression. But I could imagine all that only in Roman times. That the state councillor, who had been so nice to me and looked like everyone else I knew, was supposed to be a traitor to his country, that a young man who had walked our streets like other hundreds of students could have saved our country by killing the councillor and himself—those ideas were beyond my grasp. In addition to the fact that the concept of an assassination or execution seemed terrible to me, it was bewildering that my father had expressed himself critically about Sand in one setting but had excused him in another. He summarily answered my questions about that difference by saying I understood nothing about the matter and should put it out of my mind; I had better things to think about. Easier said than done! Wherever we looked, there were pictures of Sand. In one he was depicted at the assassination with Kotzebue, leaning on the arm of a chair, collapsed, while women rushed into the room; on others, Sand was shown at the moment of his execution. You found his portrait in every shop window, on pipe bowls, snuff boxes, cups—in short, everywhere one could place it; so I remembered the incident for a long and confused time.

The persecution of the Jews made an even stronger impression on me. The older I became, the more I noticed how my family, my parents, and all their relatives, avoided speaking of the fact that we were Jews. Isolated, strange-sounding words that I knew were Jewish[47] were sometimes familiarly exchanged among them, especially if they did not want us children to understand what they were saying; but they did not like us to hear these words. They never used them in the presence of the servants or strangers, and any questions about them were ignored. On the other hand, it was made clear to me at school that I did not belong to the majority.

When I was seven and had been praised for a good examination, the religion teacher for the upper classes, Preacher Ebel,[48] laid his hands on my head in the presence of the other children and pronounced me "You pious daughter of Israel." This made me and my fellow pupils laugh, because we connected it directly to the patriarch and it therefore seemed very funny to us. But children, and especially little girls, are as curious as cats. Once they are onto a mystery, they cannot be diverted. For a few days my friends teased me and amused themselves with Ebel's pronouncement, but they also wanted to find out what they already actually knew: I was not a Christian. They asked me who had baptized me and where my parents attended church and whether I would continue with the confirmation lessons. I answered truthfully and, since these were basically good and well-behaved children, and we liked one another, they soon stopped, because they realized that they were hurting me. I retained a thorn in my heart, however, and this became sharper, because I was not invited to the homes of those girls in the class who were my best friends when they had playmates over. Two of them, twins, who had a big birthday party every year, once told me tearfully that they were not allowed to invite me and could not come to my house either, because their parents would not let them have anything to do with Jews. We were all three very touched by that, and I was very unhappy. A whole burden of sorrow, pain, and insult lay on my poor eight-year-old heart. I could not avoid speaking about it at home, although I was ashamed and did not want to hurt my parents as I had been hurt.

But at the next small party to which I was invited, the subject came up. My parents were quiet when I told them of my experience, but I could see how unpleasant it was for them. Even if I had many other playmates at school and in the family, as well as the two daughters of the English family that lived next door to us, it did not console me for the loss of my favorites. Furthermore, the events in our city added constant reminders that it was bad to be a Jew.

Individual Jews or Jewish families seen at that time on the street were called names. Rumors of hostile acts committed in South Germany against the Jews circulated throughout our family. Although my parents were careful not to speak of these problems at home, the discussions at my aunts' and uncles' were full of concern. I heard how people had broken windows and plundered Jewish homes in Frankfurt and Würzburg and how prominent men had been insulted and assaulted on the streets. Everyone feared for my mother's siblings in Hamburg, because hatred of Jews was very strong there and the populace was said to be very brutal. Since such times of confusion in the popular mind are epidemic and are spread in some unknown fashion, our servants had also heard the rumors. Because of the gossip in the nursery I came to believe that something terrible might be done to the Jews in Königsberg one day. My father and my mother both tried to assure me that none of this was true, that what I heard was all a foolish invention; but I learned that the windows had been broken at the home of a rich merchant on the Langgasse one evening. I knew that must be true, because we children were not allowed to sit on the window ledges as usual in the evenings when we visited my aunts who lived on the Langgasse and whose living room windows faced that street.[49]

From then on I had a complete realization of the oppression of the Jews and the injustices perpetrated against them. The concept that educated Jews had to be more enlightened and better than their persecutors was already being instilled in me. The Jews at that time were reproached for their proud self-esteem, which was deemed presumptuous and arrogant. They needed this very self-esteem, though, to be able to stand tall and raise their children to work hard and to participate in the eventual emancipation of all the people. Self-esteem is undoubtedly the best shield and surest weapon of the oppressed. Generally a nation and a people who accept and suffer unjust oppression, without rebelling against it, perish in ignominy because of their cowardly submission.

In Königsberg, the epidemic of persecution was relatively mild. It consisted mainly of name-calling; when people got tired of that, both sides got along fairly well again. Everything was back on the old track and we lived just as we had before the troubles. Not so many foreign visitors came to our house as in earlier years, but the old lavish lifestyle continued. Our family's only worry was the deteriorating health of my father's oldest brother, whose chronic illness had become a serious lung disease.

[Lewald's two-year-old brother dies on the same day her mother has a new baby boy.]

It was impossible to keep his death a secret, but we were not allowed to visit our mother or to view our dead brother. They told us he looked very distorted and tried to console us by telling us we had a new brother who would replace Heinrich.

That was no help at all. Father looked pale as death and the whole house seemed different to us. Strange men, all Jews, all dressed in black, came to Heinrich's room to say the prayers for the dead. Through the windows in the nursery door, we could see that a light was burning and a strange man was sitting by the bier in the room across the hall, where the small body lay. We remembered how drolly our little brother had driven his hoop with his stick; we imitated how he had yelled "Dog!" when he became angry. The third day came, the day on which he was to be buried.

It was early morning when the hearse pulled up to the door. We stood upstairs at the nursery window as the steps of the black men echoed along the stairs, which had been covered so that my mother would not hear any unusual noises. We saw Father climb into the coach and saw it drive off with our little brother. Overcome by grief as we all were, one of my brothers ran out of the room, down to my mother, and, crying, "Mother, Mother, they're taking our little Heinrich away!" flung himself on her bed.

The shock made my mother desperately ill. The newborn baby, which she was nursing, became the victim of her illness. He died eight days later and was carried in his cradle into the same room where the other small corpse had lain. He looked like a pretty wax image with his round cheeks and closed eyes, but the coldness of his hands and cheeks filled me with inexpressible terror. He was the first dead person I had ever seen.

[Lewald's uncle also dies, and her mother is sick for a long time with mastitis.]

On my ninth birthday, although still dangerously ill and despite her suffering, my mother had not forgotten the date. I had a cake and some other gifts in the nursery, and as always on this day, I had not gone to school. Around noon, she sent for me, as she always did with us children when the pain permitted. The room was darkened, the bed stood behind a green screen. She gestured for the nurse to leave and let me sit on her bed, while she held my hands. I was inexpressibly sad. After a while, she took a piece of paper from her nightstand. It contained a pair of golden earrings, which she gave me and asked me to put on. "Wear them forever in memory of me. And if I die—you are the oldest. Be good to the children and your father!"

I felt as if I had been struck by lightning. As sick as my mother had been, as much as I had worried about her, I had thought about her death, but I had not believed in it. Now this terrifying possibility threatened to become actual, and it momentarily devastated me. I could say nothing, I could not even cry, till Mother hugged and kissed me and I began sobbing so loudly that the nurse led me out.

From that hour on, although I could still play, I was no longer a child. I had a new relationship to my family and a new attitude toward them. I had always been told to provide a good example for my siblings; now I realized that the oldest daughter must be the pillar of the family. I gained a purpose for myself. The intention to be good and, where possible, useful, naturally took root in me.

10

[Lewald's father suffers financial reverses, and the family is forced to economize. They move to a large apartment in the suburbs, with a limited staff of servants. David Markus's business is no longer in the family home, but in the city.]

Just after we moved to the suburbs, I had been promoted to the second grade. I am not speaking too emphatically when I state that learning made me happier and happier the more we progressed. We lived very modestly then, and my parents had the concept that children, especially girls, should learn how to run a household at an early age. Strangers seldom came to the house now; I was usually at home if there was not a school friend's birthday or a visit to one of my aunts. My greatest joy was being able to read as much as I wanted in the evening.

My father gave me many travel books and works of history in adaptations for children. After the fairy-tale world alone palled, he added poetry, which I particularly loved. I frequently enjoyed the sound of the words more than their meaning.

[Lewald memorizes many poems, folk songs, short lyrics, and ballads by Goethe and Schiller, some set to music by Schubert; she reads the German classical dramas and Correggio, *by Oehlenschläger,[30] but no novels. She seldom has an opportunity to go to the theater.]*

I earned my first theater visit when I could read the notice of a comedy easily. It was a production of "Cinderella"; I so enjoyed the actual depiction of a story I knew very well that I was given a small Cinderella costume the next Christmas. I loved wearing it. Later my brothers and I were taken to see *The Magic Flute,* and we played Tamino and Pamina long afterwards, walking between two rows of chairs that represented fire and water. Those are my only theater memories of those days. In the following years my parents avoided all unnecessary expense; I did not go to the theater again for a long time.

My mother was an acute observer with a great talent for imitating others, a talent which, being the kind person she was, she never used for ridicule. I had inherited the concept of wit from her, but could not reproduce it in myself and therefore only had the dangerous ability of expressing it with a quick comical remark. At school, where I was always the youngest in my group, my fellow students found this habit quite charming; at home, however, I could not use it. My father forbade me such comments, and if I made one, he would admonish me to be silent with a quiet shaking of his head. I was soon finding myself repressed by all kinds of rules, because my parents thought I was too precocious and should remain the child I still was.

They set limits to my association with the older girls. They were not invited to our house. I did not get to go to the parties at my aunts' any more, and if my cousins and girlfriends visited me, we were given all sorts of scraps of cloth and remnants to make doll clothes, i.e., to make us play like children.

All this forced play did not achieve much. I had no objection to making doll clothes, since I actually produced something, and I was proud of having made them myself. But this was not really playing; even inventing and acting out stories did not last long. We were soon tired of playing our absent aunts and uncles and of having conversations about matters that basically bored us. We had to decide on the topics first so that they would be limited to what we understood. We always came back to being ourselves, which was probably the healthiest thing, and the next few years passed without my really knowing how they went. The time from my ninth to eleventh year is the one I least remember.

11

We lived in the suburbs for only two years. My father had started a new wine business, and since his warehouses were mainly on the Kneiphof Langgasse and Kaistrasse, he wanted his home to be nearby. None of us felt the regret we had felt when we left the old house on the Brodbänkenstrasse, although we were losing the garden and courtyard. We were near our father again, he was able to come home more often, and since we had a house on the quay, the view of the Pregel and the ships compensated for the garden and courtyard.

I had become a truly voracious reader in those two years, and every ploy my mother tried to wean me from the overwhelming desire to learn and the distaste for any kind of housework, from any kind of work that was not intellectual, failed. My mother was very worried about this; she felt personally rejected. I had to be forced to do anything with her, but I was ready and glad to do anything my father undertook with me in his few free hours. I realized this; I was very unhappy with myself when Mother constantly complained about me, I tortured myself with good intentions, but still I resisted; I was reluctant and sullen when I had a task and performed it halfheartedly and sloppily. Just as Mother had formerly encouraged my bent for learning, Father now forced me to do certain tasks around the house, which I did only with strong resentment. I realized that the housekeeper could basically perform these just as well and that I was only forced to do them because I did them reluctantly and badly. Few days passed without my mother commenting that there was nothing more obnoxious or useless than an educated impractical young woman, and that I had every prospect of becoming one. Few weeks went by without my father reminding me that we had little money and would have to do without the housekeeper soon; then I would have to help my mother, who was in poor health. I could do nothing then but reassure them, weeping, that I would do whatever they wanted properly if they would let me do it alone, but to run after me, to supervise me constantly, was unbearable. I had other and better things to do.

On the whole, I was completely right. Children quickly learn whether the chores required of them are useful and necessary, and perform these quite cheerfully, if they provide a feeling of importance. They have a pronounced drive to be helpful. But if these

chores are only given them as practice, they have just as pronounced a dislike, and my parents could not see that. It would
have been fun for me to dress my younger siblings or otherwise
take care of them. But to go through the rooms, to see if any items
were left lying there, to put away the sugar after afternoon coffee,
while the housekeeper cleared everything else, made me cross.
Since my mother always complained about my behavior in front
of my father, I became very resentful of her and finally believed,
without any reason, that she loved my oldest brother and my sister
(who remained the youngest for a long time, because of the deaths
of my two little brothers) much more than me.

Perhaps it would have been better if my father had stood up
for me once in a while. But there was no appeal against my mother's reproaches or his, and since I became very emotional in my
own defense and cried easily, which my father could not stand,
the scenes usually ended with these words of warning: "Look in
the mirror and see how ugly a sullen young lady looks. Stop crying, ask your mother for pardon and pull yourself together."

Then Father kissed me. I went to ask for her pardon, without
being at all convinced that I had done something wrong, my only
resolve being to break the habit of crying and to avoid being
scolded by him. My mother's scolding had gradually become
immaterial to me, because she repeated it so often and because it
was often quite out of proportion to the matter concerned
because of her poor health. I thought my mother was particularly
unjust, as no one at school had to reproach me any more for
untidiness or laziness.

I was eleven when we moved back to town and had been
promoted to the top grade. All the other girls were between thirteen and fifteen, and my ego was strengthened by the fact that all
my report cards lauded my exemplary zeal, attention, and order-
liness. I knew I was zealous and orderly, and that made me even
more sensitive to the rebukes at home. I was happy with my
teachers and happy with my father; only with my mother, who
lavished all her love on my siblings—and me as well—was I
unhappy. It is one of the mysteries that exist somehow in all families. I can honestly say that there was never a time in my life

when I did not love my mother with all my heart; but I think she never felt as compatible with me as with her other children, although she acknowledged, even overestimated, my good qualities. We could never really see eye to eye. Since Mother could sense this unbridgeable distance between us, she never responded to my occasional effusive demonstrations of affection as my father did. For example, I liked to kneel, especially in front of my parents when they sat on the sofa and talked, and to kiss them. My father let me kneel and responded with kisses; my mother asked me to get up. She was not as warm in the outward expression of her love as Father, and since I believed she loved me less, I felt rejected by her and attached more and more exclusively to my father.

Meanwhile, a change had taken place at our school. The previous year, the boys' and girls' schools had been separated and housed in different buildings. Now there was not a dormitory with the boys' school. Madame Ulrich was therefore much busier and had almost given up all her teaching in the girls' classes. Mademosielle Anna had left, and some new teachers had been hired, a Miss von Derschau and a Mademoiselle Kohlhoff, who both, like Mr. von Tippelskirch, our new history and German teacher, were disciples of Preacher Ebel, who had been our religion instructor for some time. (He was the same Ebel who later, as I have already mentioned, reached such unhappy notoriety in the Mucker trial.[51])

Even then people noticed the nature of the Ebelians: their devotion to church attendance, the almost Herrenhut-like[52] simplicity of the women's dress, the way they kept to themselves, their prayer meetings, their extensive charitable deeds. They were called Pietists, or "Muckers," even then, and I noticed that more and more of our teachers were Ebelians. Parents of Ulrich's students really trusted his good sense; they were also aware Ebel was an excellent teacher; his students could not have asked for better instruction than that offered by him and his followers.

Since the age of eight I had taken my religious instruction with Ebel and loved him personally with all my heart. When I entered his class, he had just lost a daughter my age; others told me that he accepted me with special warmth. He was a fairly tall, slender man, with a very serious and noble face. His large dark eyes, pale complexion and glossy black hair, which he wore parted and longer than usual, gave him a special appearance. He had delicate hands; when he folded them and raised his eyes in prayer, he really looked like an apostle. His voice was spellbinding, his sermons gripping. A listener always believed that Ebel spoke with the utmost sincerity and I am still convinced that that was his ruin.

In one of my class's earliest first lessons with him, he and I had an unusual discussion. Up till then, we had read the Kohlrausch's Bible stories[53] with Madame Ulrich. Ebel told them to us himself. Perhaps it seemed to me that this new method could be interrupted or seemed like a form of conversation—at any rate, when Ebel told us the story of the snake, I said loudly, "I don't believe that. Snakes can't talk!"

Ebel looked at me and asked, "Who told you that?" I replied, "No one. I know that on my own. No animal can talk." "Certainly not," answered Ebel, "if God doesn't let them."

I was silent. That was all Ebel probably intended at that moment, but my doubts were not satisfied, and I can never remember believing in any kind of miracle.

My unbelief did not, however, diminish my fondness for Ebel nor his for me. He was always kind and friendly to us all. His teaching was very simple, without any exaggeration; his moral teachings were completely suited to our level of understanding. He did not assume any desire for self-denial in us, since that was too mature a concept for us; he did not try to deprive us of the joy and pleasure in external things, as people accused him of doing. I recall the manner in which he later told us the story of Christ, especially the Passion, as a masterwork of fiery, animating eloquence. He made us all get involved, so that we felt an empathy with the persons of the story of Christ, rejoiced over the birth of the Christ child, loved a loving Jesus, and grieved over his death as if it had happened to a contemporary. Only when we had become humanly one with Jesus did Ebel raise him from the place where we could understand him to a higher sphere, to a divine human being and the son of God, transforming our human love to a worshipful reverence. It was the path that humanity itself has taken in its relationship to the crucified one; this subtle transition did not fail to affect us profoundly as well.

[Lewald gets three more little sisters, and her father opens a small wine restaurant in their house. Her mother, though still ailing, works both in the house and the restaurant.]

Although I never lacked for anything I would have missed, I was nevertheless acutely aware that we had little money, and my father made it a point not to let me forget it. In all my learning he emphasized that I had to put forth great effort: lessons cost money that he had worked hard to earn, and besides, I would soon have to teach my younger brothers and sisters. This was especially true for music, for which I had no great affinity.

I had begun lessons when I was seven and at first had made rapid progress. My teacher, Mr. Wiebe, whom I have already described as a true romantic and a very kind person, took pains with me, and I in turn was quite fond of him: I was actually in love with his beauty, a quality to which children are extraordinarily sensitive. He was already suffering from tuberculosis when our sessions began. The illness progressed so rapidly that he was often unable to leave his room for months in the winter; so I took my lessons at his home. He lived on the edge of the Royal Garden in an old house, in a charming first-floor apartment that his mother (just as attractive, with her snow-white hair, as her son) had decorated and maintained as a veritable little jewel box. Pictures hung everywhere, flowers always bloomed in the windows, the air was suffused with the scent of mignonette—even when it rained and stormed outside it was springtime at Mrs. Wiebe's.

Each time I left for a lesson my father gave me a voucher for the teacher and an additional eleven groschen, which I had to put into a small piggy bank. At the end of the month my mother withdrew six thalers from this bank to pay for that month's sixteen hours of instruction. This little ceremony was intended to drive home to me the value of the lessons.

Even intelligent children are capable of doing stupid things, and I have done stupid things my whole life long when I was being silly. So it was that I somehow fastened onto the notion that my blue voucher for the teacher was just as valuable as currency. One day, walking to a lesson, I realized I had lost the voucher. Finding myself at the Royal Garden, I recalled that I had still held the voucher at Princess Place, and began to retrace my steps to find the scrap of blue, searching for (or so I believed) the eleven groschen my father had worked so hard to earn. As I trudged on, light snow fell and lingered on the ground, and I wandered back and forth, shoveling the snow aside with my feet in a vain attempt to uncover the voucher, tears streaming from my eyes. Eventually Mr. Wiebe became worried that I had not appeared for my lesson—my parents usually notified him if I was unable to come—and Mrs. Wiebe, concerned that I might have had a mishap along the way, sent her maid to fetch me. Half-frozen, dissolved in tears, I finally arrived at those good people's home to sob out the story of my misfortune.

A year and a half later, early in the spring, Mr. Wiebe, that lovely, gentle man died. I acquired a new teacher in the person of a Mr. Thomas, who styled himself a disciple of the English school of music and who permitted me to play only pieces by Clementi and Field most of the time. He explained that a pretty and tasteful performance was worthless; what mattered was thorough preparation. Any young lady could learn on her own to play with great feeling. I had more facility than was good for me, according to Mr. Thomas, but now I was supposed to embark on the "serious" learning of music. If I would just have patience day after day and year after year, we should soon find out what could be achieved.

His speechifying, uttered with a certain bluntness, greatly impressed my parents, who understood nothing about music. And so, to begin seriously with a serious job, they immediately bought me Clementi's "Introduction to the Art of Playing the Piano," and a totally merciless regime of scales and études suddenly became my daily affliction. I have never endured more boring hours than this music instruction. I took my lessons on

Wednesdays and Saturdays from three until four o'clock. At this hour my teacher and I had just eaten dinner. I was resentful, Mr. Thomas sleepy; I plinked and plodded away indifferently at the requisite scales and etudes, he nodded off occasionally, reviving in periodic starts and fits to pass his thick fingers over the keys a few times and to criticize me forcefully. I always gave thanks to God when he put his voucher in his pocket, signaling the end of the lesson.

But daily practice was even worse than the twice-weekly lessons. Lack of insight leads to literal interpretation, and so my father insisted on following the letter of Mr. Thomas's concept: I was allowed to play absolutely nothing but my practice-book études during my daily prescribed hour of practice. Since I was able to memorize these easily, I devised the expedient of propping a book over my music score and reading merrily away to my heart's content during the entire hour while reeling off my scales and études. If anyone came into the room, I hid the book by sitting on it. I stubbornly carried on with this procedure year after year without being discovered. Indeed, I so perfected this sort of mechanical playing that I could eventually read away peacefully during longer pieces of music, once I had memorized them and mastered their execution. Need I say what meaningless playing was produced?

Baffling to me, I progressed under this regimen. I gradually achieved Mr. Thomas's approval; he gave me a Clementi sonata as a reward for my progress and was very satisfied with his instruction. Rumor had it that he had previously been a carpenter, and someone once made this remark in my presence: because Zelter had once been a mason, became a great musician, and happened to be uncouth, Mr. Thomas believed that, because he himself had been a carpenter and was crude, he too was a great musician. As attuned as I was to wit and cynicism, this chance remark completely destroyed any possibility of my respecting the hapless Mr. Thomas.

I had no faith in my teacher from then on, and without mentioning it to others, began on my own to practice pieces other than those assigned to me. Since I could not always obtain new scores, I began to long to compose something myself. When he was at our house, Mr. Wiebe had often extemporized at the piano well into twilight, and since that had been so pleasant for me, I wanted to give myself the pleasure I had felt then. But as often as I might sit down at the piano in the twilight, I could never produce the longed-for music; even the attempt to reproduce already familiar melodies failed almost completely. I could reproduce the melody line, if it was clear and without difficult transitions, but I could not find the appropriate notes on the piano for any variation or elaboration, although I could hear them clearly in my mind and sing them aloud. It was as if the notes suddenly vanished on their way from my brain to the keyboard. For my part, I became convinced even then that I had absolutely no musical talent, and my desire to play piano declined still more precipitously after this. I told my parents and even Mr. Thomas that I had no talent, told them what I had observed as evidence of this total lack of musical ability, and asked to be allowed to discontinue the music lessons.

My father paid no attention at all to my suggestion. In spite of his usual good sense, he still considered it a misconception to think a natural talent was needed for music-making. He told me how the Russian nobility had recruited the most magnificent orchestras from their serfs, and that, giving credence to the apt Russian proverb "What two eyes and two hands have created can be duplicated by two eyes and two hands," miracles could be accomplished with the proper perseverance. The more reluctant I was to learn to play, he believed, the better and more necessary it was to force myself to do so by overcoming my qualms. There was no virtue in applying myself diligently to schoolwork; after all, I enjoyed that. If, however, I would dutifully labor at music against my own inclinations, he would see that I was happy to follow his wishes; I would also be doing what was of benefit to me, and what many a Russian peasant had done upon his master's command.

These curious notions, so logical from my father's point of view, ignored the minor fact that the Russian princes probably picked out the most musically gifted among their slaves. Besides, he judged me quite unfairly, for my aversion to music-making rested solely upon my recognition of my own total lack of talent. I loved music, immensely enjoyed hearing others play it well, was very sensitive to it and had an excellent musical memory. Just my desire to exercise voluntarily my personal love of music, as well as my wish to create something of value myself, if only the smallest piece, should have spoken for me. But my family remained convinced I was too lazy to want to expend any effort. Since Mr. Thomas reinforced my father's convictions with the remark that I had great manual dexterity and a good delivery — and would surely find the satisfaction I was missing in a closer knowledge of the music — the episode ended with a third hour being added to my two hours of piano lessons and with even stricter supervision of my daily practice.

If I found it necessary to shorten my practice hours here and there by fifteen minutes during the week because of the pressure of household chores, I had to replace this time on Saturdays. If I went to a girlfriend's house without having practiced, I had to wake up an hour early the next morning and make up the missed time before going to school. I actually had to do without the sleep I needed just because my father believed music was something mechanical that anyone could learn. I have never understood why, with such a low regard for music, he felt it so important for me to acquire it. But he put all his energy into this endeavor and, long after I was grown up, long after I was quite certain about what I could and could not accomplish in this arena — and after he had allowed me almost absolute freedom in everything else — his command to pursue music still hovered over me. For twenty-five years, from my seventh to my thirty-second year, I had to take music lessons continuously and practice every day.[54] Almost a thousand thalers as well as an unjustifiable quantity of time were wasted on my musical education, and after I had learned to play Beethoven and Chopin, Hummel and Ries and others, I still held the same opinion I had stated at thirteen. Precisely because I loved music I was especially distressed by my inability to function freely and creatively in this field.

12

[Because of financial considerations, the Ulrich school is closed before Lewald's fourteenth birthday. She is devastated and considers it the end of her "happy childhood."]

Just like me, my parents saw my exit from school as starting a new stage in my life. They told me I was no longer a child, and since I had heretofore spent all my time exclusively on myself, it was now doubly my duty to spend it on others. I was prepared for that, but no one really knew what I was supposed to do. The few little tasks required by my mother did not fill the day. I had not yet acquired the skills of handwork that would be of use to the household, because I still worked anxiously and slowly. What I was supposed to start first was music, of course. Since I constantly complained that I did not understand what I was playing, and that I would like to learn the rules of music as I had those of languages, I received permission to participate in music lessons given by a certain Mr. von Zivet according to Logier's method in a sort of music school. I had hoped to learn the thorough-bass, but the school was not worth much and after two lessons a week all winter, I gave it up. The whole school finally dissolved, and the teacher vanished as suddenly as he had appeared.

The first weeks after my leaving school went by with all kinds of trial tasks. Mother did not know how to use me properly; I roamed around the house aimlessly until I found a book, sat down in a corner, and read. That was not what my father intended, and one fine morning before the first of October, he surprised me with the following schedule, which he had made up himself. I have often looked at it since with smiling tenderness and I therefore include the original.

Daily Schedule
for
Fanny Markus

Drafted the end of September, valid until next season or until other lessons are added.

GENERAL RULES

Rising in the mornings latest at 7:00, so dressing will be completed by 7:30.

Monday

8:00–9:00	Piano practice. Practice of new pieces.
9:00–12:00	Handwork, usually sewing and knitting.
12:00–1:00	Reviewing old text books: i.e., French, geography, history, German, grammar, etc.
1:00–2:30	Rest and dinner.
2:30–5:00	Handwork as above.
5:00–6:00	Piano lesson with Mr. Thomas.
6:00–7:00	Writing practice.

Tuesday

8:00–9:00	Practice of new piano pieces.
9:00–10:00	Domestic handwork.
10:00–12:00	Instructions in thorough-bass.
12:00–1:00	Like Monday.
1:00–2:30	ditto.
2:30–5:00	ditto.
5:00–6:00	Practice of old piano pieces.
6:00–7:00	Writing practice as on Monday.

Wednesday like Monday; from 5:00 to 6:00 practice of old music pieces on the piano.

Thursday, Friday, and Saturday like the first three days of the week.

Sunday is completely at Fanny's disposal except for piano practice from 8:00 to 9:00; but lessons unnecessarily missed during the week must be made up, and the hours not spent at the piano because of going out or visits replaced exactly.

Fanny will try, by following this schedule precisely and otherwise demonstrating good behavior, to prove to her parents that she deserves further lessons and to be given good books by her father to read in her leisure hours.

Visits outside the house will occur once, and, only upon exceptional occasions, twice a week.

This schedule, with its curt commands, seemed neither unusual nor harsh to me. I had been accustomed to a specific schedule and discipline from childhood on, and I am sure the plan was a relief for my mother as well as myself. It took care of the problem of what to do with me and removed my unease with her changing attempts to occupy me. But this winter was extremely monotonous for me.

Five hours every day I sat at a specific place at the window of the living room and learned to darn stockings, repair linens, and try my hand at tailoring and other work. Two hours I spent at the piano, an hour I bored myself with the contents of my old school books, which I already knew by heart from A to Z, and another hour I copied poems to improve my handwriting. In between I walked from the kitchen to the dining room and from the living room to the nursery. I watched my three youngest siblings now and then and had the depressing feeling at night of not having accomplished anything all day. I bitterly envied my brothers, who went quietly to their Gymnasium, did their lessons, and did not spend nearly the time on them I did on mine. Their whole existence seemed preferable to mine, and with the longing for school, the desire to become a teacher arose in me, so I could have a career in which I would not be constantly worrying about how to spend my time.

I would not have dared to express this idea to my parents, for it would have strengthened my mother's concept that I did not have the proper feminine sense for domesticity and the family, that I had more brains than heart, and that my whole trend toward intellectual pursuits was a misfortune for both of us. If she had been consistent in this attitude, it would have been the end of this idea for me. But while she reproached me about it one day, she would show delight in my talent and knowledge the next. My father usually was justified in having great confidence in her keen powers of observation, and he now wanted to make me domestic and "feminine" with his somewhat stubborn dogmatism. It was my mother, on the other hand, who, moved by compassion, tried to get me more freedom. I was really very unhappy that winter, but did not want to complain to my parents, because they were doing this out of love and according to what they thought was best for me. My mother was not conscious of her own jealousy toward my whole development; my father realized even less how she felt. I did not even see the weakness in my mother then. I only believed, with all sorts of other unreasonable ideas, that she loved me less than my siblings. As in most families, no one was perceptive enough to see where the real problem lay in the relationship between me and my mother. My father arrived at the truth many years later, but the rest of the family still thought our conflicts were my fault. No one wanted to see how much injustice, how many serious wounds had been inflicted unwittingly on me by my mother just in those years where my heart had still been so soft, my resistance so weak, that I could not express my feelings, let alone explain myself or understand how to defend myself against any psychological damage.

Young people are more vunerable the more sensitive and defenseless they are. Every blow to the heart forces them back into themselves and accustoms them to a lonely inner life. Such insularity can become quite dangerous for certain natures, even though it may be healthy for tougher types. As far as jealousy of parents of the better education of their children—a problem that is more common than people realize—I have tried to depict that literarily in one of my novels, *Wandlungen*,[55] in the characters of old Brand and his son.

But it was not only with my mother but with my siblings as well that I had lost the old carefree relationship of my childhood. Usually, girls develop far earlier than boys, and I had developed more rapidly than usual. I had as completely outgrown my ten- and twelve-year-old brothers as I had my eight-year-old sister. My three little sisters still gave my mother much work at home, and she was pregnant for the tenth time. Her health was poor. Despite all her worries, though, she had arranged dancing lessons for me that winter, which took place in turn at our house and those of the parents of three other girls. Nevertheless, I felt the pressure of family problems. But this was another matter I did not dare mention, and without the tender friendship I had with one of my former schoolmates, I would have been desperately unhappy at this time.

This friendship had begun in the fourth grade. We had attended school together for almost four years and remained close friends throughout our youth, until our different religious persuasions finally separated us.

Mathilde was the daughter of a Major von Derschau and three years older than I. She had lost her father at an early age. Her mother, a woman of excellent character and masculine uprightness and veracity, held a position in a local women's religious foundation. Mrs. von Derschau lived on a moderate pension and the interest from a small inheritance. She and her oldest daughter, who also resided at the foundation and had been one of the teachers at our school, both belonged to Ebel's congregation, but a certain robustness of their natures protected them from the extreme other-worldliness of his other adherents. Mrs. von Derschau's open mind always connected to life and the world around her without prejudice. Even her preference for literature was not influenced by her later religious inclinations. She busied herself with the Bible and didactic writings, but she did not hesitate to go to performances of her favorite play, *Intrigue and Love*.[56] After she had perused her hymnal, she liked to listen as we read aloud poems by Schiller or other writers, which were appropriate to our age and our penchant for the sentimental and pathetic.

Mathilde was thirteen when I met her. She had been attending another school, and since learning was not her strong point at the time, had difficulty, despite her other excellent qualities, in adjusting to the discipline and seriousness of our institution. Full of goodness and cheerfulness, always ready to laugh, with her already well-developed figure, her large eyes, and her glorious light brown hair, which could not be restrained by a conventional hairdo, she gave the impression of a charming and lovable girl. Her whole person, her arms and hands, were beautiful; her teeth, which her laughing mouth constantly revealed, were incomparable. In contrast to me, who was never good at any physical exercise but dancing, she excelled in all athletic games. It was a pleasure to see her run, leap, throw a ball, or climb. What brought us both together was Mathilde's wish to have help with her lessons. We soon formed a strong attachment and loved being together.

Mathilde was as much at home with my family as I; similarly, I was very comfortable in her mother's small rooms. Although we were in straitened circumstances, she found more life and distraction in my home than hers, and I, who always lived in a swarm of children, found something very appealing about Mathilde and the quiet of the remote churchyard and her mother's little rooms. We would work at a table, while her mother, dressed in her inevitable black wool frock and her modest white cap, sat knitting beside us. We drew from nature or slipped into Mathilde's sister's room, when she was out, to tell each other everything that we knew or thought.

We liked to share whatever we had. If one of us received something from our parents, the other asked for something similar, if possible, and since both families had to limit their purchases to essentials, our wishes were appropriately modest. If we could discuss it in advance, we dressed alike, and the first verses we wrote when I was twelve were about the bourré silk shawls our parents had given us, with which we felt as rich as princesses.

It was a special treat from when we finished all our work on Saturday afternoon to Monday morning at either her house or mine. It was part of the pleasure of being together that it was basically uncomfortable at the foundation house, that everything was sparse, that we had to suffer small inconveniences for one another, because self-sacrifice is one of the elements of youthful friendships.

When I was at Mathilde's on Sundays I would go with her and her mother to Ebel's church. We sat together, sang from the same hymnal, listened to the same sermon of our mutual teacher. I believe that it was I who in those days found the greatest exaltation. On summer afternoons, we took walks with her mother, frequently visiting the grave of a daughter who had died as a young woman. On those summer evenings we played on the field used during the day for bleaching clothes with the other children who lived at the foundation. Among them, our favorite companions were the four sons of the widow of an attorney, Mrs. Richelot, who were all older than we. Several of them were already in the upper classes of a Gymnasium.

I had brought this friendship home from school with me; the older we got, the more important and devoted we became to each other. Mathilde's cheerfulness and youthfulness were an essential supplement for me, while my participation in serious matters, my joy in reading benefitted her. Although I began to consider myself an adult even earlier than would have otherwise occurred because of my relationship to an older girl, she was so modest and basically healthy that I could have found no better friend in the whole world. She hated all brooding, all reflection; melancholic emotions were a burden to her, and by nature she was nowhere as out of place as with her own family. Beside her serious mother, beside her churchgoing, contemplative sister, she always looked like a threatened bird. With them she maintained an anxious silence. The life would go out of her. Only at the home of her brother, who was married to a beautiful and lively woman, or at our house, did she breathe freely and happily.

Everyone in our family loved her. Her personality was much closer to my mother's than to mine. My father sometimes chided her because she laughed too much and too loud, which he did not like. But she would only break into further laughter on hearing the cry we heard so often, "Don't laugh so stupidly, don't laugh so much, that's indecent!" and could not stop, till we were sent to our room. Finally Father had to laugh himself about the good humor and childishness with which the beautiful adolescent girl accepted his scoldings. We all missed Mathilde if she could not visit that week.

The two of us only had one problem, the unhappy fact that she went without me to her religious instructions and would be confirmed without me, because I was not a Christian. My mother shared my distress. I had heard her state a thousand times that she regretted, out of regard for her family, not having converted to Christianity, when she encountered so many obstacles to her marriage; a thousand times I had heard her complain that she did not really belong to any church or religious denomination and that we, as she put it, were growing up without a proper religion.

On Sunday and other Christian holidays, it hurt her to see families go to church with their children, because she did not have this edification. I have no doubt that my mother would have considered it the greatest gift if my father had decided in that period of our lives to convert to Christianity. It would have given her spiritual support and stability to have had a positive religion and guidance from a higher world to look up to.

I doubt that she ever expressed such a desire to convert to my father. She probably did not realize how much she wanted it. But for us, she constantly reiterated the wish to let us become Christians, for which she gave two reasons. On the one hand, she told our father that it was sad for us to dangle between two religions. We knew nothing about Judaism, we had received Christian religious instruction in school, we had more connection, therefore, with Christianity, and it would be a blessing for us to be told what to believe, because a person should have a faith. On the other, she presented the fact that we would have the same split in our day-to-day lives as in our religious ones. She did not want to let us associate with the Jewish families; the prominent Christian families, however, rejected Jews just as they had ten years previously. A large part of society and a number of advantages were closed off to the Jews. The thought of knowing we would be in such a painful position as Jews all our lives was difficult for her. She was convinced it would have made me happy to go to religious instructions with Mathilde, and since my father's brothers and sister in Breslau and their families had already converted long ago, she would have considered it a blessing if he would have chosen the same way for his own family.

At this time she was not to get her wish. My father felt not the slightest need for religious edification or church affiliation. He was not interested in belonging to anything not open to him. If he may have wanted to convert out of love for my mother, he also saw the disadvantage because of his business affairs, which brought him in constant contact with orthodox Polish Jews. So nothing remained for us for the time being but to deal with our faith and our religious needs as best we could.

We had little of religion at home. We said a paternoster[57] in the evenings out of habit, and that was it. My father usually avoided discussions of religion with the remark that such casual conversations led nowhere and were not subjects for polite society. If there were mentions of the nature of man or the immortali-

ty of the soul, my father would put an end to them by saying that
it was useless to speculate about matters about which we could
know nothing and foolish to discuss a state that we would only
reach when all our abilities to perceive and evaluate were gone.
Every moment used to speculate about the hereafter was stolen
from the present. An "I have" was worth twice a thousand "If I
had's"; since action was of the essence, you should do your own
job properly and not worry about the hereafter. Man gained spiritual immortality from his own deeds, and earthly immortality
from his children. The Old Testament said nothing about the possibility of life after death; that is why the Jews laid such great
emphasis on an early marriage and a large progeny, so that their
memory would live on after their death.

Beside this rational and practical concept of the nature of
mankind and immortality, which was very illuminating for me, I
had constructed my own religious world. Although my father's
ideas were very clear and reasonable to me, they did not satisfy
the part of my being that found nourishment in Christianity. The
great doctrine of love and denial of self in Christianity lured me;
Ebel's teaching, added to that of the previous lengthier one by
Mr. von Tippelskirch, had roused in me the longing for an ideal
for which I had to have a model. Neither the historical figures of
ancient times nor of more recent history offered me what I wanted. I could admire the deeds, the courage, the strength of purpose, and the devotion of such heroes, but they did not embody
the ideal love and striving for self-fulfillment I longed for. Even if
my teachers had not already told me of Christ, my present association with the Derschau family would have sufficed to make
Christ, the All-Loving, who had sacrificed himself for mankind,
my ideal.

It was not the Son of God I venerated, because I had always
rejected the idea of the only begotten son of God as I had the
incarnation of the Greek gods. It was the human Jesus Christ,
the Saviour born of my people, the historical Christ, whom I
revered and whom I wished to emulate, without actually knowing the name of this doctrine or anything about the disputes aris-
ing from it. Where I lived and in the circumstances in which I

grew up, neither a particularly sharp intelligence nor a special gift for divination was required to arrive at a point of view that was in the air anyway.

Since I was accustomed to use my reasoning ability from early on, I was not prepared to believe unquestioningly. I cannot remember ever having believed in a miracle, in having anything but a mythological impression of Christian miracles. Every now and then I tried to consider them at face value, but if I did not succeed, I told myself that all ancient peoples had believed in miracles, and that was that, something now past. The stories of the Old Testament had a great attraction for me, with the adventuresome journeys and deeds of their people and heroes. The travels of the Jews through the wilderness, the episode of Joseph and his brothers, of Saul and David and Jonathan, the stories of Ruth and Esther, the splendor of the Ark and the Temple in Jerusalem, the betrayal of Absalom, and the story of the heroic Maccabeees had occupied my imagination greatly in their time, until Christ gained victory over them all and became my ideal.

Later, when I was about sixteen or seventeen, the reading of Goethe's Easter scene in *Faust* took the place of my own inner Easter cult. I had read *Faust* when I went to school, and it had become part of my life since then, something from which I gained more and more as I matured. When my brothers grew older, we celebrated a kind of spiritual spring festival by reading the final scene of the first act of *Faust* together and revived our hearts with the joyous "Christ is risen!"

Most of my life I preferred the stories of the Bible to those of Homer, in which the repetition of the adjectives and the events bored me. I was revolted by the descriptions of murder and battle; I recall that my father had to force me to read and recite to him a certain assignment from the *Iliad* every day. He became very annoyed once about the stubbornness with which I asserted that it made no difference to me if they thrust the spear through one man's teeth or another's body. They were just committing murder for no good reason whatsoever. It was most unreasonable that two nations should fight to the death and destroy a city just because a woman had run away from her husband—I could not admire that.

Only an occasional story like that of Hector and Andromache kept the *Iliað* from being totally abhorrent. Killing and dying, without the idea of dying for mankind, were intolerable.

I was always scolded severely for such utterances, which my father considered willfulness and rejected completely, but I could not suppress them, because that is the way I felt. I could not pretend admiration for something that was antithetical to my very essence. It was part of my aversion to the inhuman, and a forerunner of the dislike I later had for representations of the torments in Dante's *Inferno* and all paintings of martyrs. Even now I have to make myself look at the Laokoon group[58]: it has always consoled me that Apollo Belvedere is his neighbor at the Vatican. I will stand looking at the Apollo, while my friends are busily studying Laokoon.

13

A few weeks after my fourteenth birthday, my parents' last child was born, and this event marked my entrance into practical life.

For my mother's previous confinements, a housekeeper had been hired; this time I was to perform this function, and I assumed it with trepidation. My mother had instructed me in the necessary tasks, but she was constantly afraid I would not be able to meet my obligations. I was therefore doubly afraid when she went into labor one morning and I was faced with my fears for her in the midst of a large family, in the midst of a household, in which everyone was accustomed to the security and experience of a mature woman, and in which I was suddenly supposed to handle everything.

My father brought the basket of housekeys out of my parents' bedroom, and although he was also worried, he said encouragingly, "Be brave! If God gives someone a task, He also gives them understanding. Above all, keep the children quiet." Then he kissed me on the forehead and I became confident that it would work, because it had to work. And it did work, although the running of such a household was no easy task for me then.

At that time our household comprised seventeen people; my parents, eight children, of whom the youngest four were scarcely a year apart and therefore completely dependent, three clerks, an apprentice, a cook, the old nanny (who had returned to us for the care of my little sisters), and a baby nurse. This was a group that had many needs and was all the more difficult to take care of since there was a certain system in middle-class households forced like ours to economize that cannot be used in large cities and probably is not even current in Königsberg any more. The idea seemed very practical—to buy in quantity where the low cost of space made storing provisions possible—but was undermined by the impractical desire to make everything you could yourself at home. You acted as if you lived in the country, but had all the inconveniences a farm wife suffers in being far from town, while paying city wages and prices for servants and food.

An average Königsberg family put up ten or twenty bushels of potatoes in its cellar in the fall. Several bushels of fruit were peeled and laid out to dry by the baker. The amount of vegetables required for the whole year were obtained in the fall, and stored, according to their type, in beds of coarse sand in the cellars. In the same way, whole barrels of sauerkraut and pickles and pots full of beets and marinated herrings were prepared, not to mention the finer fruits and the jellies and fruit juices necessary in case of illness. Even chamomile, elderberries, and calamus were purchased in the summer from the herb gatherers for such purposes and stored for the winter.

But that was not enough. Every week the rye bread dough had to be baked. If there was a birthday or holiday, the cakes were baked at home. We bought the milk as it came from the cow, to skim off the cream ourselves; the beer came in barrels and we drew it off into bottles. If you wanted sausage, you made it yourself, once a year, at home; hams and all kinds of corned and smoked meats were considered better if they were not bought from the butcher. To have a proper selection, you bought half a mutton, calf, or pig according to the season. I need not even mention that, with those ideas, all poultry was fattened at home, plucked at home, that we collected and stripped the feathers ourselves, and that naturally everything possible was knitted, sewn, and tailored at home. The fad for self-fabrication went so far that daughters were not only instructed in tailoring and millenery, but that, for a while, we even had shoemakers come to the families, so we could learn to cobble and be able to make women's and children's shoes at home.

There was certainly a charm in having such a household. There was a pleasure in being so well-prepared, if you had the means to do so. The full storage rooms and cellars with their stoneware jars, barrels, crates, and drawers were lovely to behold. The dried fruit on strings, the marjoram and onions, along with the spices, gave the storeroom a delicious odor. The sprouting vegetables in the cellars were wonderful. You had a comfortable feeling when everything was gathered up. Now winter could come! You would not be embarrassed in the least by any unexpected guest. As everywhere when you have worked extra hard, you were inclined to want some reward for it; and for the children, there was much pleasure in the baking and fruit-drying, preserving and sausage-making, which we all looked forward to. The men, however, had to pay out more money than usual for this kind of economy, the women were often taxed beyond their strength, and no one who helped out, as we all did, had much time to think of anything but the household and the family.

It was obvious that a middle-class Königsberg family had to have much room, that cellars, attics, closets, and a courtyard were indispensable, and that many servants were required. You must add to that the fanatical cleanliness of my fellow Prussians, for whom it was dogma to scrub every room weekly, a benefit that was bestowed on floors and stairs twice a week. The mirrors and even the windows (if the cold permitted) were polished weekly, and the rooms wiped down with a damp cloth every morning and swept and dusted after every meal if possible. Added to the necessary cleaning up of the kitchen, the pantries, and the multitudinous dishes used for all these supplies, this all amounted to a never-ending labor and activity and an atmosphere of moist cleanliness in which orchids or water fowl, depending on the season, would have been more at home than we poor human beings.

As busy as the women were, the maidservants had it even worse, and all of them complained about it at times. But any housewife of that period—we are speaking of a generation ago—who would have dared to lighten her burden, who would have bought her bread from the baker, her dried fruit from a grocer, her processed meats from a butcher, would have been considered a heretic, a criminal, who was shirking her domestic duties. It would have permanently damaged her reputation and done irretrievable harm to the happiness of her marriage and her family.

People always stated, with some accuracy, that everything not done at home was shoddier and more expensive. But they did not consider the costs of a large residence, servants, heating, and the value of the time expended on these questionable activities in the house. They also forgot that their prejudices made it impossible for the merchants to depend on a large volume of sales, thus making all price competition impossible. We find the same problem today, thirty years later, when we want to explain to the majority of women that it is not practical for lower-income families to waste fuel and the services of a maid on a meager lunch.[59] I was certainly not convinced of the efficacy of the Königsberg system while I kept house at my parents' home. There is nothing more limited and obstinate than women who withdraw behind the walls of sanctified custom instead of using their good sense. They make custom a matter of showing their sensibility and concern for their family, and their prejudices become the symbol of family happiness, a holy shrine of social order. As much as I like to take care of my own home and hearth now, I am happy that the kitchen stove is not an essential part of our family happiness and the cooking spoon in the housewife's hand is not a symbol of her dignity, a veritable scepter, without which a woman cannot assert and fulfill her role as spouse, mother, and housewife.

I have always taken pleasure in overcoming obstacles I felt capable of handling. Particularly at this time I was helped by ambition and eagerness, and I felt cheerful and confident. This attitude, which I had developed after my youngest sister was born and my mother was out of danger, was accompanied by the happiness of being able to care for my mother, of keeping my father, siblings, and other members of the household from being deprived of any necessities, and of proving to my parents that I was not impractical and useless.

I approached my new job with considerable trepidation, but after the first eight days I felt fresher and happier than ever before, although my tasks were spiritually and physically difficult for me. My father teased me later about finding me in front of the big linen closet in tears because, even standing on a chair, I could not lift the heavy tablecloth. I did not want to call for help, for that would have revealed my weakness and ineptitude to the servants. I was fourteen years old.

But I gained strength—and I had finally rid myself of that boring schedule! My mother was satisfied with me, my father took pleasure in my success, and my little sisters, who often annoyed me despite my love for them, became much dearer to me since they were the objects of my care and efforts.

In addition, it was spring. The bay sparkled under our windows and was reflected in the ceiling, ships came and went, and we could bring the first bluebells and cowslips to my mother's bed and hang garlands of cut calamus and fir shoots around the wardrobes and chairs, since she loved their odor. The baby in her cradle wore the little cap and jacket I had made for her before she was born. I will always remember that spring with happiness, and with good reason: for the first time I was enjoying the pleasure of true charity, the strengthening that independent action gives us along with its responsibility.

I felt like a grown woman, and, as though my physical powers were maturing along with this realization, I began to grow quickly, became stronger, gained color, and soon looked, as was the expression in Königsberg, "complete." One could no longer force me into the role of a half-grown girl, which I had always found uncomfortable, like all halfway matters.

The summer which followed was quite as pleasant. My tasks at home diminished greatly as my mother grew stronger, although my father had wanted me to continue. It would have been better for both her and me—preserved her strength and developed and increased my abilities. But Mother found her own strength and her true element in running the house and could not bear the thought of losing her one superiority over me, if I were to continue my independent stewardship. As soon as she was able, she took over the reins. She was used to checking everything she asked anyone to do, just to make sure it was done properly. I soon lost any pleasure in doing anything around the house because I could not avoid thinking that she might as well have done it herself. This anxious mistrust in the performance of others is a very common failing in men as well as women, and the reason for it is the belief in the unreachable excellence of your own achievements. All the complaints about the bungling and unreliability of inferiors, which you so often hear, are based on this belief. It seems so natural for anyone in charge of a project to issue clear orders, depend on the efforts of your subordinates, and make them responsible for work poorly done or neglected. Too few people understand this, because jealousy usually prevents them from considering themselves dispensable.

If I had had the insight and patience at fourteen that I possessed twenty years later, I would have helped voluntarily everywhere I could have been of use, without requiring any acknowledgment. But back then I considered my little tasks, which really were only fetching and carrying, a waste of time. I did not want to do anything without results, and because I had to do these petty chores anyway, I did them reluctantly. My mother was constantly complaining, and with good cause, that I was peevish as soon as I had to do something. I did not then and still do not feel as culpable as she considered me. It just made the matter worse that my father again, as he had done previously, supported my mother in her accusations, while I knew that he was actually on my side in his heart.

This caused a kind of quiet complicity between me and my father which hurt my mother and put her in a worse mood than ever, since she soon sensed it. She knew how much my father loved me; she loved me very much, too, but the realization he had a part of his nature with which she was not compatible and that I could and would fill this gap eventually made her unhappy. It gave her behavior toward me an irritability that I found unfair, one which finally clouded my relationship with my mother all my youth (really, all my life), while my five younger sisters and my brothers could and did love her unconditionally.

When I was having fun, when I showed pleasure with pastimes, dressing up, and parties, Mother was always satisfied with me. She found me feminine and natural then, and I could have spared both of us many unhappy hours if I had been clever or devious enough to conceal from her the serious side of my nature, which she considered "masculine and uncouth."

Despite these conflicts with my mother, after running the household I gained more freedom to chose my own activities — provided I first completed my sewing and knitting chores for the family and practiced my music. I did not have to study the "old school books" at certain hours, I could read any works of history or other subjects that I could find in my spare time, and I had the same free choice among Scott's novels,⁶⁰ which my father was reading at the same time and with the same suspense.

Now that we were living in the Kneiphof again and I was permitted to go out by myself, I often visited my youngest aunt, my father's sister, who had been married against her will to a wealthy but uneducated merchant and who was very unhappy. She was as intelligent as she was good and sensitive, and she loved poetry. She had an excellent library, from which she let me make my own choice of what to read to her when I visited, so I liked to go there. My memory of her is associated with many poetic experiences of that time.

Among Goethe's dramas, my father especially liked *The Natural Daughter*.⁶¹ It was therefore one of the first I read; as a matter of fact, I had read most of it aloud to him. He had pointed out the lofty and simple beauty of the language, which I sensed myself, but he had also emphasized the plot and the denouement and used the character of Eugenie as an example of a person who could both make decisions, but also subordinate herself — qualities and virtues doubly important in women.

This play left me totally cold. The long conversations, all

dealing with the fact that an unfortunate girl had been married off against her will, did not attract me. Young and mature people have very different ideals, and young people (luckily) do not understand about moral compromises. I felt only aversion for my father's ideal of femininity, for Eugenie and her resigned attitude. I would have found it far more natural for her to leave her homeland than to marry without love because of the uncertain possibility that she might one day be able to help the relatives who had rejected her.

When I told my father that, he reproached me by saying that he should not have let me read the drama, because I obviously was not mature enough to understand it. But I would see its value when I became older, and in the meantime, he would save himself an explanation. This was obviously intended to arouse my curiosity and to make me want to read the work again. But when I did this, I disliked it even more, so his plan failed. And the secret thought that my father's fondness for Eugenie was based on his belief that every woman should marry, and that the more educated a woman was the more readily she could adapt to an unsuitable or undesired marriage, made me loathe the resignation of that illegitimate daughter even more.

One day, when I was at my aunt's, I turned the conversation to Eugenie and to the fact that my father found her and her decision so noble. My aunt listened to me with her sad, friendly face and then said briefly, "Don't let them talk you into that. They only say it because it's convenient for them."

I had already expected to hear this, but my aunt stopped suddenly as her husband entered, unpleasant equally in appearance, speech, and manner, and demanded something of her. After he left, she said, "It's nonsense to think that a woman can get accustomed to something which is repulsive to her. Have I become used to my fate? I knew I was signing my death warrant when I married, and I told them so. But they all talked me into it, all of them — and now they all pity me!"

She said that with a bitterness completely alien to her, and the accusation she uttered with her words against her much beloved brothers, against my dead uncle, and against my father,

who all had forced her into marriage with their persuasive arguments, made me very sad. I was even more shocked by this sudden clear view of my aunt's unhappiness, which had been no
secret, although she bore it patiently. The thought that someone
could force me into a similar situation completely dismayed me.

On that day when I was fifteen I resolved firmly that I would
never be persuaded to marry anyone, except someone I was certain I loved. On that day I first realized fully that a child has certain rights in respect to its parents, that I had my own innate
independence, even from my father's wishes, something I never
would have dared to believe before; and my ideas extended, as if
with a magic stroke, beyond the parameter of home and family,
far out into my own future and a wide world.

The conviction that is the basis of the plots of many of my
novels arose in that hour. This is why recollections of your childhood and youth are so important; they have hidden within them
the seeds which later ripen into and form the convictions and
character of the adult. The world and our relationships with others not only develop new characteristics in us but enhance and
strengthen those already created and present when we leave our
childhood.

14

A fast coach runner was seen in Königsberg that summer. My
parents told us that in earlier times, all the important families had
runners in front of their coaches, who hurried ahead of them.
Although my father decried this luxury so demeaning to human
beings, he decided to take all of us to see the demonstration to get
an idea of how fast a man could run.

To watch this we took an omnibus wagon to an inn on the
Bülow Gute Kalgen, which was on the main road, approximately
halfway along the course the runner was to take. There was a
crowd of all sorts of people in front of the inn, and since the students made their presence felt considerably in Königsberg then,
some of them were also present on horseback or in carriages.

Soon some officers accompanying the runner came riding from the direction of the city, and among them you could see a scrawny, average-sized young man, dressed in a fluttering page's uniform of faded pale blue and white satin, running by quick as an arrow, while the wind blew the tall feathers on his beret back and forth. I was standing with the others, including Mathilde, who usually came with us on such occasions, in front of the inn door. When the cry of the crowd announced the arrival of the runner, I stepped up onto the base of one of the wooden pillars supporting the balcony of the second floor. I had hardly reached my post, when one of the group of students turned around, and, after seeing me, said to a companion: "That girl has the loveliest eyes. She's going to be a real beauty some day!"

My face aflame with inexpressible pleasure, not shame, I slipped off my perch. That runner could have come by ten times; they—my father and another man—could have discussed even more vigorously whether it was right to permit such exhibitions as the run. It did not matter to me at that moment. The idea that someone thought I was pretty, the possibility that I could become even prettier, made me very happy. As a child, I had been teased at school because I was so pale and thin, and I always felt unattractive next to Mathilde. I had finally decided, albeit with a heavy heart, that I would have to find approval through intellectual accomplishments, but my deepest longing was to be tall, slender and beautiful like the heroines of the books I was reading, although there was not the slightest prospect of that.

The young student who brought me those glad tidings and now lives as a well-respected and hardworking man on his estate in distant Masuria, obviously had no idea what a wonderful thing he did for me that afternoon with his comment. He freed me from the pedantry threatening to develop in me because of my seriousness. At that moment, I would have traded a library full of books for a becoming straw hat, and all my small store of knowledge for the pleasure of hearing him say once more that I could become pretty.

The mood stayed with me and made me very happy. I no longer had an excessive drive to learn; I only wanted to please.

Instead of the intellectual zeal I had had as a child, the longing for a doctorate and a professorship in Bologna, I now had the wish to enter the world as soon as possible, that is, go to a ball—but more precisely, to find satisfaction for my newly aroused vanity. Actually, though, at that time there was no question of a ball, because my father thought I was too young. Luckily I had just found a social group that offered me entertainment of various kinds and gave me sufficient opportunity to meet young men and girls.

While I was still at school, I had met the children of the most prominent Jewish family in Königsberg, the Oppenheims. Its head, the old banker Oppenheim, lived with his wife, a very lovely matron, on the Kneiphof Langgasse, in a stately house, magnificently decorated in the style then current, right next to the house that my maternal grandparents had occupied for thirty-six years. The oldest daughter, who had married a Mr. Friedländer, lived with her sons and daughters at her parents' home. Two other daughters, one married to a banker, the other to a consul, and the only son, who had a very gracious and beautiful wife, all lived in great prosperity in Königsberg and formed a family circle and society, the equal of which I have seldom encountered.

As was often the case then in Jewish families, the women were far better educated than the men and thus extremely adept in social matters. Since the family had far-reaching business connections, it constantly had foreign visitors. All renowned artists visiting Königsberg called on it; and because the women were pleasant and the hospitality of the family extensive, some of the officials and academics of the city also took advantage of the opportunity to stop by. The Christian mercantile aristocracy, with its strong anti-Semitism, kept its distance from the Oppenheims as it did from all Jews. Only to the balls of the young Christian merchants and the other balls given collectively by the merchant aristocracy, the officials, and the nobility were the Oppenheims and one or two other rich Jewish families invited—an advantage which I greatly envied, although it only proved the truth of Lessing's words: "The richer Jew was always the better one for you!"

All four families founded by the Oppenheim children employed bright young academics as tutors and French governesses. The third generation varied considerably in age. The oldest grandson had taken part in the campaign of 1815 as a seventeen-year old; a brother and a very lively and sweet sister were close to his age, and a whole swarm of young people moved around these three, some of whom were older, some the same age as, and some younger than I. Wednesday and Saturday evenings and all day Sundays the whole family gathered at the grandparents' home. The tutors and governesses, the private teachers, the friends of the various sons, daughters, and grandchildren, and a number of outsiders were usually present. It was really fun to go through the house on those days and see how the various groups were amusing themselves, while old Mrs. Oppenheim in her old-fashioned silk gown, her lace cap and pearls, her black silk shoes, and white silk stockings, which she wore even in coldest winter, went around, her head trembling, to check that everything was all right.

Up in the room of the grandfather, who always wore felt slippers in the winter because of his gout, some old people played whist; in a granddaughter's room, friends were reading companionably, and in the big back room, we younger ones had our games, played with dolls when we were children, later played "jeux d'esprit," or danced with our male counterparts after we got tired of childish games. I spent many happy hours and days in this circle.

In the summer the various families moved out to a great country estate close to the city in the direction of Karlsruhe, the grounds of which included three or four houses and cottages. Although it was crowded and cramped for space, there was even greater hospitality there than in the city. We young people could have not asked for any happier life than was available to us on that estate, where I stayed occasionally as a guest for several weeks.

[Two other families the Markuses are friendly with are the Kählers[62] and that of her nemesis and model, Eduard Simson.]

Although the Simsons had moved in to the front part of our house on the Kneiphof Langgasse, while we lived in the back on the quay, we had retained some rooms of this front part for our own use. I had already left the nursery and shared a room with my sister. Now I received my own room. It was a gloomy, cold, and totally sunless room, it had only one window looking out onto the court, but three doors that all led to cold chambers. On the flat roof over my room was a large balcony, a so-called look-out. Underneath was one of my father's wine storerooms, the odor of which always penetrated my room. But I was still very glad to have it! I collected my small treasures there. They were not many. My own framed mediocre pastel drawings over the extremely uncomfortable sofa hung along with my even-worse still lifes of fruit.

It was either having my own melancholy room, which made me feel quite important, or the reading of *Rosalie's Legacy*, by Friedrich Jacobs,[63] that suddenly made me eager to keep a diary. Until then, I had been satisfied to note a few places from the books I was reading, but now that was not enough. I really liked the young men and women of Jacobs's novel, which I had read with Mathilde. The gentle mixture of noble feelings and pale blue sashes, of balls and religiosity, of love, consumption, and pious sentiments of death, appealed to me. Since I had been made systematically sick at this time because of the prevailing idiocies of medical practice, and had to suffer all sorts of illnesses and complaints, it was very easy to lose myself in Rosalie's atmosphere.

Oddly enough, this was connected to the stir that the advances in the area of orthopedics had created. Up to then we had all grown up like our mothers and grandmothers, without anyone considering watching our growth pattern. If you were not deformed, you were considered straight, and I cannot remember any fragile or deformed women in the circle of my contemporaries or schoolmates. We all sat more than was necessary and did completely useless fine handwork, for example, petit-point in frames—and we were eager to use the finest white canvas, which only aggravated our eyestrain and was even worse for our posture. But we were doing quite well, since young bodies adapt easily, when all at once, the newspapers, or God knows what, spread a panic among our mothers about the deforming of their children.

It did not reassure our mother or help us that we walked straight and looked normal. Every family began inspecting their daughters for damage, a veritable misfortune came over us, and before we knew it, we all were deemed fragile and decimated so that it was necessary to provide cures designed just for us. Three of my cousins in one family were sent to the newly opened Königsberg Orthopedic Institute, two girls from the Oppenheim family were brought to Blömer in Berlin, and others of my girl friends had to wear amazing devices at home and were strapped to stretcher beds at night; in brief, it seemed our mothers would only be satisfied if one of the doctors assured them that they too were unfortunate enough to have incipient cripples among their own children.

For my part, I had sat as much as the others, had been just as foolish about embroidering in petit-point on fine linen, but thanks to my mother's carefulness, I had always carried myself very straight, and since I had very good eyesight, had not suffered from my unnecessary and tedious handwork. But this caution in my mother's attitude also made her subject to infection by the orthopedic epidemic. She began to undress me and to look, and one day made the unfortunate discovery that I was crooked. Her brother, my doctor uncle, and a Dr. Ungher, director of the surgical clinic, were summoned. I was turned this way and that, and it was finally determined that, although I had a flawless skeleton, my right shoulder was higher than my left, and that I should hang from a sort of rack every day for a while, lie an hour on my back on the floor, and have four to six leeches applied to my shoulder every two weeks.

Naturally my father considered all this very foolish, but either could not contradict the diagnosis of these prominent doctors or was unwilling to assume such responsibility. At any rate, I had to hang from the rack, getting blisters and callouses on my hands, and had to waste a good hour every day lying on the ground, which hurt and was terribly boring. After an extended period, in which I also had to endure the application of leeches, which damaged my health, they began to wonder why I constantly complained of headaches, dizziness, and palpitations of the heart, all probably the result of the leeching. Instead of realizing that, they ordered me to do vigorous exercises—my father had me pump water for a half hour every day—and instead of feeding me properly, because I had become very thin, they gave me a vegetarian diet to thin my blood.

It was only natural that I should end up anemic and very nervous. I was more emotional than ever, was filled with a new and sudden penchant for the elegiac, and thought a great deal about my own death. Mathilde, who had lost several siblings at our age, helped me as best she could, although she looked extremely healthy and did not have to endure any orthopedic tortures herself. What I did not accomplish in the way of raptures during the day with the horde of children and the household all around was confided evenings to the secret pages of my diary by the sparse light of a candle in my ice-cold room. Following good Ulrich school habits, I had bound the book prettily in blue paper and provided it with a blotter, sewn in according to regulations.

I kept this with great satisfaction for a long time. If I froze at night while I was writing, obviously because the room was so cold, I "felt the wings of death hovering over me." If I was sleepy and could not see well because of the inadequate light, "my eyes closed, faced with the false light of the world." In brief, every word I wrote was trite or an affectation. Although I loved to dress up and to enjoy myself, although every compliment paid me was savored and I was basically very satisfied with myself and my achievements, I had filled two fresh quarto books with such drivel by the second autumn. One evening I was sitting there, "to collect my thoughts, before I closed my eyes on one of my days again." The brilliant thought came to me, of looking over everything I had written to see what I had experienced and felt. I did want to see how my confessions would affect those surviving my death, and moved to tears, I began to read—and read and read— and the scales fell from my eyes!

There was not one honest word in anything I had written for a year and a quarter. I had spoken of spiritual suffering that I did not know, of a longing I had never felt. I was embarrassed and felt idiotic. I found myself obnoxious and ridiculous at the same time. I wondered what was the matter with me. I would have been delighted to find out that I was actually in love with someone. But I was completely clear-headed, and my good sense told me, bitterly, how unworthy it was to assume such borrowed finery. My reason added that it was very ungrateful to consider myself unhappy without cause. I can only use the expression that I used then to describe my condition; I seemed like a counterfeiter and terribly *malhonnette*. This was a word my father used for such dishonesties. I had no peace after seeing myself so clearly, until I had burned every page of this chronicle of lies.

That was the end of my self-admiration for all times. Through this experience, I gained such an aversion for all such self-deception that I never kept a regular diary again. If I occasionally made a note for myself in later years, it was only to remind myself of something I had read, or of a temporary situation, or to retain a comment for the moment. I did not even begin these almost factual entries again until 1834, when I was given a journal by a relative as a present for my twenty-third birthday; by then I felt more secure about my inner truthfulness.[64]

I learned something from this experience about the questionable value for young people in keeping a diary. Whenever I looked at systematic diaries kept by girls or women, I always noted that they were untruthful and a misfortune for their owners. The lives of most women are not complex, their range of ideas is frequently limited, and their thoughts are usually concentrated on their own small world, which must be handled simply and lightly, if it is to be presented in an entertaining and sensible fashion. Typically, though, if a girl plans to write something every day, she first looks to see what she can find in herself and others that is special. Then her everyday obligations become important duties; the pleasant and unpleasant things people do assume great significance. Even the most ordinary young women then fancy themselves misunderstood souls and noble sufferers. I have never discovered a happy, joyous, healthy feminine diary; they are all useless and, like mine, good for nothing but fueling the stove. Mothers who encourage their children to keep a diary are making a grave error, but it is very sound for adolescents and women to write down excerpts from what they have read and to broaden and enrich their meager store of ideas with thoughts of great and mature thinkers.

15

Although I was growing intellectually and beginning to find my own place in the circle of my friends, the strict discipline of our household and my father's iron will continually loomed over me. I could think and feel whatever and as much as I wanted, but I had to perform my chores, and the freer I seemed inclined to develop within, the more inexorable and harsher became the demands my father made of my obedience and the execution of my duties.

Not the slightest negligence was ever ignored; nothing I had undertaken could be abandoned. I remember two characteristic examples of my father's way of treating me.

For years I had wanted to embroider a petit-point purse for my mother, as was the fashion then, but I had not been able to gain either permission or the money for it from my father. Finally in the summer of 1826, when I renewed my request before my mother's birthday, I had to make a cost estimate. The canvas, the embroidery floss, the pattern, borders, ties, and the silver amounted to six or seven thalers, a large sum for a luxury item. Because I had a distinct pride in surprising my mother with such a gift, I received the money and began my task. However, I could only work on it in the mornings, before she arose, and afternoons from two to four, when she napped.

Unfortunately, in order to make my purse particularly beautiful, I had picked such fine canvas that a pattern large enough for a big sofa pillow was concentrated into a very small space. While I indulged in the thought that the pattern (a dove, framed by roses and forget-me-nots, with a wreath of summer flowers on the reverse) would look as if painted, I saw one day after another pass, and likewise I saw the possibility of finishing this work by the twentieth of August for my mother's birthday diminish.

Not to finish a project you had begun was something my father would not tolerate. Although I was not quite sure what would happen if I failed, I had an ominous feeling of impending disaster that I wanted to avoid at any cost. I arose very early—always very difficult for me—and took my embroidery frame with me whenever I visited anyone; my whole mind was concentrated on the dove and its roses. My father saw the problem I was having, but said nothing. Finally, one afternoon about eight days before Mother's birthday, he came in as I was embroidering and asked when I would be finished.

With great apprehension I showed him my work, admitted that I had not even finished the first half, claimed I had done everything within my power but had underestimated the time it would take and that it would not be possible even to complete the first side before the birthday.

My father's face did not change. "If the first side is not complete by the twentieth, I will cut it to pieces so that you will have a reminder that a sensible person never begins anything he cannot complete. Act accordingly."

I just sat there. I knew my father well enough to realize that the destruction of the work, my pain, the unnecessary expenditure, were all of no concern to him if it was a matter of imposing his will and teaching me a lesson. If I wanted to avoid the threatened fate, I had no choice but to do my work during the night. So I did this, even though it was a sin against my eyes. I was able to finish at least the first half by the deadline and had the satisfaction of seeing my mother's pleasure and hearing my father say he was glad I had pulled myself together.

In the same period of my life, I had gotten into the habit of not closing doors completely or even leaving them open if I was in a hurry. I had been warned, but I would simply forget. One evening I was having a wonderful time at a party at one of my aunt's. There was dancing and I felt quite the lady. Suddenly the maid came in with an announcement that our footman was there to say that my father had requested that I come home immediately. Very frightened, convinced that something had happened to my mother, who was already frequently ill then, I rushed out.

The footman could not tell me what had happened. Full of concern, I flew up both flights of stairs and into the living room. There sat my father quietly reading on the sofa, my mother knitting by his side, and my siblings doing their homework at the table. Without permitting me a word, my father said calmly, "You left the door open again when you went to the party; close the door." I stood transfixed, tears flooded my eyes, and I wanted to take off my cloak and hat quietly and stay at home, but my father would not allow that. I had to put on my clothes again, the footman accompanied me, and with a feeling I cannot describe, I went back to the party; to be sure, after an hour, the pleasure of the games and dancing won out over my deep humiliation.

Such Draconic measures were not caused by mere whims on my father's part, but they were intended to make me responsible, dependable, and independent. If I had an intense dislike for something, I had to do it. If there was a household chore that feminine sensibility found too repugnant, I had to tackle it. I still remember that I had to pierce my little sisters' earlobes, after an old woman had demonstrated it for me on a few poor children. If I even dared to refuse a job like that, he would say, "I have to train you as a model for seven younger children. If I give in to you, I'll have to begin all over again with each of the others, and since you have the good fortune to be the oldest, you have the responsibility of aiding your parents' task in raising the others."

I cursed the "good fortune" of being the first born hundreds of times because of such moments. If I did not want to eat fish, which I really loathed then, I had to pretend to enjoy it to set an example. If I hesitated to touch a frog or a spider, my brothers were told to press it into my hand. If my father saw that certain sounds like the screeching of a knife on porcelain bothered me, my brothers were allowed to play a concert on the plates. My father dealt inexorably, not only with these external manifestations but also if I betrayed any mental weaknesses, a fright, a sign of indecisiveness, or a loss of control. His own sisters reproached him for it, and I heard the oldest tell him once that one needed to be considerate with feminine weaknesses and that he would ruin me for life with his experiments in toughening me.

"Be so good as to leave that to me," he replied curtly. Today, as hard as his harshness often was for me then, I bless the fact that he did not show me needless pity, that he had no mercy on any of that weakness which women cultivate in themselves as feminine tenderness, and that he never considered making the days of my youth easy, only of making me capable of leading a life useful to myself and others.

I never even considered that my father was being harsh or unjust to me, because I had unquestioning faith in him and his judgment and deep respect for his self-control and untiring labors. His customary benevolence and temperate fairness were so predominant and overwhelming that I can only call the feeling that I and all my siblings had for him reverential love.

He never lost his temper with or said an abusive word to us; after I was an adult, he never said one word of reproach to me unless we two were alone. He even tried to avoid scolding me in my mother's presence, since her nervous nature was easily irritated and she would add complaints and reproaches that had nothing to do with the case in point. All his admonishments had as a basis this maxim: "A person cannot live his life over. There is no point in speaking about what has happened in the past, except to avoid doing it in the future."

Tears, remorse, and contrition were offensive to him in the highest degree. everyone should look at himself in the mirror once a day, to be lord and master over himself and his countenance. So he led us to the mirror whenever we wept and felt humiliated.

"See how you look! Don't ruin your face. The matter is done and over with; do it better next time." These were the words with which he almost always dismissed us after a reprimand. Then he gave us his hand and kissed us. His only desire was to make thoughtful people of us, ruled by our own good sense, exercising goodness and justice because goodness and justice were the reason for our actions. He also endeavored to strengthen our self-confidence. Even as children we were not allowed to accept the smallest gifts of money from our aunts and uncles. He thought only your father should give you money; other than that, you should never accept anything you had not earned. "You behaved well." "You dealt with it sensibly;" these were the highest words of praise we ever received from him.

Consequently, the discussion to correct children's behavior were unusually short and infrequent. It was impossible for us to hear the kind of nagging reprimands that call for a defense and lead to futile arguments between parents and children, the kind that have become fashionable in raising children under the title of "meaningful" discussions. My father did not consider children his equals. Even in later years, when he knew in his heart that we were of age, he always made us feel that we could do nothing we could not justify to him.

In addition to the serious dealings he had with all of us, he gave me serious books to read when I was very young. I was sixteen when I read Kant's anthropology[65] for the first time—and with great edification. My whole life, my whole upbringing, had prepared me to find the simple definitions enlightening and valuable. Even more, as my father had probably expected, the chapters about greed, about the character of a person, and of the race affected me. To free yourself from bad qualities so that another person has no hold over you, to supervise and better yourself so as to become free and independent, were teachings that struck me deeply. The clear definitions of character qualities and flaws made me think of my own in a beneficial way and led me to the firm determination to learn to control all aspects of myself, so others could not control me.

Discussions specific to certain issues such as the nature of women puzzled me the most. The book said feminine characteristics are usually considered weaknesses; they are the subjects of jokes that fools find humorous. But these traits are just the levers by which women guide men and help them to fulfill their potential. A man is easy to read, but women do not reveal their secrets, although (because of their honesty) they are not good about keeping those of others. Men love domestic peace and are happy to submit to its regimen, so they can carry on their business without hindrance. Women do not avoid waging domestic battles with their tongues, for which purpose nature equipped them with honesty and persuasiveness to disarm men. A man bases his right to rule on his strength, by which he protects the home from outside enemies; a woman, on her weakness and need to be protected from men by a man. She defuses the exasperation of the man by reproaching him for his lack of consideration.

All this gave me a distinct aversion to so-called weak femininity. I firmly decided neither to arouse pity in men by my weakness nor to manipulate them by weaknesses burdensome to them. Instead of my childhood desire to learn as much as the boys, I now became determined to be as active in my circles as the men were in theirs, and to gain their recognition and respect instead of their protection and chivalry. Since sensible ideas often have little unreasonable side effects in young minds, I conceived an intense dislike for certain forms of masculine courtesies. I could not stand it if someone offered to carry my parasol or shawl or perform some similar service. These seemed like activities unsuited to a man, which he only carried out because he considered us helpless children. The more I built up an idealized concept of manly worth, based on my father's qualities and youthful charm of various fictional heroes, the more I wanted to be worthy of the love of such a man and to become a suitable wife for him.

My father vigorously encouraged these ideas, when he encountered them. He found the position of women sad; whenever we happened to discuss such a subject, the Jews knew what they were saying when they thanked God every morning for having been born men.[66]

[Here Lewald quotes a passage from Goethe her father would recite to illustrate this point.[67]]

He only said this to keep us from struggling against what he considered the inevitable, that is, that every woman must marry, that a married woman, no matter how bad her lot or unsuitable her husband, was still better off than an unmarried one, because she was doing what was natural. A woman who believed in herself and cultivated her own inner life in addition to doing her natural job could always be happy if she performed her duties to her

husband and raised her children properly. She would then possess all the elements necessary for satisfaction, to be completely
what she should be. Besides, it was certain that that woman was
the best who was not recognized or spoken of outside her home.

He always said this as a form of praise for my mother, but
never considered that all the guidance I received from him tended to make me her complete opposite. He constantly reminded
me that I was destined to be a pliable, domestic woman, dependent on her husband, as Mother was. Ironically, though, he had
long since imbued me with an independence and strength of
character, which he underestimated because my love and respect
for him made me completely obedient to his wishes. Yet I already
felt justified in not sharing his opinions, and I absolutely did not
agree with him in his plans for my future marriage. On the other
hand, while I never intended to let myself be forced into an
unwanted marriage, I did not dream of ever marrying or making
any other major step without my father's consent. I felt myself
completely his possession in this regard. But to give me to someone else if I did not want it—that was not within his rights.

16

It was during this time that I met a young man who was to have a
great influence over my life and development in the next few
years. At this time I was taking dancing lessons with five of the
Oppenheim girls and two daughters of the Kähler family. Our
partners were students, with the exception of a young lawyer, and
since the lessons were only once a week and held in the various
Oppenheim homes, there were always small soirées afterwards
for the guests, which the hosts tried to make very lively and entertaining for us. We formed "tableaux vivants," improvised apho-
risms, and even presented comic skits three or four times during
the winter, which were performed by the members of the dance
class and some of the unmarried women and men of the Oppenheim family. (I took no part in these comedies, because my father
did not permit such masquerades and performances.) My mother

had been ill that winter and moved into my room with me for the quiet; I usually had to leave the parties earlier than the others, but that did not really bother me. During the day, all I thought about were the dancing lessons, and I dreamed about them at night, talking in my sleep and disturbing my mother.

In the spring as the lessons drew to an end, there was a party at the Kählers as a last meeting for our merry group. Attending were friends of the son, who was a student and had been one of our dancers, friends of the daughters, some relatives, and some young men attending Dr. Kähler's course of lectures. I did not know many of the guests. Since dancing was not allowed in that house, we played games and the evening passed quickly, because the whole atmosphere of the family was intellectually stimulating and pleasant. The next day, I had a great deal to relate to Mathilde, who had not been there. I told her that when I climbed into my friends' coach to leave, a very tall young man had pushed the servants aside to help me in. She asked me who he was, but I did not know his name.

A few days later I received a visit from one of the Kähler daughters, one of the loveliest creatures you can imagine. Her golden curls, her pale blue eyes, her well-shaped nose, and her beautiful complexion gave her an irresistable charm, and her great vivacity made her seem as light as a bird, since she was very small. She came laughing into my room; as soon as we were alone, she asked in her light-hearted way, "Well, don't you want to get married?"

I looked at her in surprise. Although she was only seventeen, just a year older than I, we were already accustomed to all sorts of presumption from her. However, she put on a serious expression and said, "No, I'm not joking. Did you see our relative, Leopold Bock? He just about declared he wanted to marry you or no one, and he's a man who keeps his word! You know what you have to do now."

We both laughed about it again and again and were very amused by the whole matter. She told me that Leopold was to take the examination for his theological degree soon and was a tutor for a businessman's family. We were most amused at my girlfriend's joke that I would never be able to "support" him as his wife, because I was too short to reach even his elbow. We treated the matter just as we had treated the relationships in our make-believe families five or six years earlier, because actually we were still almost children, despite the many things we had learned and the serious thoughts we were capable of having, when we were so inclined.

However, my friend's information made an impression on me even if we joked about it. I could not explain to myself why I was unable to recall what the young man looked like, although he was a visitor more of her parents than of the children and had only taken part in our games occasionally. In the following weeks and months I saw him only now and then with other young men I knew. My girlfriends' teasing continued; I learned from them that Leopold came from the Harz region, that he was the son of a country parson, and that he was of a very pure and idealistic character. All his fellow students held him in high regard. I was as curious to become acquainted with him as I was intrigued and flattered by the thought that I had made so strong an impression on this paragon in a quite superficial encounter.

Finally, at the end of spring, my parents had a picnic for us in front of the city gate, to which some of my girlfriends and other young people were invited. We had spent the afternoon merrily playing childish games with my siblings, the youngest of whom still had to be carried, and had just sat down to devour our supper when Leopold suddenly appeared, and a few of the young men with us got up to greet him. One of them, a relative of ours, introduced him to my father, and my mother, not knowing how I felt about him, hospitably asked him to join us. He had not come by chance; some of his friends had told him of the outing. They made room for him next to me, and I really saw and spoke to him for the first time.

He was very tall and slender and had the clear olive complexion you often find in the dark-haired people from the Harz in spite of their blue eyes. He had a pleasant voice and was unusually serious for his age. I was surprised by the shyness that came over me; the seriousness with which he spoke intimidated me, so that I lost the openness and confidence I usually felt with others. There was none of the polite chatter or gallantry most young men employ when they want a girl to like them. I did not know what to think about him. We broke up early, because we had the younger children with us, and he accompanied us on the beautiful evening walk home. Sometimes he strolled with me, sometimes with my father. In front of our door, he asked for permission to call on us, which was given without any hesitation, because my father had a high regard for Leopold's employer. Father knew this man would only have entrusted his children to someone hard-working and reliable.

That evening (I found out later), Leopold had to retrace his steps back completely along the way we had come and go even further into the countryside because the family with whom he lived resided during the summer in a fairly remote country house. I did not see him often until the following fall. I heard of him, however, through acquaintances. When he came on his infrequent visits to us, he asked me about everything I had done and what I was planning, as if he had a right to do so. Women have such an instinct for dependency, that when they are young, they involuntarily feel they are the possession of the man who has the will to treat them as his own. I, at any rate, was dominated by Leopold long before I knew it, and although I tried to resist this domination occasionally, that resistance was only due to my innate need not to give up my own will completely, not to lose my own personality entirely.

In the autumn we moved out of our house on the Pregel to the front house on the Langgasse, so that my growing brothers could have their own room. This location was also much more convenient for my father, because he could reach us more easily from his office and warehouses. With this move, my eleven-year old sister and I gained not only the large beautiful portico in front of the door, which belonged to us all, but a friendly little room in the entresol, a "horizontal room," which was mine until 1845, a year before my father's death, when I visited and lived at home for the last time.

This room was at the corner of the house in which now we

lived. One window looked out on the side street, which went down to the Pregel; the two others were on the Langgasse side. With my sharp eyesight, I could see all the way down the Brod-bänkengasse to the cathedral square, at the entrance to which Leopold lived with the family of his wards. My sewing table stood by the window. Each day at noon, when Leopold came up the Brodbänkengasse with his pupils for a walk, we saw and greeted each other. That was the high point of the day for me.

He was very busy in those days, his friends said. He wanted to take his second examination in theology. He himself said nothing about that. However, he was coming to visit us several times a week by this time and soon, because of his pureness of thought, his enthusiasm for everything great, and the naive simplicity that softened the seriousness and strength of his character, my parents and siblings were as fond of him as I. He demonstrated in his person the value of the German Student Association, which suffered such heavy persecution and with which the worthiest students had allied themselves.[68] A deep love for our country, an equally deep commitment to the humanism inherent in Christianity, a strict moral code, a veneration for women, a feeling for the broth-erhood of man, were all so basic to him that nothing trivial, facile, or unworthy could touch him. Although he was gentle and good toward what he trusted and honored, he became very agitated or icily angry whenever he encountered dishonesty or frivolity.

I have often been puzzled since then as to what made him notice me, what attracted him so suddenly. I assume it was solely my appearance, because I had none of the attributes he prized in a woman at that time. I was geared to external success and had a burning desire for an exciting life in the world; a ball with won-derful dancers was much more on my mind than the quiet life of a remote parsonage. I hardly knew how to value a love like his, and I certainly did not appreciate it at first.

We were never alone together. We did not have anything to say to one another that others could not hear, anyway. Leopold reproached me when I showed my enjoyment of Heine's bold and frivolous writings or of French novels, which were contrary to his more mature and nobler mind. He deplored my passion for dancing, because he did not like to dance. He told of his father's parsonage in the Harz region, he spoke of the wonderful life in nature with great warmth and of his parents, whom he venerated, of his brothers, all older than he, of his father's wish to have him as his successor, of all the domestic details of his home, and even about his family's two white Pomeranian guard dogs. When I said I did not like dogs, especially Pomeranians, because they barked so terribly and always bared their teeth, he consoled me by replying that they were intelligent and very friendly to everyone belonging to the household. That reassured me and made me very happy, because it showed he considered me part of his family already.

After a while, Leopold directed my reading completely, which was greatly to my benefit. My reading became more serious, not because the subject matter was so—my father had already seen to that—but because it was more suitable for a young girl. I had always had a special fondness for Körner's *Lyre and Sword* and his heroic drama *Zriny*,[69] which I had received as a gift quite early in life. Now I learned to know Körner's love poems, and the idea of love and my German fatherland began to melt together in me, as they had melted together in Körner and as they dwelt in Leopold's heart as an entity. Until then, I had known that virtue and morality were proper and necessary. Now I began to feel that they were beautiful and sacred. The memory of the battles for the freedom of our country, which had only been great historical events for me earlier and had always featured the figure of Napoleon, either as victor or loser, took on new significance for me. I saw them as a civilizing and elevating force, and recognized them as the elevation of a whole people against an uncivilizing tyranny. I owe my complete commitment to a united Germany to my first love.

Instead of *Rosalie's Legacy*, which had inspired my foolish diary, I read the biography of Pastor von Meinau's wife and similar works. It seemed to me I was growing in his eyes when Leopold made it clear to me what an extensive and productive influence a woman can exercise within a small village congregation and the confines of her home and family. He made fun of me when I told him of the striving for intellectualism I had had as a child. Because he made it clear to me that I was, or could become, all that his idealistic love saw in me, he made me very submissive to himself as he educated and enlightened me. Those were wonderful days!

17

My brothers were about thirteen and fifteen when my father called them in one day to announce that he had decided to let them convert to Christianity. We were all very surprised; I, because I was not included, and my brothers, because there had been no mention of it heretofore. This had always been my mother's ardent wish. She had taken part in the decision and seemed delighted. When we children had overcome our first astonishment, my elder brother declared he would never convert if his parents and siblings did not. He did not want to live spiritually separated from them or lose his close association with them. Since he was closer to my mother than the rest of us even then, they were both equally emotional and moved. My other brother, a strong and passionate person, who showed his qualities more in physical activity than in independent thinking, was basically indifferent. He was thinking of long journeys to foreign countries, of battles with savages and wild animals; he had a longing to go to sea. Despite his good mind, he hated school. Which church he belonged to or where he would be buried was of no concern whatsoever to him. In addition, my father, who had recognized the passionate nature of this son early on, had decided to break his spirit instead of guiding him to the right path. So Moritz feared Father although he loved him passionately; despite great affection on both sides, this brother's relationship to my father was never totally free, and the violence done to his character as a child was a disadvantage to him all his short life.[70]

I usually also had little courage when I was confronted by my father, and the declaration that I was to be excluded from the conversion was doubly startling for me: first, because it denied a certain longing I had cherished for a considerable time, and second, because it seemed a bad omen for the future of my love. Driven and encouraged by this, I ventured the question of why my father would not let me be baptized.

"Because baptism binds you, but frees your brothers," answered Father firmly. "I've considered everything thoroughly, so don't think about it any more! The matter will be handled as I say. If I let my sons become Christians, I make them free masters over their own future. They can chose any career for which they are suited; they will gain equal civil rights and can marry either a Christian or a Jew. After all, every reasonable man does what seems of benefit to himself. Women, however, can chose neither their career nor their mates and will do best to remain in the circumstances in which they were born. If a Jewish woman should want to marry a Christian, it can then be decided what to do." He added finally, "It doesn't suit me for me and your mother to be baptized. You'll finally realize that such an action is no separation from the family and will have no disturbing influence on its love."

Then he kissed us. My mother, who would have loved to become a Christian, and my oldest brother were very moved. Since I, however, had developed that sense of isolation from my own family that romantic attachment creates in women, because they will eventually have to commit themselves to a new family, I gained the happy conviction from this discussion that my father would place no obstacles in the way of my future with Leopold.

[Lewald spends the summer in the country with her family and sees little of Leopold until the fall.]

Soon Leopold's visits became more frequent. Instead of coming a few times as in the previous year, he came almost every day and finally, every evening, without my parents seeming to find that unusual. His behavior toward me changed, too. He sat next to me, even if other people were there; he arbitrarily scolded and praised me in my parents' presence; he jealously repulsed all my old acquaintances and childhood friends if they approached me. I enjoyed all of this because I loved him, but it was embarrassing, too. My older girl friends joked about our "silent love"; some of my younger friends teased me being so unusually tender and submissive. Nevertheless, with the changeable attitude of a moody child, I decided one day not to let Leopold order me around any more.

It was in November, on my father's birthday, which was celebrated like all such days and considered particularly important. As my parents were not very close to their families, most of the guests were invited for the children. We had also invited six or eight of our friends and decided to dance. Leopold did not dance, however, and I had hardly stopped playing for the dancers in order to join them when he came up to me and said, "Don't dance!" I looked at him and said, "Why not?" "Because I don't dance," he replied. "As if that were a reason!" I cried, and I wanted to take my cousin's hand when Leopold held me back with the words, "We're through, if you dance."

That stopped me, but it also made me angry. I did not dare to dance, but I still had to have a reason not to for the others, and to leave and help the situation, I hurried upstairs with the excuse that I did not feel well. Up in my dark room I began to cry without realizing why. I was happy that Leopold considered me so much his possession that he scolded and did with me what he wanted, but I felt a rage toward him I had never felt against another human being. "I hate him!" I said to myself, while knowing I had never loved him as much as now. I resolved not to go downstairs again, to torture and frighten him, to show him that I would not take orders from him and he had no right to give them. Yet I was miserable because I was sitting in this dark room and crying instead of being with him and the others.

These are circumstances that every person, man or woman, has experienced. It is the battle of independent young people, who are afraid to lose themselves to another being. I believe that the strength of this battle shows with certainty what that person will eventually accomplish. You have to be something to be able to give up something; however, you have to possess yourself to be able to give yourself away. Defiance in love is only the March storms that precede the coming of spring.

In the midst of my tears, Mathilde entered and, cheerful as always, she asked me to be sensible and come downstairs. I was just happy to have found someone to whom I could angrily express all the rage in my heart. I complained about Leopold; I called him egotistical, self-righteous, and tyrannical. I assured her that I had received a lesson that I—I was only seventeen—would find useful the rest of my life. Everything Mathilde tried to do to calm me made me angrier. After she had finally exhausted all her reasons, she said, "If you promise not to tell anyone, I will tell you a secret your mother asked me never to reveal. But give me your word, that you'll not give it away."

I promised and Mathilde told me the following: "Soon after Leopold had come to town, he visited your father and asked for your hand. He told him that he loved you and he could not live without you any longer. He therefore wanted to accept a teaching position, which had been offered him, so he could marry you. Your father told him there was no question of that. Leopold would have to get his degree in theology first. Then, after he had been assigned a church, he would be welcome to call again. Your father had Leopold give him his word of honor not to tell you of the proposal nor to declare himself in any way, because you were too young and emotional, et cetera."

I was stunned, dazzled, as if I were stepping from the darkness into a bright light. My rage was gone; I was not angry at anyone but myself, no one was wrong but me, but I felt the position into which my father had placed me for the time being was untenable and had been imposed without any consideration of Leopold's character—and I still believe that!

I returned to the party, happiness in my heart, filled with a desire to make up with him, feeling there could be no real problem when people are in love. Just as we had found each other without words, we understood each other without words, and the time now passed with us being together in joyous, quiet peacefulness daily.

[Lewald's father, for reasons never explained, develops an antipathy to Leopold, and the latter's visits become more and more infrequent.]

A few weeks later I was in my room one evening and heard the doorbell ring. The door was opened, I recognized the step on the tile floor and I put up my handwork to go down to the living room, which would now be opened. But I did not hear this sound, the doorbell sounded again, the kitchen doors were banged shut, and everything remained silent. I did not understand. I hurried down the stairs. I asked in the kitchen, who had called. They said it was Leopold, and upon my second question, if he were in my mother's sitting room, the kitchen maid answered, "No. The master came home and ordered that if Mr. Leopold called, he was to be told that the family was not at home."

I had not expected this. Leopold would never believe that "the family was not at home"; my parents never went out socially, except on the two evenings a year they attended parties at my aunts'. Besides, the light from the living room was visible in the hall through the glass doors. I really did not know what to do and I was very sad. I desperately wanted to help myself, to do something, to write to Leopold. Then I thought that that was Leopold's responsibility, not mine. I did not have the courage to defy my father.

The days passed, I do not know how. Leopold came down the street at noon as usual and greeted me; that was all. At the end of the week, my father came into my room, stood in front of the stove, asked what I was doing, and looked through the books lying on the chest of drawers. Several were Leopold's and were inscribed with his name. My heart was in my throat. My father put the books down and spoke of something else, but I hardly listened. He never came up to my room in such a way, in the evening and alone, and I expected a reproach, an explanation, a resolution—but in vain.

After Father had been there a while, he started to leave and only then said, "I see you have some of Leopold's books. Send them back." "I'm still reading them, Father," I replied, just to show I was still alive. "Send them anyway; you can finish them some other time."

"But why, Father?" I asked with great self-control.

"Do I have to give you reasons?" he said. "That is usually not necessary between us." His voice was soft and emotional; he left, and the next morning I sent the books back without a word, without a line. I only left a small piece of paper as a sign and reminder, marking one of the Körner poems that we had often read together and loved.[71]

[As a consolation prize, Lewald's father agrees to let her be baptized. She is instructed by the family friend Professor Kähler.]

In February, my teacher pronounced me sufficiently prepared to receive baptism. The twenty-fourth, my parents' wedding anniversary, was set for this religious ceremony, and Kähler now asked me to prepare a profession of faith, which I would acknowledge in the presence of the friends I had chosen as my witnesses.

I sat down to write this, when I suddenly realized, thinking to myself, that I did not believe anything of what constitutes the essence of ecclesiastical Christianity, of what forms the actual articles of faith (the Apostles' Creed). I did not believe in the divine parentage of the Savior, I did not believe in the "only Son our Lord, who was conceived by the Holy Ghost, born of the Virgin Mary, suffered under Pontius Pilate, was crucified, dead and buried; on the third day he arose again from the dead, he ascended into heaven, and sitteth at the right hand of God the Father Almighty; from thence he shall come to judge the quick and the dead." I did not believe in immortality, let alone the resurrection of the flesh; I believed neither in original sin, for which I, though I bore it without guilt, would have to atone, nor in the concept of being redeemed from a sin I had committed through my own volition by the death of a sinless ideal of mankind, crucified eighteen hundred years ago. I did not believe in the redemptive power of Holy Communion either. In short, I believed none of that I was soon formally to profess; I was in utter despair.

I had taken several days to compose my profession of faith, and every day that passed heightened my sense of futility. I was appalled at the thought of uttering a falsehood ceremoniously and of thus committing perjury at the baptism. I was also afraid to tell my revered teacher how far I had stretched the freedom of the rational, humanistic interpretation of Christianity to which he

had generously attributed a certain amount of credit in his explanations. I imagined what an impression it would make on
Leopold, if he learned—and he would undoubtedly, through the
Kähler family—that I had refused finally to convert to Christianity. He would remember everything we had discussed. Everything
I had often told him would seem a deliberate lie to him. He, my
teacher, my parents, Mathilde—none of them would know what
to make of me, and I did not know, either.

If you do not want to start doubting yourself in such situations, you end up doubting others, and my instinct for self-
preservation led me in that direction. I began to ask myself if my
teacher had really revealed the last inner core of his faith to me.
Did the ministers of the Christian church act just like the heathen
priests they deplored in respect to dogma and the mysteries, giving laymen the symbol instead of the truth? I asked myself how it
was possible that a man of such sharp intellect as Kähler, a man
who strove as earnestly after truth as Leopold, could believe in
the mysteries of Christianity. This seemed impossible to me; so I
told myself, audaciously, that it was obviously impossible for
them, too, that they would have to acknowledge some other
truth, see a deeper meaning within the standard dogmas or the
pure spirit within the form. A religion which was based upon a
mystery valid for every person must also allow each individual
his own mystery. If the teachers of Christianity thought they
could compromise by using silent knowledge equally with a spoken confession, why could I not do the same as they, if I found
myself in a like position?

Soothing myself with such thoughts, I went to write my profession of faith. It was a sorry example of enthusiastic casuistry. I
avoided, as best I could, making any positive declaration, and
because of the vagueness with which young girls usually tend to
express themselves about abstract matters, this probably seemed
not very unusual. For me, however, who had achieved control
over my thoughts and their expression even then, this profession
was a product of pure calculation, and was so repugnant and
alien to me in later years that I finally burned it so I would never
have to look at this evidence against my honesty again.

Now came the day of my baptism. It was to take place, as had my brothers, in the Kählers' apartment, because we did not want to call attention to it at our house; an evening hour was set. I had chosen the witnesses myself: two older men, acquaintances of my parents', whom I cherished; Mrs. Kähler, the model of a noble and educated matron; and my friend Mathilde. My parents and brothers were there. The baptism and confirmation were celebrated in due form. My mother was very happy that she had saved one more of her children from Judaism, and my father said, "I hope this will be good for you." That was all.

As I stood there, however, taken into the covenant of the Christian community, as my friend and my brothers congratulated and embraced me, as I told myself that I was getting closer to Leopold with this step and further from my parents—I found that I had put more distance between Leopold and me by my lack of belief and was tied more closely to my father by my convictions than ever before. It was one of the few moments of my life when I felt in conflict with myself, and I was very unhappy because of it.

I was very conscious of the fact that I had carried out a decision, originally made with good faith, love, and confidence, with a hypocrisy usually foreign to me; but I lacked the courage to admit to a mistake and to place myself in direct opposition to those I loved most. I had trespassed against myself out of fear of others and love. Although I could not see any other positive purpose in that hour marking a definite stage in my life, I did vow to myself that this would be the first and last time I would stray from the God of truth and fearless veracity. I think I have kept that vow. The meaning and spirit of Christianity as the purest teaching of freedom and brotherhood only became apparent to me at a time when the days of my youth lay far behind me.

19

[Lewald's father, a political liberal, makes her aware of the revolt against the monarchy in France in 1830.]

The names of the great English and French statesmen had become well-known to us because of Father, and we had heard of the advantages of constitutional government from childhood on. When the news spread of the movement against the reactionism of the Bourbon regime in France, my father lived and breathed his partisanship for the French liberals, and conversation centered more and more on political events. Although the businessmen realized the possibility of a new French Revolution in the wake of the announcements,[72] Father placed great hope on this revolt. I remember very clearly his shining eyes when he talked of the July Revolution.

We were sitting with Mother and her oldest brother, the doctor, under the shadow of the awning over the portico, when Father came quickly up the steps. He held a newspaper in his hand and said, "The revolution has broken out, Charles X has fled, the Liberals have won, the Duke of Orleans has been proclaimed General-Lieutenant of France, Lafayette, Casimir Perrier, and Lafitte have the rudder in their hands. That will bring fresh air and movement everywhere."

Father was excited, enthusiastic, and happy, but my uncle, considerably older than he, shook his head resignedly. The earlier repression of the Jews had made him timid; he was the kind of citizen despotic governments love. He was completely satisfied if you let him pay his taxes, work in his profession, and do as he pleased at home.

"Don't talk so loudly about it," he said to Father. "What's all that to you? You are a man with a wife and children. How does that concern us? Be quiet and shut your ears; that's always the best course."

This last was a favorite remark of the doctor's and was possibly even more maddening for my father than the opinions behind it. He answered rather brusquely, my uncle left, and Father let us read the newspaper reports aloud to him one more time, to get double pleasure from them: by remembering the first French Revolution and its early middle-class proponents and by thinking with warmth of the possibility of a free constitution for Prussia, too. The July Revolution was just the kind of revolution he liked;

it brought an educated bourgeoisie to the fore, it placed power
and control into the hands of the class to which he belonged, into
the hands of intelligent businessmen. He really could not see
beyond that or wish for anything better. If he had lived through
the 1848 period, if he had still been in full possession of his
capacities, he would undoubtedly have strongly opposed 1848's
strivings for a broader democracy. He was a just and provident
master to all his subordinates; they stayed in his service for a long
time; they were all very attached to him and revered him. So did
the artisans he employed. But the thought that his clerks, his Mr.
Jürgens, his Mr. Ehlers, his workers, his servants would be as
franchised as he, that his barrel maker, his wine drayman would
vote at his side, that they would have an equal voice—he would
have rejected such an idea as foolishness, as an insult to his dignity. He was a person who believed in command and the exercise
of authority. Even in his relationship to his family, you sensed
some of the old tribal chieftain. If he had been born a nobleman,
he would have been a rigid aristocrat. He was always an example
to me of the fact that even people with clear minds and noble
hearts find it difficult to escape the limits of the time in which
they are at the height of their powers.

The 1830 French revolution, however, made a deep impression on me, because, in comparison with the Greek revolution,
the heroes and deeds of which had appeared to me as a child like
visions from fairy tales, it was the first great event I experienced
with clear understanding and with my mind prepared for it. I
knew of the heroic deeds that had been performed through the
millenia by many peoples to gain a suppressed freedom; I had
developed a great enthusiasm for the German Wars of Liberation
against the rule of Napoleon. It was the small things that I understood, those that were emotionally close and accessible to me,
which aroused my interest, rather than the great matters distant
to me. Since I loved and was fluent in French and fairly well-
read in French literature, I followed closely the events of the
July Revolution, then beginning an involvement in public affairs
in general, which I have continued all my life.

My father did not find much agreement among his siblings

and in-laws with his delight in the July Revolution. They were not as educated as he, and our relationship to our relatives had become rather peculiar anyway. The times had long passed in which all our extended family lived in similar circumstances. There were no more visits after supper, as there had been when I was a child; we did not live near enough to one another to chat over a glass of punch or a toddy, depending on the season. Our economic situations also differed. Some of my mother's sisters were rich, or at least well-to-do, another was no more prosperous than we, and my father's sisters had constant money problems, since their husbands did not know how to overcome their financial losses. Although everybody tried to help and support each other as best they could, not only the life-styles but the degree of education, the social interests and the training of the children were very different in the various families.

My mother always maintained a good relationship with her sisters, only one of whom had children, her whole life long. My aunts valued my father and loved us children. Still, they constantly criticized the way we were raised and considered it too grand—although my mother's eldest brother-in-law, a very rich and well-regarded man, did not stint in providing a good education for *his* children, who were partly younger and partly older than I and my good friends. My cousins, however, had the prospect of being rich one day, and we did not. So I often had to listen to my aunts and uncles say that I had been educated far over our circumstances, that I would never find a suitable husband, since my father only entertained scholars and educated men and no young Jewish businessmen at all. After I had converted to Christianity and the affair with Leopold had ended, the main topic of conversation was what my father was to do with six overeducated daughters, a question with which my childless aunts and uncles constantly assailed me when I visited them by myself.

They never asked my father such questions, because everyone realized that he would reject them outrightly, but my mother did not know how to defend herself and would be very cross. She raised us with the firm conviction that education was the greatest happiness she could give us. She watched over our outward behavior, over our speech and posture, with a delicacy of feeling and an untiring patience, as if she had had the same advantages in her youth. Still, she could not readily say how she pictured our future. I admit that her most fervent wish was that we should not marry Jews and to remove us, if possible, from any contact with Jews, but that was something she could not overcome in herself.

I spoke up with our relatives and always defiantly. I knew that none of the complaints about my being spoiled or overeducated were valid. (Such complaints could only concern me, since all my sisters were still young children.) I sewed, worked, and did as much for my family as any other girl. I tailored clothes for everyone at home, I helped everywhere necessary in our household; but since my mother had trained us to be properly dressed from early to late, and we never "got comfortable" for our labors, and because we accidentally had pretty hands, which work did not hurt, our relatives always commented that we probably never put our hands in cold water—so as to keep them white for the piano and social affairs—and made other remarks about lazy women.

Far from defending myself in this case, I was actually pleased about the comments. If they said I was too conceited, I said I would be even more conceited when I was master of my own actions. If they told me I would not be fit for any man of our class, I explained that it had never occurred to me to marry such a person anyway. If they reproached me because I had not come to greet them properly at some event—which they considered a subtle snub—I laughed in a way they could interpret as they chose. I loved to irritate them, because they were unfair to me and made me angry, and since they actually meant well by such remarks and really loved me, I have always thought of them with some embarrassment in later years.

It was at that time that Börne's[73] writings began to gain great attention. His way of thinking was somehow typically nationalistic and touched us all; his ideas were rousing and did not let the excitement produced die down. You had to remember back; you had to think forward. Every single one of the Börne sketches was a glowing spark. In each one of his works, you could feel with what strength his reasoning power strove to master his fervent heart. Even his smallest work was a cry for release from some form of prejudice, a cry for freedom. Just like his thoughts— strong, fresh and courageous—his style had become freer, and the language with which he spoke more fluid and energetic. Not only was I surprised by the spirit of Börne's writings, but his language made such an impression on me that I never tired of reading him aloud over and over, simply because of the sound and liveliness of his style. I finally knew individual sketches like "The Novel" and "The Temple of Janus" by heart.

I think no one has ever given sufficient credit to Börne and Heine for what they did for the German language. They gave it back flexibility and quick-wittedness, which made it suitable for usage in political and social debates at the least. They stamped new coinage from the gold ingots of our linguistic treasure, heaped up by Goethe and Schiller, and made an accessible and useful common property of what had previously been the exclusive possession of a privileged few.

The Belgian revolution followed on the heels of the French; the world had come into motion; we constantly heard new and exciting news and wanted to have more and more of it. The question "What news did you hear today, Father?" had become the usual greeting for him when he came home for lunch from the stock exchange. We were usually sitting with Mother in the little anteroom on the street, to be able to go to the living room and the table when Father arrived. We were waiting for him there doing our handwork one day in September. Mother was at her customary place on the window sill, I, opposite to her at the same window, my sister at the other window, my brothers and the younger children in the room, when my father entered and we asked the customary question.

"Yes," said Father, "I have some news, but not good news... something very sad." Frightened—this sort of announcement was not Father's style—we looked up at him. His expression showed that he himself was very upset. With a tremor in his voice, he added, "I have just found out that Leopold has died in Braunsberg."

We were all silent. Everyone looked at me, and I sat there more quietly than the others. I had heard quite clearly what Father had said and even understood it. I had heard my friends say that Leopold's fever had returned repeatedly, and that tuberculosis was suspected. I had never thought about him being really sick, though, let alone on the point of death. I remembered him as strong and full of life—and now he was dead. I just could not grasp that. I was stunned; I felt nothing but an inner numbness.

Mother asked about the details; my brother, who had loved Leopold very much, was shattered; my sisters all spoke kindly and regretfully of him; I sat there silently. Finally we were supposed to go to lunch, and my parents asked me if I would like to eat in my room. I said no and went quietly with the others to the table. Human beings are strange—I still remember every dish I ate and that my father told his employees of Leopold's death, while I kept sitting there as if without thoughts or feelings.

After the meal, I usually went to my room, and I did so on that day, too. My sisters and brothers had gone to their school and Gymnasium. I sat at the window from which I had always gazed when Leopold came down the street with his pupils in the early morning and greeted me. Today he was not coming—and he could never come again.

I deliberately called up such thoughts now because I wanted to cry, wanted to escape the lifelessness which had seized me, but to no avail. I could not cry, and in the midst of my numbness, I was seized by a despairing remorse, because I had followed my father's orders blindly and without will, like a machine. I should have listened to the advice of my girl friend and seen him again, when he asked to visit me. A feeling of guilt I could not suppress, a rage against my father, tortured me in addition to my other emotions. And yet I still felt numb. These were hours I still remember with great pain.

The visit of a friend who had also heard of Leopold's death brought me out of this stupor. Her pale face, the tenderness with which she embraced me—her tears evoked mine. I cried and began to speak; I realized what I had lost—and I was so young that I thought I was through with all the wishes and hopes for my life. Tragedies strike young people with special force, because they do not yet realize the restorative powers of life, so that every loss seems irreplaceable, every destroyed hope the only and last one. It is quite wrong to consider youth the time of courage and hope, because both are far more the fruit of experience and an achievement of maturity.

Neither my father nor my mother ever uttered one syllable about Leopold to me after that day, nor I to them. My older siblings and some of my girl friends consoled me as best they could and gave me the opportunity of talking about him. I never found out how he spent the last period of his life or how he died. It remained dark and mysterious for me. Only my loss was clear to me. I had lived and suffered through an entire love affair without ever speaking to my partner in it other than in the presence of my assembled family. I had seen a whole future looming before me without any basis except my faith in my beloved, and it had collapsed without my understanding where the destructive blow came from. I stood at his grave and could hardly show I was mourning. I had gained only one thing—the strength to live an inner life without showing much on the outside, the strength to rely on myself and to pull myself together.

20

People were still occupied with the events and consequences of the French and Belgian revolutions when rumors of great problems among the people of Poland began to spread among us Prussians, and the progress of the cholera epidemic toward the European border of Russia created much concern.

We knew of the conditions in Poland, of the hardships that the Russian government had imposed on the country and of the individual terrible injustices of the arbitrary and bizarre tyranny exercised by Archduke Constantine, the Czar's viceroy in Poland. Although commerce between Poland and Prussia had been curtailed, we understood the hatred of the Poles against their Russian masters quite well.

My father had stayed in Warsaw for extended periods of time in the course of his business dealings, and he really liked the city, its social life, and the energetic character of its men and women. We had all known some Poles since childhood, since a number of them had continuing business relationships with my father. Among these land owners, who brought their farm products for sale in the local markets, there were frequently handsome and pleasant men. The men and the women had more relaxed social customs than I was accustomed to and a warmth of expression, a capacity for enthusiasm that I found very appealing. They liked me, too, because my partiality for them and my liveliness were obvious. An older Polish lady, who was having an extended stay in Prussia because of her sick youngest daughter, had considerable influence on me, because she made me aware of how harsh I was judging other women and girls and what a prude I was myself. She was a serious woman, an excellent mother, and, as her compatriots told me later, had an unblemished reputation. It thus surprised me that when I was her guest for a week at a sea resort, she approached the wife of a Königsberg professor in a friendly fashion and spoke to her. All the other ladies were avoiding this woman because she was supposed to be a former mistress of Prince August. I asked my Polish friend that evening if she did not know that. "Oh, yes," she replied, "everybody has been eager to inform me. But the woman is here to recuperate, she never gives any offense, she was very friendly to my daughter on the beach the other day, and it is not charitable to remind her unnecessarily of a past that she would probably like to forget. The virtue of German women must be very fragile if they are afraid it would be damaged immediately by mere contact with a poor, confused person!"

Another time, when we came back to this conversation and I explained to her how strictly we observed the maxim at home that you should avoid even the appearance of an indiscretion, she threw in this remark: "They are about to make you into a complete prude, and that would be too bad. It would be better to tell you that there are situations in which women should not avoid assuming the appearance of wrongdoing, if this serves a greater conviction or purpose. A woman's reputation is very important and well worth considering, but it is not the final criterion of her worth. And think about how easy it is for you to tread the straight and narrow path with the support of your parents. What do you know, what do those other women who turn away from the professor's wife so judgmentally know, of the ways of her past? It is Protestantism that makes German women so uncharitable. Protestantism doesn't recognize forgiveness of sin or absolution and has no pity for the sinner. Only in Catholicism can you find love and the charity to forgive."

Later in the fall, the Polish Jews, the main agents of the trade between Poland and Prussia, brought the news whenever they came over the border that matters were "uneasy" in Poland. Finally, at the beginning of December, the first reports of the revolution in Warsaw arrived in Königsberg.

The proximity of this revolt made it touch us more than the revolutions in the West; since we were unaccustomed to the unusual, people were more frightened or hopeful than the probable events justified. The main concern of the businessmen was, naturally, what effect the revolution would have on border and customs regulations, and the demands of the aggressor Poles as well as the Russians soon made it necessary to loosen the control of imports. I do not know whether the Poles opened the border formally or the Russians just ignored the traffic, but suddenly there was such a lively increase of trade in Königsberg that the town was as full of Polish Jews in the winter as it usually was in the summer. We could earn money from and with everything.

My father knew just how to use such an opportunity. The work in the wine warehouses increased immediately, both day and night. During the night, the workers rinsed out barrels and bottles in our courtyard, and since it was cold, we had to prepare coffee and beer soup at night for them. My father was gone frequently. He went to Danzig and Stettin to increase his stock of supplies from their stores; he went to the various border towns several times to supervise the transport of the merchandise. The more the revolution spread in Poland, the more active the traffic in goods became in our city. Against all previous practice, the family was drawn into helping in our business.

My father had always wanted to give his children some practical business skills. When I left school, he had me trained, for example, in tailoring and all kinds of mending. He had always wanted the boys to learn a trade. He thought of sending them to a bookbinder or glazer, but the few free hours left to the schoolboys were insufficient for the learning of such skills. In the preceding spring, Father had used the opportunity offered by a Frenchman traveling through Königsberg to have my brothers instructed in the distillation of liqueurs, eau de Cologne, and perfumes, which were made by the cold method.

One of the storage rooms behind the living rooms of our house was converted for that purpose, and under the direction of M. Jeannillon, my brothers and my eldest sister made brandy and mixed volatile oils and bone-black until they derived satisfactory combinations. After Jeannillon left, small amounts of liqueurs were made under Father's supervision to keep the three young distillers in practice. Our sales representatives were able to dispose of them quite easily when they traveled through the province. Now, after the outbreak of the revolution, all kinds of merchandise was profitable and our little distillery was expanded. It was a pleasure to see how the two schoolboys and my sister hurried to their laboratory, after they had finished their homework, and then worked, black as charcoal burners but happy as larks, because they were being useful to Father. Mother, I, and the younger children had the simple task of cutting the labels and pasting them on the bottles. In such a way, a small profitable business, which depended largely on the efforts of those three siblings, had arisen next to my father's major enterprises. Another time, my father bought a whole load of oranges, which we unpacked at home and wrapped individually. The profits from this transaction, with which we all helped, were turned over to Mother to buy a satin coat, since she had deprived herself of all luxuries in the years Father could not pay his bills. He was so consistent in this regard that, when my oldest uncle gave me a black silk dress for my fifteenth birthday, I had to put it away for several years, because Father could not afford to give Mother silk dresses. It would not have been proper for me to show off in a gift silk dress. Later, when Father could once again afford silk dresses and a higher standard of luxury for personal expenditures, the silk dresses my relatives gave me as birthday presents were no problem and gave me great pleasure, because I loved pretty clothes.

[Lewald meets Johann Jacoby[74] for the first time.]

About six months before the cholera epidemic broke out in Königsberg, several young Prussian doctors had gone to Russia and Poland to learn about the disease and to help in the hospitals. One of them was Johann Jacoby, who was then only twenty-five. Shortly before his departure, I met him at a party. We girls were surprised that someone could be so happy and dance so merrily, when he had such a serious mission and dangerous task before him. I did not know him well then; our friendship began at a much later time; I really thought he had a prejudice against me and found me very superficial. That would not have been surprising, because I cultivated all sorts of ridiculous habits at the time, which he probably saw clearly. I answered him the way he addressed me—sharply and briefly. I thought we repelled each other and would do well to avoid further contact. The quiet deliberateness characteristic of this man from early on, which separated him from his contemporaries, demanded a respect I was not prepared to give such a young man, because I had not seen it in any other of my male acquaintances since Leopold's death.

[The cholera epidemic causes some rioting in Königsberg and Lewald's father decides on a name change.]

After the outbreak of the cholera epidemic, my father surprised us one day with the information that he had requested from the government permission to change our name from Markus to Lewald, a name his brother had already adopted twenty years earlier. The matter of whether Father had decided to take this action at this time because he wanted to complete it before the epidemic might take him from us, or had chosen this moment because such a decision would attract less attention at a time of crisis, is immaterial. Suffice it to say that this intention was announced to us just as arbitrarily and suddenly as the baptism of my brothers. But that action had been a joy for my mother, and the name change created great concern in her. She fell around my father's neck in tears and begged him not to insist on it; they had been happy together for twenty years under this name, and it seemed to her that he was tearing away a piece of her life if he took away her name.

My father was very indulgent of her emotional reaction, but it did not change his decision one bit. His heart was very warm, but his reason preserved him from all softness of feeling as long as he was in his full powers, and only later, when he became sick, did that weakness come out in him which is often falsely called "feeling." He reassured Mother kindly with sensible reasons. He told her that it was very inconsistent of her to want to get away from Judaism as much as possible but to resist shedding a Jewish name. He asked her if she would not have married him if his name had been Lewald twenty years ago. When he noticed that there was opposition to the name change among the children, particularly from my eldest brother, he said seriously, "The important thing is that I consider the change appropriate, even necessary. You two boys will attend the university this year and the next. Why would you want a Jewish name? What good will it be to you in your life? —Quite aside from the fact that you would have a name different from that of your family if you ever met my brothers who live abroad and their children. Don't even think about it, I know what I am doing and you will realize it one day and thank me."

On the following day, the name change was announced in the papers. I have never discovered how the name Lewald came into our family or how one great uncle, who had married a Christian artisan's daughter thirty or forty years earlier and had first called himself by it, had come to choose it. It was not a name among the Prussian bourgeoisie. The noble family that bore the name spelled it "Lehwaldt," and so our name in its present form seems to have been an invention of my uncle. It had the advantage for us of giving us a unique name that became what a name should be—a positive distinguishing mark.

21

[Lewald has many diversions and meets interesting young men at parties, but worries about her own frivolity in not mourning properly for Leopold. She also writes some bad poetry.]

I do not own one page of these poems any more. I burned them many years ago, because keeping useless papers is foolish and impractical. Even as an adult, I have only written bad poetry and with the exception of occasional poems for my own use (birthdays, anniversaries, etc.) I have written very little verse. Besides a few short poems I wrote on a trip, which my cousin August Lewald published in *Europa*, none of my poetic productions has ever reached the public, and ten years later, when I learned I could write prose, I dropped poetry completely.[75]

22

[She writes of her brothers and sisters, her life in the household, and of the ups and downs in her father's business. She never knows what their economic situation really is, but has been taught to be thrifty at all times.]

It was therefore a great surprise for me when my father called me into the room he shared with Mother, a few days after my twenty-first birthday, and asked me, "What would you say if I took you on a trip with me?"

My father had been planning a trip since the winter to purchase wines on the Rhine and Neckar, and this had recently been set for April.

It was the first extensive trip my father had made, and at that time, the western borders of Germany were far more distant from Königsberg than now. I myself had never seen a city other than

Königsberg and had only left its confines to make an occasional visit to acquaintances at the sea resort Kranz, five miles from town. When my parents and my brothers and eldest sister had made an excursion a year ago to see Frauenburg and its cathedral, and Elbing and Marienburg with their magnificent castles, I had stayed home to keep the house and take care of my little sisters. At that time, Father had told Mother, who felt sorry for me, "Don't fret, dear Mother. Fanny will one day see more of the world than you are seeing now!"

But that had been no real promise, and although I often sat at the window in the winter, looking at the snow on the roofs sparkling with the red glow of sunset and thought of such light on the glaciers of the Alps, or declaimed Mignon's "Thence, thence!"[76] or recited the words of Joan of Arc about "the mighty flowing Loire" to myself as I was sewing, I had never hoped for or expected such a trip. It lay far above everything I could expect from my parents and beyond any demands of daughters considered justified in the circles of my more prosperous relatives. I did not know how to respond to my father's proposal, other than to look at him and Mother joyfully.

And we were all beaming with joy: Father, because he was able to give me such an unexpected pleasure; Mother, whose entire devotion and sweetness came to the fore in her pleasure over my happy face; and I myself—I felt not only as if I would see part of the world, but as if Father were giving me the whole world! And a lovely piece of the world and of life was disclosed to me by that first trip, which paved the path for my future—a path neither my father nor I could foresee at the time.

Things became very busy at our house. My father gave me thirty-four thalers to outfit myself. I had never had so much money in my whole life, and it seemed that I could buy a whole wardrobe that would even be suitable abroad. But a simple green marceline dress (the first colored silk dress of my life and thus a real acquisition), another summer dress, a travel hat, several morning caps adorned with lace and pink ribbons (giving me what I considered to be an irresistably romantic look), a few embroidered collars and new shoes—purchasing just these had

quickly exhausted my colossal fortune. At home, we began to
sew and tailor new clothes and to refurbish and alter old ones; we
could scarcely draw breath!

All at once I had become a new person for my siblings. I, too,
looked at them with different eyes, because I was to leave them
and Mother for an undetermined time. That "we children," who
had always thought of ourselves as an entity, could be separated,
that I was to leave now, right now, felt like a completely new concept to me, as the time approached, although I had thought about
it earlier in connection with my marriage to Leopold. All foresight
is colorless compared with the power of actuality and the present.

We were all indescribably happy. We seemed more important
to ourselves than usual, because one of us was going joyfully on a
journey, and yet Mathilde and I cried, and even my brothers did,
when we thought of being separated. There was much discussion
in the family. The childless aunts and uncles saw in the planned
trip only a new way of spoiling me, a thought they clung to until
they came upon the idea that my father intended to marry me off
to someone somewhere. That was within the scope of their thinking; they often told me that Father probably had an eligible
"beau" for me, and they warned me urgently to climb down off
my "high horse"; if a decent man wanted me, I should marry him
sensibly, without worrying too much about love, which did not
matter as much in marriage as it did in the courtship.

That was very reasonable, but I was not particularly recep-
tive to this kind of prosaic thinking. It had no effect on me other
than strengthening all my ideals and making me long even more
to be in a position where such offensive comments could not be
made to me. My relatives fortunately had no idea of the hurt
caused by their tactlessness.

My childhood and school friends, of course, thought differently. They had not forgotten that our teacher dubbed me "the
author," nor my beautiful occasional poems. They said that my
father was taking me along so that I could become a writer. They
were as unaware as I of how directly opposed to my father's
plans for me this idea was, or how making me a writer would
actually come about.

I swam in a veritable sea of rapture! Everything enchanted
me: the new clothes and the farewell visits; my trunk and the love
of my siblings; the passport, which had my name as well as
Father's; Mother's untiring goodness; and all the small new items
added to my travel outfits. I floated back and forth from the most
superficial to the most essential. Over me shone the light of the
most golden hopes. I do not know what I really expected. But I
was full of expectation, and this condition is the closest thing to
pure happiness.

The days passed rapidly and it was time to leave. I cannot
describe how we said goodbye or how we went to the post-coach.
Nor can I describe the bliss and pride with which I rode in the
post-coach through the streets at the side of my beloved father.
The pleasure of being able to greet all my acquaintances! The
pleasure of seeing the green veil of my straw hat fluttering in the
bright morning of April thirteenth!

And now, tears again, as I saw Mother and my brothers and
the younger children crying on the balcony and the clerks, the
coopers, and the workers standing in front of the cellars and saying goodbye! And then the triumph of driving by the houses of the
two aunts, who had wanted to marry me off so badly—and telling
myself I would not marry yet, and never, if I did not want to!

Then, a last look at the Pregel and its ships, at the houses of
the suburbs and the old Haberberg Church, at the pump with the
small, carved, brightly painted figure of Hans von Sagen, the
brave shoemaker who had once defended Königsberg against the
Poles—and now, out to the city gate onto the long limitless highway—which led everywhere!

I had left Königsberg and my home for the first time. My
father gave me his hand. "Well, Fanny?" he said. I kissed his
hand. He, himself, led me out into the world, into a life that was
to take me on the most circuitous routes to a happy ending.

BOOK TWO

The Years of Suffering

1

[Lewald enjoys her first long trip and is excited by Berlin.]

Everything enthralled me. I had a room to myself for the first time in my life, I was living in a hotel for the first time, I was served by waiters, I had red silk curtains and a beautiful carpet over the whole floor, and (this was the main thing) I had nothing at all to do, no duties to fulfill. I was there completely for myself and my pleasure; everything that happened did so, to some extent, for my sake. This satisfaction of my egotism was very pleasant. I basked in the feeling of freedom. I thought about home, my room, Mother and my siblings, who were at work or in school, only to rejoice, because I did not have to do anything. I was very happy on that morning, and I seemed so important, so interesting to myself, that I still think about it with pleasure. It was as if life were only now really beginning for me, as if the whole world lay open before me, and as if I would encounter the best and most beautiful things immediately. As I sat at the window in my new negligee, foulard robe, and a little cap with pink ribbons, and gazed with wondering eyes at the old-fashioned splendid palace, the Elector's Bridge and the statue of the Great Elector,[77] I was convinced, deep in my heart, that Berlin would find me as attractive as I found it. I would not have been at all surprised if some noble and beautiful young man had appeared at the window of the palace and fallen in love with me at first sight.

People tend to underestimate the childish romantic vanity of a young girl, because they do not realize how naive she usually is, and because most women are later so ashamed of this naiveté that they will not admit to it. For my part, I mistook my feelings for the feelings of the people around me with the greatest ease. I thought I excited surprise and pleasure because I felt such emotions, and a newcomer to such a life needs some self-deception.

The ten days we spent in Berlin did not do much to advance my self-esteem or to satisfy the expectations I had of the society in the capital and which I had hoped to fulfill in my first visit. When we spoke of Berlin at home, I always heard about the linden trees, of all the beautiful elegant streets, and of the brilliant intellectual scene. I rode through the lovely streets of the city the first few days and knew the names of all the families that had the best salons. But after leaving the hotel, I did not live in the elegant parts of town, but with one of my aunts on the ugly and noisy Münzstrasse, and the circles I longed for were not open to me. I was dependent on our relatives and my father's business friends. These were fine people, but their companionship was not even up to the level of my friends at home. Added to that was the fact that my relatives did not like me nearly as much as I had expected. They tried to change me: my clothes did not have the proper cut, the bodices were too short, and my hair was not styled in accordance with the current Berlin fashion. I had curls; with black hair, they supposedly made me look old. I was as proud as Samson of my hair and my curls, which I had had since childhood. After my appearance had been duly criticized, they went on to my behavior. I was supposed to be more extroverted, more naive and sometimes not so sure of myself, because the way I was, serious and certain and sure, would not attract men. I should try to please men, because it would not be easy to find someone who would chose as his wife a girl with so many unmarried sisters from a relatively poor family. The worst of it was that none of the women giving advice inspired any confidence or even respect in me. They were older than I, much older. But mere age had never impressed me. It does not excuse superficiality and lack of culture. I was mostly dealing with half-educated and therefore usually arrogant women, who had no idea of the seriousness of my nature and my desires.

My father was not entirely without responsibility for the advice given me. I heard him say to an acquaintance once how happy he would be if I found a suitable "beau," as that was one reason he had brought me along. I could have screamed with shame and rage at that moment. I felt like faulty merchandise that you bring to market because there is no buyer for it at home; so I compensated by becoming even more naive, merrier, and eager to please. I had to exercise the greatest self-control to hold my tongue. A visit made to the family of a privy councillor, an in-law of my father's, was not calculated to make me feel better.

The councillor, a Jew who had converted to Christianity, received us coldly and formally. That was stupid, because he could have chosen not to receive us at all. I think he was very aware of his own dignity and appearance because of his new position, and he could not let any opportunity slip by to demonstrate his magnificence. Ten years later he had changed greatly because of the liberal education of his children; he became more relaxed and benevolent. He was not the only man I knew who was reeducated and changed by his children after he had guided their early education. I always compare this in my mind to the foliage of a tree, which grows out of the tree, draws its first nourishment from the tree, and then fertilizes the earth around the tree so that it can derive strength for new leaves and growth.

My father was amused at the pretensions of the councillor, and he spoke laughing about them after we had left him. The man had a discouraging effect on me, because I was already hurt and depressed, although I had enjoyed my father's quiet dignity during the visit and was pleased by the contrast between Father's good looks and social grace and the councillor's homeliness and stiff awkwardness. I told myself at the time, however, that there was no escaping the problems I had suffered at home, so it mattered little whether I was unhappy there or in Berlin. Then, on that morning of painful discoveries, we went to the newly erected Schinkel[78] museum.

From the hot spring day, from the noise of the street, we stepped through the as yet unpainted and unpeopled, columned passage into the cool, still rotunda of the antique gallery, illuminated from above. I had never seen a noble structure or a work of sculpture. It seemed to me as if I had been suddenly transported into another world, of which I had had vague visions in dreams as of a distant home. I do not know what happened to me; I could not have said what I was thinking. Tears came to my eyes; I folded my hands, and only the presence of my father deterred me from kneeling in rapture. For the first time I enjoyed that freeing of my soul which I so often felt in later years from observing the beautiful, or art in general. Even now, when I step into the rotunda of that museum, unfortunately marred by the tasteless statue of Frederick William III, I feel warmed and refreshed by the memory of that first impression.

I realized that there was something in the world for me, something that was higher than all the incidental matters touching and hurting me. Regardless or not whether people liked me, whether or not I married, whether I was dependent or free, or whether society received me kindly or disdainfully—there was beauty in the world and I could partake of it!

[Lewald sees Rahel Varnhagen[79] at a theater.]

On the evening when I saw *Corregio*,[80] I was made aware during the intermission of a lady sitting in one of the boxes. She was small and elderly, wore a strange and not exactly fresh or pretty headdress, and was conversing with another woman sitting next to her and two men behind her, who were leaning toward her. They were listening very intently, but she often turned her head toward the stage while speaking, with great vivacity. I could see that she had a dark complexion and very serious dark eyes. She was unmistakably Jewish, and I was told that this was Rahel Levin, Mrs. Varnhagen von Ense. I had never heard of her, but she interested me because of Varnhagen. I mentioned to my companions that we had brought a letter of introduction from my aunt in Hamburg, Dr. Assing's wife, to her brother, Mr. von Varnhagen, but had not used it, upon my request, because the visit to the councillor had been so unpleasant. Our friends tried to persuade us to visit the Varnhagens before we left, citing Rahel's kindness and Varnhagen's humanity, but I was hesitant about it and my father was busy; and so we did not do it. Later I would have given almost anything to have met Rahel, who became the object of my warmest admiration and love because of her legacy of letters, to have been received into her own home, and to have heard words from her eloquent mouth, if only once.

[From Berlin, the Lewalds go to Leipzig, Weimar, Frankfurt, Darmstadt, Heidelberg, and other cities. Lewald is pleased because she is sometimes taken for her father's wife, not his daughter. She is appalled at the conditions in the Frankfurt ghetto.]

In Frankfurt we again sought out the birthplaces of Goethe and Börne. The appearance of Jew Alley, where Börne had been born, was still was appalling in those days. I hardly recognized it when I revisited it in 1848. Even the distorted physiognomy of the inhabitants, which struck us then in their contrast to the looks of the frequently handsome Polish Jews, seemed to me later to have moderated in the younger generation. The demoralization of the race in Jew Alley was really something terrible in 1832, and we could not forget our impressions for a long time.

2

[The Lewalds arrive in Baden-Baden to visit her father's youngest brother, Friedrich Jakob Lewald and his large family. Friedrich Jakob is full of tales of Goethe and his patron, Karl August of Weimar. She meets Ludwig Robert, Rahel's brother, and his wife, as well as Ludwig Börne.]

Börne lived not far from us in Stephanienbad. When we went from our house to town, we passed by his home, where he often sat in front of the door with his friend, Mrs. Wohl, and her companion. He was small and thin, his hair already lightly touched with gray although he was still in his prime. The well-known etching of Börne, made from the portrait by Oppenheim, is very like him. The characteristics of Börne's outward appearance were reserve and calm. He had problems with his hearing, and there was something alert, listening, expectant, in his face, when others spoke, which then faded as soon as he spoke. His clothing was very clean; you could see his appearance was very important to him. A large long watch chain was the only inappropriate item in his attire. We always thought it was an inheritance or had been given to him by someone who did not know him personally.

The discussion and mood of those days before the Hambach Festival[81] was excited and passionate. Börne would listen quietly to everyone's opinions, and then interject some pertinent or decisive comment. It was touching with what happy satisfaction Mrs. Wohl looked at him then and how delighted she was about the impression Börne's enlightening and important words made on the listeners.

We had arrived at Baden-Baden on the twentieth of May, about a month after our departure from Königsberg. After meeting several of my uncle's friends, we became aware that we were much closer to the political movement and excitement, the beginning and growth of which we had only followed in the papers till then.

The names of Wirth and Siebenpfeiffer[82] were on everyone's lips. Siebenpfeiffer and thirty-three other citizens of Neustadt had invited all the men (and women, married or single!) of Germany to a national festival at Hambach Castle near Neustadt; this invitation received a greater response after the government had first forbidden the festival and then had permitted it again, for fear of greater unrest. The government declarations against the festival, and those of its proponents in its defense, followed one another quickly. Ludwig Robert saw the approach of a devastating revolution with this event. Everyone either looked forward to or feared the unpredictable results of the May festival, depending on his political belief.

My father had to go to Neustadt on business; it had been one of the original reasons for his trip. A wine auction was to be held there, and since its date was so close to that of the Hambach Festival, he decided to attend the festival as well. I wanted to go with him very much, and my uncle tried to talk him into taking me. But Father thought I would be very uncomfortable at such an event, the outcome of which was unpredictable, so he went without me. Börne also went to Neustadt a few days before the festival and returned very elated. I was present when he spoke to my uncle and several other gentlemen about it. When he noticed me, he said, "You should thank me. I took your father, with whom I spoke only yesterday, under my protection at the festival. People were in a very anti-Prussian mood, and I told them this was a Prussian, whom you could admit to the festival without any fears. This was no spy."

This was a joke, but only in regard to my father, because Börne had spoken the truth about the feelings against Prussia. People confused it with Russia and several times in Baden, I saw signs in public houses with the words "and no Prussians!" written in under the usual sign, "No dogs admitted." Such signs were usually quickly removed, because this attitude was not very promising for the unification of Germany, which the Hambach Festival was trying to achieve.

My father returned from his business trip to Neustadt a few days later and told us about the festival, the first folk festival he had ever attended, with great enthusiasm and warmth. He brought home Siebenpfeiffer's opening speech, titled "The German May," and a number of printed papers. Among these were the first issues of a newly published newspaper, also called *The German May*, and many songs composed for the festival. Everything had a passionate style and had (the papers, which I kept as souvenirs of my trip, are lying now faded and yellow on my desk as I write this) all the characteristiscs and shortcomings of the demonstrations for which they were composed. They set loose a flood of emotions, without building a channel to direct it, so that it could be dammed to provide a driving power. If such a direction is not there, the high tide of enthusiasm runs off into nothing without any effect or results.

About thirty thousand people gathered at Hambach Castle. Enthusiasm ran high. "You German men," the end of Siebenpfeiffer's speech exhorted, "let us forget all differences, all distinctions and separations. Let us carry only one flag, the flag of our German fatherland, and remember at all times what we should be and want to be. Let us swear allegiance to only one law in our hearts, the sacred law of German freedom. Let us look toward only one goal, the shining goal of German national unity, German greatness, German power. When all German men finally grasp this one thought completely and strongly, then I swear by Thuisko, the god of free Germans, that that which we all strive for and for which we are now laying the cornerstone will arise in radiant strength—a free German fatherland! Long live a free and united Germany! Long live the Poles, allies of the Germans! Long live the Franks, brothers to the Germans, who respect our nationality and independence! Long live the people of every nation who break their chains and swear the oath of freedom with us! Long live our fatherland—the power of the people—the union of the people!"

Everybody had worn the German colors (red, gold and black) in Neustadt and had gone home after the festival past border markers painted with all sorts of other colors, with which the rulers of the various German principalities fence in their territories from one another. Matters were the same then as now. It is not the fashion any more to swear by Thuisko, god of the free Germans; people are satisfied with Arminius the Cheruscan,[83] who is also sufficiently remote. Now, however, we do not have any names like that of Ludwig Börne, whom everyone knew and respected.

Father had much to say about the reverence Börne encountered everywhere. Wherever he had shown himself, he had been greeted with friendly cries; the students in Neustadt had brought him serenades, and women had thrown him bouquets. Without stepping forward, he had been the focus of the festival.

All these reports and experiences made me feel as though I were peering through a telescope. Distant worlds, the existence of which and influence on our own lives I had been vaguely aware of, without actually seeing, now suddenly appeared on my horizon, dazzling me with their scope and aura. I could hardly follow the experience with my mind, but I liked the change in my vantage point. What was best, there in Baden, was that the people I met liked me. They let me have my own way, were interested in me and encouraged me. I was very happy to be treated so well by people I respected far more than those in Berlin.

3

[Lewald also visits Strassburg, to see a part of France. David Lewald returns to Königsberg, but sends Fanny to his oldest and favorite sister, Minna Simon in Breslau, to have a greater range of experiences abroad. She travels there in the company of a rich great-aunt and finds she is received far more favorably in Berlin because of this.]

Since I did not know the streets and my great-aunt liked to visit people, she accompanied me almost everywhere and I could not avoid thinking that the universal approval I now received was based on the coach in which we rode, the hired footman who announced us, and the wealth of my aunt, who chaperoned me with her companion. My uncle in Baden-Baden had also generously given me several costumes made in the newest Parisian fashion. So my bodices and dresses were short enough, my boots the best style and nut-brown, my sleeves as full as sacks, the white capes with their high, stiff edges disproportionately big, the ascots very ornate, the pink silk bonnet with a French rose properly tiny, and the parasol as generous as an umbrella. This whole ensemble of items too tight or too wide, which was completely unharmonious, found such acclaim from my former feminine critics that part of it rubbed off on me and I rose several degrees in their estimation. I liked this, because I needed to find approval and good will, but I knew precisely what had caused this change of attitude and what it was worth.

4

[Lewald visits her father's relatives in Breslau and falls in love again, this time with a cousin, Heinrich Simon, son of her father's eldest sister.]

Aunt Minna, as my father called her when he spoke of her, was the eldest of the siblings and was beloved and revered by all. It was unanimously and unequivocally felt that she was a superior being. She and her household were the ideal of both my father's other sisters; even my great-aunt spoke of "Minna" with a whole different tone of voice than of everyone else. It was Aunt Minna and her family whose companionship Father had promised me when he wanted to reconcile me to a prolonged absence from home.

I had already been required to write my aunt and her daughters for many years and a friendly correspondence had resulted from that. My cousins, some of whom were younger, some older than I, knew as much about my life as I did of theirs. Sometimes my aunt would insert a brief note and I considered that a special favor. Aunt Minna was very reserved and unintentionally received many of the benefits connected with this kind of personality. Only those who have suffered as much as I did from having an emotional nature really recognize an inborn trend toward reserve as a major advantage for the ones who possess it.

We had to go a long way before we came to the summer garden residence that the Simons were renting in front of the Schweidnitz Gate on Konrad Street. Although we were tired and had just arrived and Uncle Friedrich Lewald was back in his own house with his extensive family for the first time in a year and a half, he and Uncle Simon immediately took me to visit his oldest sister on the same evening. The whole family seemed to find this completely normal. I was already prepared to love and revere this sister of my father's; these feelings (and the suspense of waiting to meet her) were heightened by this special homage of my uncles.

The house lay surrounded by a large, shady garden. My heart pounded as we entered the gate. My cousins came toward us from the house and I saw my aunt step out of the conservatory and look at us with her lorgnette; she was evidently very nearsighted. She came down the steps as she recognized us, and as she stepped forward, I noticed that she limped slightly; but since her walk was quick and unusually light for her age, this weakness, the result of a case of smallpox, did not detract at all from her appearance.

She embraced her brother and then me, and said with her soft voice—squinting slightly to see me better—"Welcome, child.

You look very much like your father." I was immediately touched and won over by her look, her voice, her few words. I kissed her hand and felt a sudden empathy, the kind that seldom deceives, before I ever suspected how much I would love her and what a great influence she would have on me.

My aunt was probably in her early fifties then and was of medium height and slender. She resembled her siblings, although her features were not as beautiful or noble as those of my father and one of his other sisters. She was scarred from smallpox and pale and had light eyes—you could see that she was myopic when you were close. Her melancholy expression only changed when a pleasant experience or a joke she was privy to made her happy. Then her face became animated and winning. It was primarily her quiet voice, the way she expressed herself, and the fine lineaments around her mouth that made her so attractive when she spoke. Just as there are noble and beautiful rooms that seem to forbid a person to utter or even think anything petty or ugly in them, my aunt exercised a calming and authoritative effect on everything around her.

She was a totally serious woman, a term that can be applied to very few of our sex. All the small tendencies present in most women, all the weaknesses and follies they consider charming in themselves, were foreign to her. She did not like fancy clothes, although she was very fastidous about her appearance. She had no need for diversion, because her inner composure satisfied her. She did not long for trips because her house was her world. She had almost no contact with strangers, because she had raised her children to be completely satisfying company for her, able to meet all her intellectual needs. This way of life explains why months often passed during which she did not leave her house for even a few hours. In the summer, when people moved to a garden residence or went to the Silesian spas, she walked in her own garden, since she loved nature and could lose herself happily in the contemplation of a small bird or a beetle or even the most insignificant flower in the grass. In the winters she walked up and down her room daily at twilight for exercise; then it was a pleasure for us all to hear her soft voice chatting with someone or, when she was happy, her equally soft laughter. Her reserve was not something selfish, because she participated and helped where she was needed, without participating or helping needlessly just to keep herself busy. Because she was not curious about petty matters, she had an uncommon eye and understanding for the universal. To escape from excessive concern about her children, which could have led her to curtail her own development by sacrificing herself for them and thus not able to raise them properly, she had resolved early in her marriage to set aside a few hours a day aside for herself and for reading; she then instituted and firmly maintained this practice. Every afternoon she withdrew to her room to rest; you can understand and work out many problems in this way, if you limit your readings to great and important books, as she did. She was always conversant with the newest literary works and was vitally interested in the cultural and political events in Europe. No one offered better proof than she of the progress and the success with which reason prevails over prejudice or freedom over suppression in all spheres.

Her inclination toward quiet and the constant, probably imaginary illness of a daughter kept all types of social events from her house. She did not call on anyone, and no one was invited to come. Now and then there was a single short visit for a few hours or her daughters came to see her. Only the father, who was unusually well-educated for a businessman in those days and had a happy, outgoing personality, went out—to the Resource every day from five to eight—but was always home for the family supper. Of the six children, four still lived at home, including the oldest son, Heinrich, who was much involved in the political development of Germany at the time and was preparing for his bar examination.

The family had told me a great deal about my cousin Heinrich on the trip, in the many days we had to spend chatting in the coach. Uncle Lewald called him a very good and hard-working person, the women in the family raved about his good looks, his personality and his charm. Their descriptions surrounded him with a certain romantic glow, which was enhanced for me by a sad event in his life.

Heinrich Simon had been provoked into a duel in Brandenburg on the Havel when he was scarcely twenty-three and had
had the misfortune to kill his opponent, a Refendarius Bode. He
had given himself up to the authorities immediately and, after a
lengthy investigation, had been sentenced to a long prison term
at Fortress Glogau. I believe some general amnesty freed him
before he had finished the sentence. When I came to Breslau, he
had been back with his family some time.

He was not at home when I came, but his mother and sisters
spoke of him, and when Uncle Lewald offered to take me with
him to his home in town, they would not let me leave until I had
met Heinrich. Finally, when we could wait no longer, his sisters
said he would come to see us early the next morning, but Aunt
Minna insisted I return to her for breakfast, so she could enjoy
my company as much as my other relatives had.

I went out to the garden on time the next morning, but Heinrich had already left for an appointment with the law court and it
was noon before his sisters happily announced that he was coming home. The youngest sister went to welcome him, and I wanted to also, because it seemed the natural thing to do. But I was
beset by mistaken ideas about feminine dignity and restraint,
which I could not abandon, even when dealing with a close relative. Adding to this hesitation were the many conversations my
great-aunt and her companion had had about Heinrich's attraction for women and how much they spoiled him. That was probably the only way those two good women could interpret him. I
resolved on my part never to spoil him. To maintain this resolve
right from the start and to show the appropriate dignity and
restraint (which in most cases are completely calculated and only
provocative affectations—as they were with me) I remained sitting quietly next to my aunt, although I was terribly curious
about my cousin and already inclined to love him, since I liked
his family so much and they loved him greatly.

It may have been my virtuous restraint that moved my cousin
to embrace me formally when he entered and not to address me
with "Du" as the others did. That embarrassed and irritated me.
When I gazed up into his handsome face, the thought came to me

that he had looked at a person with those eyes as he aimed his pistol and had murdered him with the hand he gave me in welcome. (I did already have enough sense in those days to find a duel, murder for the privileged, abhorrent.) That frightened me. I could not understand how he could talk to his family so easily or how he could tease his sisters endlessly. When he turned this joking on me, I did not like it at all. Since he was far superior to me in every way and more mature because of his experience, my precocity and intelligence smacked of the nursery and schoolroom to him and seemed comical. He dealt with me in a somewhat playful manner that day, which hurt my feelings intensely, because I thought I was not being treated with the proper respect.

Back at my uncle's home, the main question was how I had liked Heinrich. "He is handsome and intelligent, but cold and distant," I said. "He may be able to be very gracious, but he did not seem that way to me, and I can't get past the thought that he shot someone." My uncle, who seldom said anything bad about anyone, but let people go their own way in most cases, deviated from his usual habit. He maintained that it was unreasonable and unfair to consider a person's misfortune a crime and added, "If you knew how that poor man is still suffering from the result of that experience, you would find it very commendable that he conceals this suffering within him and always shows a happy face to his family, who worried so much about him and made many sacrifices for him. I have sometimes come into conflict with him because he is haughty and unbending, but he is still an extraordinary and excellent person, who cannot be judged as simply as you have just done."

It was the first and only time my uncle rebuked me, and since such rebukes usually make the recipient pass their guilt and unfairness on to the person who caused them, I was now even angrier at my cousin. I knew why I had not found him as attractive as everyone had prophesied. I felt I was an exception to my sex and a particularly beautiful and worthy exception. But while I went to bed with commendable self-confidence and told my roommate (my great-aunt's companion) of all the things I had not liked about my cousin, I could not get rid of the inner conviction that I had never met a handsomer man in my life, nor ever found his equal.

5

[Lewald tells about her relatives' prosperous life style and the famous personages she meets in their social circles, including the poet Hoffmann von Fallersleben.[84] *She also discovers her uncle's extensive library and the group of men that gather there.]*

I could reach the library from my room by a covered corridor without going through the living room. After I had been sent once to my uncle in the library on an errand by my great-aunt, and had been well-received by him and his friends, I often went there on my own, since he had invited me to do so. To hear men conversing freely with one another was something new to me. At home our male guests had usually been of our age, and the older and foreign people who visited were always careful in their conversations, because the presence of young girls and my mother prevented them from speaking of serious matters. Each discussion had limits in its scope and subject. If it became more serious than my father deemed suitable or if it touched on areas of which he did not want us to hear, he ended it quietly with the explanation that he did not want to speak about that.

It was different in my uncle's library. The times were agitated; the German newspapers and journals brought stimulating and exciting news every day and were always available, along with the *Revue de Paris* and the *Revue des deux mondes*. Politics, literature, and social and religious questions were freely discussed. Because I was serious and eager to understand what they were speaking about and what the situation was, they easily forgot that I was a young woman and carried their conversations on to their conclusion.

We were then at a period of history in which the lives of the people (and thus, the life of the individual) seemed to have gained a quicker and livelier tempo. In France, the Romantics had come to the fore, with all their shining and passionate exaggerations, with their bizarre but intellectually stimulating works; they had, for the moment, eliminated the calm and contemplative. Victor Hugo, Balzac, Lamartine, George Sand, Janin, Dumas, Eugène Sue, Alphonse Karr, and Emile Souvestre[85] had a tremendous influence on those who had previously clung almost exclusively to the classical examples of German literature. Those writers offered a glimpse into the conditions and mores of French society that should have revolted and frightened the reader. Under the pressure of political circumstances, intellectual life in Germany did not develop freely, lacking the necessary content and offering men no real scope for the development of their powers. Thus in the foreign literature, German intellectuals mistook excess for strength, lack of self-control for freedom, and confusion about morality and every mistake and crime created by them as acknowledgment of the individual. Even good persons who would not have hurt a fly could not prevent a shiver of delight when *Han d'Islande* raged before them, when *La Histoire des Treize* revealed its terrible secrets to them, when Quasimodo and Lucrezia Borgia and the horrors of *La Tour de Nesle* and the dying and insane on the Salamander[86] gave them that delicious feeling of terror, which Bettina[87] named a *grauel-plaisir* (shudder-pleasure) in similar cases.

Despite the overwrought prose and the purely materialistic interests aroused in the reader, there were a number of deep thoughts in most of these works. Their psychological observations were acute and their language so flexible and powerful, so tender and fiery at the same time, that every work had both an intoxicating and a dazzling effect.

In Germany also a new generation of writers had sprung up. Heine's *Travel Memoirs* and *The Situation in France*, Börne's *Reports from Paris*, conveyed French life to the Germans and brought the longing for freer involvement of the individual with his government, for freer self-determination in personal relationships, more vigorously to Germany. Gutzkow, Laube, Theodor Mundt, Gustav Kühne, and Wienbarg[88] spoke a language never before heard in Germany. Although we may have outgrown some of these writers, as they themselves outgrew their earlier styles, we who were young then as they were must bear witness, albeit reluctantly, that we generally greeted all those youthful works of the so-called Young Germany movement with surprise and total acceptance. Even more mature people than the Young Germans and their youthful readers did not deny the persuasive and progressive power of the young world-attackers, even if they were far from approving or admiring their basic tenets and innovative phraseology as much of the rest of us did.

Besides these new books, my uncle's friends retained their deep admiration for our classical writers, and even the German Romantics, who did not appeal to most of the group, had a fervent admirer in Dr. Eppstein. It was he, an unmarried man, living for his muse and thinking himself destined to be a poet—without ever having written anything worthwhile—who had been introduced to the Tiecks[89] in Dresden and had become a frequent guest at their house. He thus became deeply attached to Tieck and his daughter Dorothea, and consequently made him an enthusiastic admirer of the whole genre of literature represented by Tieck. So the works of Tieck, with which I was previously unfamiliar, those of Novalis and Waiblinger, the novels of Heinrich Steffens, and the poems of Anastasius Grün and Zedlitz[90] became part of my reading. After my interest had been aroused, I would bring all the books discussed by my uncle's group from the library to my aunt's room to read them at leisure and copy excerpts from them.

It makes a strange impression on me now to scan those excerpts and note what small individual fragments shaped my knowledge and opinions and how many unlikely pieces laboriously collected from the most diverse corners and ends formed the mosaic of my life and rounded it into an independent whole. I feel the old regret that even today women are not given that thorough scientific training in school or career education that is regarded more or less as an absolute essential for men of all classes and occupations.

If it were not such a serious matter, it would be comical: the confidence with which men place the running of their household, the partial representation of their position in society or partial control of their income, the care and education of their children, and finally their own happiness and honor into the hands of young persons equipped for these most important tasks only by their good intentions and the blind faith placed by men in love on the worth of the women they have chosen.

No one employs a servant without knowing if he has the proper training; every apprentice, whether to a craftsman or an intellectual superior, has to have an education for many years. A master is not recognized nor a teacher, contractor, carpenter, professor, or attorney given a job or position without having proven his ability. Yet we usually entrust the most important task of life—the founding and maintenance of a family, the education of human beings—to young, inexperienced creatures who have basically been denied the proper training for their job. It seems to be the common opinion that only women are made useless for fulfilling their duties by being systematically taught the kind of knowledge that almost every man has to prove he has acquired to be admitted to the exercise of any kind of profession.

This is an underestimation of women, a complete misunderstanding of their place and purpose in human society. The ones who will suffer the most from this are the ones who are guilty of this sin against women and against the human race. The number of truly happy marriages, the number of women and mothers who can be a real support to their husbands and children in every sense of the word, is therefore much smaller here in Germany than one admits. Neither happiness nor success is often found in most marriages where husband and wife only coexist peacefully because the husband, feeling guilty, does not demand from his wife what she is incapable of giving. He has decided not to expect too much; an immature creature, prepared neither by experience nor insight for human relationships and married life, has not become mature or acquired judgment, merely by having found a man to make her his wife.

So that there will be no doubt at all about my challenge: it is the emancipation of women that I demand for us, that emancipation for which I have striven and have gained for myself, the

Heinrich Simon, Stadtarchiv Frankfurt.

emancipation to work, to work seriously. And such work is completely available outside, and even more within the family, if we make it possible for a woman to understand what is involved and to perform what she recognizes as her job. But more of that later.

[Lewald writes more about her readings and criticizes Goethe for upholding the sanctity of marriage at any cost in his novel Die Wahlverwandtschaften *(Elective Affinities).[91]]*

6

I felt very much at home at my uncle's. He and his wife made me aware that they enjoyed my company. If my aunt or great-aunt had a criticism, they gave it in a friendly fashion. Moreover, since the daughters of the house were still quite young and I was the only young woman in their circle, the men who visited the house were very attentive and friendly to me. I gained in self-confidence and soon seemed so rich in literary knowledge because of my constant reading that I felt like a real nouveau riche, constantly playing with the gold coins in his pocket because they are so new to him. My fortunate memory easily assimilated everything I read, I had quotations by the score in my head, I thought out ideas quickly. Since one of the visitors at the house quoted endlessly and another threw about witty sayings all the time, I imitated both as best I could; I was less satisfied with myself than with the indescribable feeling of being able to do and say what I wanted. I was like a pupil who had been kept strictly disciplined at school, who feels as though he has to break loose when he gets to the university to prove his freedom.

I do not know what my uncle's friends thought of me; I hardly knew what to think of myself. Sometimes I worried about what my father would think, if he knew of my immoderate reading, or how he would rebuke me if he heard how decisively I was judging matters that I did not sufficiently understand. But that never lasted long. I always reassured myself by recalling that it was my father who had sent me here against my wishes and had turned me over to my uncle, or, so to speak, to myself. He had thus given me my freedom, declared me of age, and so I was now my own master and could read and speak, do and leave undone what I wanted, as long as I took my two piano lessons a week and practiced an hour daily.

We had hardly returned to Breslau when I received an order from my father to begin my musical studies once again, and the Lewald children's music teacher was engaged for me. According to all reports, Mr. Freudenberg was supposed to be a very well-educated man musically and was, I believe, an organist at a

church. His tall lean figure, his yellow hair, his outer air of help-
lessness, his old-fashioned buff tail-coat, and his soulful eyes
made him a very extraordinary apparition. Music was an ideal to
him, something divine, which he would have most liked to enjoy
with a few chosen disciples in quiet reverence. He thought—and
not without reason—that virtuosos and concerts were generally a
horror, a type of immorality. I feel remorse in remembering the
poor organist (who was a true Jean-Paul character)[92] because he
was condemned to teaching me and my uncle's completely unmu-
sical children.

Actually the music lessons and practice were not nearly as
bad or as serious as at home. I saw to it that I and my teacher did
not suffer too much. I took my lesson at a piano in my great-
aunt's room. When I practiced, I chatted with the good old lady,
who constantly complained about a headache whenever music
was played; she was delighted when she was able to announce
that my practice hour was over. When my teacher came, we
spoke much about music (better for me than playing it!) and to
this conversation I diligently tried to hold him. After we began
the actual musical instruction—I usually had to play fugues,
which I did not understand at all at that time—he corrected my
playing and praised my beautiful hands and arms, and my great-
aunt used the time to tell him about her childhood friend,
Baroness Eskeles, who had far more beautiful hands and arms
than I and was wonderful to behold when she played the harp. In
between, we would occasionally play a little music—that is, the
teacher played the fugues (which sounded quite different under
his hands than under mine) and my great-aunt would scold him
because he had conducted a few quartets with his friends in front
of his wife's bedroom immediately following the birth of their
baby, to give her pleasure and a delightful surprise. He maintained that for a musical soul like his wife, music could only have
a strengthening effect. My aunt's companion, who would also listen to the lesson and was already at the age when single women
with tender loving hearts find the lot of women sad and gush
about spiritual pleasures and music, also rebuked the teacher for
his carelessness and selfishness. She did admit a woman whose

husband took such interest in her spiritual progress was to be envied. A little piano playing also accompanied this conversation, but there were often visitors at this time and so the poor knowledgable organist naturally finally gave up—with reluctance, for he was, despite his airs, the model of a good man and earnest teacher. He could not help it that my great-aunt and I were no friends of piano lessons and would always try to shorten them as best we could.

I soon became tired of enjoying my freedom by excesses and a tasteless demonstration of my intellect. That was really not my nature, and if my own good sense had not prevailed, the life in the Simon household and the attitude there would have soon brought me back to the right path.

The society of my cousins, because of their ages and education, was really more compatible than the circle of men I encountered in my uncle's house. I felt at home in the strictly disciplined family life, and an attraction soon developed between me and my cousins, which bound us together for many years. Even more than my other cousins, my Aunt Minna and my cousin Heinrich won my love and an influence over me and my entire future.

From the first days I had seen him, I had thought about him. He was about twenty-seven then and, as I have already said, one of the handsomest young men I had ever known. His tall strong figure and his posture were very noble; the physiognomy, which in later years so resembled Michelangelo's head of Moses, the ideal Jewish type, still held something of suffering despite all his other strengths. On the beautiful forehead, surrounded by a mass of black, curly hair, lay an air of deep melancholy, which could be alleviated by an expression of illuminating clarity when he was in a good mood. Even when he was older, he put everyone into a good mood when his face was happy and his bright laughter rang out. He was a master of all kinds of manly activities: a good gymnast, a good rider, a good shot, and an excellent swimmer. His young colleagues and his superiors considered him an excellent attorney and untiring worker, his friends a true friend. His sisters loved him with a kind of pride, and he was obviously the light of their days for his parents and his brother.

A new life came into the family each time the eldest son entered the garden, and still his mother said to me one time with a sigh, "I am so sorry that you didn't know Heinrich earlier. He was such a happy person!" His sisters also always looked at him with a kind of sadness, which I could not really understand since he always seemed cheerful, unperturbed and ready to talk and to give himself to his family with complete love. He went walking in the garden with his mother, brought his ailing sister to her favorite seat, carried his little niece around with him, as long as she demanded, and knew something to do for everyone, so that all of us, even the old servants, loved him and were full of praise for him.

His temperament was basically serious, however, and his thinking far-reaching and intense. He had read and learned much and was almost the only one in the whole group upon whom the brilliance of the new literary works made no impression. He sometimes used a quote from Heine, because, he said, "It was convenient, just as unclean and much-handled small change can be convenient at times," but he rejected Heine's cynicism and the writer himself, because Heine "was not serious with the holiest matters." That last criticism was also directed against many of the other writers that appealed to me. "They are only pretending," he would say, or, "They would do well to refrain from actually doing what they profess in their books. I can sense it in them; they are not consistent." At that time his judgment seemed harsh, but later I had many an opportunity to realize how correctly he saw and judged them.

He was completely consistent, a self-confident person who consciously and unconsciously worked on perfecting himself. He carried in his heart an ideal of masculine excellence and dignity that he strove to reach, an enthusiasm for the beautiful that made him aspire to educate himself to be a person living in beauty. He had within him a kind of fantasy and romanticism, demonstrated by his love for Jean Paul and Byron, which came out in his predeliction for carefully planned jokes and mystifications. He loved to pull these on us, especially on me at first, with youthful high spirits, when he was untroubled.

The interchange between us two was already very lively after the first few days. We seemed a pair of good comrades to each other, liking to wrestle, because we considered ourselves well-matched. One would challenge the other and the latter accepted the challenge. Our close relationship removed the pressure; we teased each other constantly, everybody in the family enjoyed the bantering, and even my aunt was often amused.

[Lewald learns all the details of the duel in which Heinrich Simon killed his opponent, and he speaks to her of his resulting depression and guilt.]

From that evening on I began to care about him; and what we care about grows into our hearts. I was happy that he enjoyed my company and that I distracted him. I think my aunt loved me more because of this, and upon the request of her and her children, I moved out to the garden house with them completely for the last weeks of the summer.

Those were happy days. My cousins and I developed a great affection for one another, and the whole family loved me as I loved them. For the first time in my life I was able to express myself freely and openly to a woman whom I respected totally. That was impossible with my mother and father. I could tell my aunt of my longing for a good education, without hurting her feelings as I had with my mother. I could tell her of my desire for independence, to become better acquainted with the world and its people, without being reprimanded; I could state that I felt that a marriage solely for convenience was debasing and immoral, and that I would never submit to such. I told her of my affection for Leopold and she listened quietly. She knew far better than I how close I was to forgetting that silly first love forever. I gained a mother in my aunt and had a second home at her house for many years.

All aspects of my personality were satisfied by this part of my family. As highly as my father valued German literature, as deeply as he sensed the beauty and sublimity of the art of writing and its results, and as much heart and feeling as both my parents had, the atmosphere at home was still strict, because every action and deed was constantly submitted to the test of reason. To say or do anything in my father's presence that was an exaggeration or bordered on the fantastic would not have been possible for me or any of us. If you never let yourself go when you are young, if you never abandon yourself completely and freely to the charm of a passing mood and do something spontaneous, you will always remain on your own leading strings, lose the ability to soar and give up a large portion of your originality and capacity for happiness.

None of the Simons, neither my uncle nor my aunt nor any of the children, had any particular talent for poetry, but they were nevertheless poetic people, and had the tendency to shape their own lives poetically, something which actual poets often cannot. When I was older and met most of our poets and writers, I often asked myself how it was possible for people who could depict the fates of literary characters with so much warmth and beauty could let their own lives pass in such a boring and ugly way. On the other hand, I have met other people and families and wondered why they were not poets, since their whole lives were works of art and poetry. I have found the number of people who have the courage to live for themselves and not the opinion of others very limited. But this courage was very evident in my aunt's house without much discussion of it or statements about the right of self-determination. Although none of my aunt's daughters had ever left the almost too tight family circle, I breathed an air of freedom in their presence that was invigorating and liberating for me.

In the fall, when they moved into town, I learned to know the family in its total seclusion and the conventlike regularity of its days. My uncle and Heinrich were gone for certain hours because of their professional responsibilities. The apartment was not large; the rooms lay close together. Next to the living room on one side was my cousin's room; on the other a bedroom. My uncle's room was separate. One of the women kept constant watch in the bedroom of the daughter who liked to play the invalid. Whatever hour you might come, it was always as still as death in the house, because the invalid did not wish to hear any noise, and I was sure to find my aunt with her work and her pleasant, melancholy face sitting at her place by the window, either sewing or with a book. If the front door bell sounded, you could tell who the visitors were by the ringing. After lunch, after my uncle went to his club toward evening and Heinrich came home from the coffee house where he had spent the afternoon reading the papers, the same complete silence reigned as in the morning.

At twilight, my aunt usually walked up and down the living room arm in arm with one of us; we heard Heinrich pacing back and forth in his room, too, and then we seated ourselves at the table in front of the sofa with our handwork. I could hear when he pushed his chair back from his desk, when he arose to get something; I could hear the clock in the living room count off the quarter hours, which he would spend working until he came into the room at the stroke of eight for supper; it was a real joy for me to be able to expect him.

We did not jest with each other so much any more as at the beginning, but my whole mind and senses were soon focused only on him. I could read every mood on his noble face, I enjoyed and suffered only what he did, and my love for him soon made me indifferent to the lively society I was part of at the Lewald house—which had so attracted me for a while.

I did not know what to do when I first realized how much I loved my cousin. With the naiveté of youth, I had completely accepted the one great love that fills your whole heart and life as an article of faith; I was amazed at myself. I was surprised, happy, and proud, and also very elated. Because I had found a beautiful love when I was still half a child, without asking for it, I thought my love would always be reciprocated. Far from realizing that the first shy love of our youth is the most beautiful flower of our heart, everything I had felt in the past seemed pale and lifeless to me in contrast to the strong joyous feeling that permeated me now. Some poor-spirited natures exhaust their powers of love permanently with a youthful love, sick and wretched and weak like a tree that only blooms once and never can bear fruit.

We saw each other every day and still not so much that his absence did not make me happy to see him again and again. There were only six years' difference in our ages; we had been raised similarly and enjoyed each other's company. We were united in our devoted love for his mother but were nevertheless different enough to attract one another. Heinrich Simon was not the man at twenty-seven that he would be in 1849: the man who accepted an office in the regency of the Reich with the full knowledge that he was sacrificing himself for a temporarily lost cause, because it had become a necessity for him to be true to his convictions.[93] But there was already something powerful in his character that I felt and that won me over.

I am sure he soon knew how much I cared for him; he would have not been any kind of man if he had not found that attractive. If he ever asked himself that winter what he felt for me, I do not know. He liked me, as his family loved me, he trusted the power of my personality as I trusted his, and he and his mother had a precognition that there was more in me than I had developed or proved up to then.

"If I were your father," my aunt said to me once, "I would have you write every day." "What?" I asked. "Whatever you wanted. You have an obvious innate need to express yourself, and, as I have seen, you become much clearer to yourself when you do so." "I talk too much for you?" I asked again. She smiled. "I only mean," she responded, "that you still do not say everything you think and if you wrote it down, you would be able to reflect longer and more deeply than when you speak and thereby gain an advantage."

Another time my cousin said, "I think you will have to suffer much in life, because it seems to me you could bear it resolutely, and such natures do not have an easy life. I'd like to know what will become of you? You'll certainly not embroider and darn stockings forever!" "I assure you that is not my intention, but my fate," I retorted. "Haven't you ever written poetry or something else?" he asked. I told him this question was ridiculous, although my heart was really set on proving myself through poetry.

7

The fall and winter passed too quickly. I hardly noticed how I was changing. Only when I received letters from my siblings and

Mathilde did I realize that I had become older and more mature than the actual months I had been gone, and had gained other ideas and interests than they. When I read Mathilde's letters, I perceived an air of resignation she had never shown before. She had fallen in love with a distinguished young nobleman, a love which was reciprocated (but apparently not to be consummated). She seldom wrote of it, but thought about it constantly, and when I finally confided in her that spring how painful it would be for me to leave Breslau and my cousin, she urged resignation and submission to the will of God, who would do what was best for me.

This was no consolation at all. I was afraid that the Pietism in her family and friends had become her master, now that she did not have me and my rejecting convictions as a balance. I consoled myself with the hope that I would be able to bring her back to reason when I was around her again. I had not yet realized that it is much easier to darken and confuse a clear mind than it is to clear up a confused and darkened mind and to bring it back to reason.

At first, the plans had been that I should stay away from Königsberg a year. My father therefore wrote me in February that he would come to Silesia in March, if it were not too cold, to fetch me. I watched unhappily as the cold abated in February, the melting snow dripped from the roofs, and the thawing ice began moving on the Oder in March. With each day, the idea that I would not be able to see Heinrich any more, nor live in his presence, became more appalling. I had hours when I was convinced that he loved me because I felt how much he enjoyed being around and trusted me. He sometimes spoke about himself with unguarded openness, he was tender and emotional, and I told myself that men of his temperament only act like that when there is true feeling involved. Such moments did not last long, however; he quickly mastered his emotions and gained self-control, and when he had regained his equanimity, my suffering began again.

In the meantime, my father had arrived in Breslau, and I was shocked to find that I did not feel any pleasure at his arrival, as much as I loved him. Everything he told me affectionately about Königsberg, of my mother and siblings, only made me afraid, because it reminded me that my home was not here in Breslau.

With my new love also the thought of leaving soon became more actual with the arrival of my father. My aunt, who noticed my distress, spoke confidently to me of returning soon, of being together again. My uncle gave me a lottery ticket and said, laughing, "Be sure you win and get rich; then you can choose your own husband!" My cousins surrounded me with love; Heinrich was friendlier than ever and was unhappy with my father, because he had not permitted him to accompany me to Posen. Heinrich had offered to do this, when my father had earlier suggested this plan to my uncle, so that the winter journey and his absence from Königsberg would be shorter. As a form of self-preservation, I told myself this was all for the best and the way I wanted it. At twenty-two, you are completely unwilling to accept the fact that a situation is hopeless.

And why should I not hope? Why should my cousin not love me as I loved him? But what help was it if he did love me? I still had to leave him. He was as helpless as I; he still had to take his examinations, was working very hard to start a career, and even after he had passed, would not have a sure and steady income. What could he do with me? That is what I told myself when I was being sensible—that Heinrich wanted to educate himself as much as I did. I had often heard him speak of traveling extensively, but never of marriage or a home. I knew he had not come to grips with life, was not clear about what he wanted and was unhappy. I was desolate about this because I loved him—but paradoxically wanted to see him even unhappier, if possible, because he loved me. Of course, in his situation, this would have caused him even greater problems and worries at best. But the whole blind egotistical sophistry of passionate love had overcome me. Hovering between unfounded conclusions and unfounded hopes, I suffered tenfold, because my reason often showed me my foolishness and my heart would not subordinate itself to reason.

Finally, the day of departure came. We were to leave Breslau in the evening with the express post-coach. In the afternoon I visited my Aunt Simon to bid her farewell. From there I was to go to my married cousin, who had promised to bring me home and to my father.

In tears, I said farewell to my aunt. "Just consider youself one of my children," she said. I kissed her hand; I embraced her emotionally. Heinrich accompanied me. It was the eighteenth of March; the sky was already dark and the streets were dry. We had to go a few blocks; he gave me his arm and we went the whole day without speaking. I was so sad I did not even notice our silence. When we reached my cousin's house, he asked, "Why aren't you talking?"

"I can't," I answered briefly. I raised my hand to pull the bell. He held me back.

"Wait," he said and now we stood, facing each other, neither able to utter a word. All at once he cried, "Nothing can be done! Goodbye!" We fell into each other's arms and wept bitterly. Then he pulled himself together, we shook and we separated—to find each other again as friends only after many difficult years for me, to form a bond of trust and faith until the death of that unforgettable man.

I hardly remember how I lived through the evening. There were many people there, guests and friends of my Uncle Lewald, and visitors for my other uncle and my father. I conversed with them, I was given all sorts of farewell presents; I might not have behaved very well. As we sat in the express coach, left the city and drove out into the darkness, I felt completely shattered. It did no good to remind myself I was with my beloved father or to think of my mother, my siblings or my friends at home. I felt removed from them and removed from Breslau as well.

[After an unpleasant journey home, Lewald finds herself in the same restricted family circumstances that had oppressed her previously. She is also very unhappy about her abortive love affair.]

8

I have never been able to be unhappy without doing something about it, and the profound feeling of remorse toward my family for my attitude when I returned home brought me to my senses.

They were not at all responsible for my problems. I had much less to bear than Heinrich, who was able to put aside his deep pain and accept the love of his family cheerfully and gratefully. I did not want to be inferior to him, I wanted to come to grips with myself, endure quietly what I could not change and perform my familial duties.

The worst of it was that there was nothing to do. I did not even have to keep house as I had done when I left school, because I was now supposed to alternate these duties with my sister month by month and be free the first month. This was a bad freedom for me, and I almost longed for the return of my old schedule with its strict regimen.

Naturally I had to take two piano lessons a week again and to practice an hour daily. I also had two drawing lessons a week and occasionally attempted to draw from nature; but the instruction was bad. I depicted the people I was trying to draw fairly well, but I never achieved any improvement or freedom in the matter. I took as little pleasure from my drawing as from my piano lessons, and my pleasure in music was completely destroyed because I had to teach two of my little sisters; although they honestly tried, they had even less talent than I did.

So began my life as a typical young middle-class unmarried woman. I could do what I wanted, but I did not know what I should do with myself and my time. I was in my father's house, did not have to worry about my next meal, and had no vital responsibilities except sewing for the family—there was naturally much of this for a family of eighteen. We had learned alterations and fine mending from a special teacher several years earlier, and I did not mind sewing; anyone with a strong urge toward activity is happy doing the kind of work that produces something tangible. But I did not want to spend the whole day doing nothing but sewing, knitting, and mending. I was not compatible with my old friends, either, so I had no particular interests that attracted me and therefore spent much of my time brooding over what I would have done better to forget if I wanted to live a healthy life.

I had used my leisure time the day I arrived in Königsberg to write to Breslau to thank them for a letter and a ring they had sent. This I had done with a thousand heartfelt tears. The answer came quickly. My relatives had become as accustomed to me as I to them and, in that quiet household, must have really felt the absence of a cheerful daily visitor. They wrote me to that effect; even Heinrich, who had caught the flu right after I left, expressed such sentiments as that and connected his illness with my departure. And I, deluded by my wishes, took his remark at face value. Rereading the letters later and more calmly, I realized, with some embarrassment over my mistaken ideas, he was gently jesting with me.

These first letters began a lively correspondence between me and my cousins which had the dangerous advantage for me of indirectly providing news of Heinrich, even if he himself did not write me. This letter exchange was my real life at that time. Without any obvious reference to Heinrich, I tried in these letters, which I knew from my experience with his family he would also read, to find out anything I wanted to know or hear about him. Besides these family letters, I also continued my correspondence with him, if not as frequently, although he, as Goethe's mother wrote about her son to Bettina, really had better things to do than to write me letters.

I occasionally read to my family items I deemed suitable from the letters I received, but I showed no one the letters I wrote. I kept an ideal separate life for myself, although my adult siblings soon became my confidantes and my passion for Heinrich Simon was hardly a secret to anyone in my family.

My siblings did not like him, although they did not know him. They saw me suffering and blamed him, because they were young and inexperienced. They did not know how easily a woman needing love can lose herself to a man and had never experienced how sweet it is to be loved, how difficult it is to remain hard, cold, and indifferent to an open, warm heart that is offered proudly and joyously. That is what they could not assess at the time, what deceived me and did not leave me in peace for many years.

[Lewald is more compatible with her mother and adept in society, but still very unhappy.]

9

[One of Lewald's sisters is very ill and loses an eye as a result of an infection. In general, however, the Lewald family flourishes, especially economically.]

In our home life and in our social situation, things had changed for the better. My father's income increased steadily. We had become better acquainted with the families of several professors, partly because they had been at the seaside resort with us and partly because of my brothers, who were now students. We also had the company of several intellectual university lecturers who had moved from Berlin to Königsberg. Since we could now spend more on the household than previously, we entertained frequently without diminishing the quality of our hospitality.

We still did not eat extravagantly, even on Sundays, when, as had become customary, we usually had one or two guests. We had soup and a roast, drank beer, and that was it; even if more guests were invited, which caused a certain change in the menu, the importance was placed on everything on the menu being of good quality, not of unusual or great variety.

That is what made our guests feel at home. They saw they made no extra work and they were received informally and cheerfully. My father had let us fix up one of the storerooms, which was attached to the other rooms as a dining room. The dishes, the linens, and the silver had been refurbished, and we daughters given freedom to replenish our wardrobes as we wished, because my parents liked to see us well-dressed. Now and then they would tell our relatives that such luxury in dressing was spoiling us, but my parents were of the opinion that being deprived of things made you want them all the more; girls and women who had been prevented from satisfying their desire for pretty clothes and jewelry when they were young, would in later years put far more value on them than those who had been able to satisfy this need. My parents were correct as far as their six daughters were concerned.

For my part, I loved company and pretty clothes more than

all my sisters. The mental stimulation from the conversations, the physical movements in dancing, were distraction, refreshment, an actual need for me and a means to be happy with myself. I felt I was born for socializing with people and for intellectual exchanges. It gave me great pleasure to devise an attractive outfit for myself and even greater pleasure if it turned out well. I could look at myself for a long time in the mirror with a satisfaction that was half vanity and half artistic; in those melancholy days I particularly liked doing it when I felt miserable.

With the self-tormenting pleasure of passion I then bemoaned my fate. I admitted that I looked well, I knew in advance what one or the other of our guests would say to me, that they would like me. I was very angry that my cousin Heinrich did not recognize my charm and was angry at the same time with those who did. I found consolation in my belief that I deserved to be loved in every regard and to be proud of myself, and found it doubly hard to believe that I was so rejected by the object of my love. As foolish as Heine's words—"I wanted to be either infinitely happy or infinitely miserable and now I am miserable,"—might sound, they express the intemperance of youthful passion excellently. I often quoted them to myself when, with a flowered wreath in my hair and dressed for the ball, I left my room. Now I know that every feeling of that period of my life contained an element of self-deception; but you cannot free yourself of these violent moods easily until you are completely mature. And so I suffered.

My father, who had set his will and his prohibition so strongly and arbitrarily against my youthful attraction for Leopold, let me go on with this infatuation without question or warning. Looking back, I can only explain this to myself as a sign that he either underestimated the power of this love or else recognized it and respected its strength. In the first case, he would have tended to let time take care of it; in the second case, he would not have put himself in a position where his patriarchal power could be challenged. He saw it as his prime responsibility to retain his power over us as long as he was able.

[Lewald gives an account of the "Mucker" trial, which aroused great interest in Königsberg and all of East Prussia at this time and which involved her former religious teacher at the Ulrich School, Pastor Ebel.[94]]

10

In our family life, in the meantime, many good things were happening. My father, who had been a city councilman for many years, was elected city magistrate, and we were all very proud of that, especially my mother. To receive a post because of the confidence of his fellow citizens is surely the greatest honor a man in his bourgeois circumstances can experience; and my father was a man who looked at it that way. He already filled his place on the city council with great pride and had been very involved in all its activities. His transition to magistrate fitted his personality even better, because every mature man has the desire to exercise his influence beyond the scope of his family to his society. Men who do not have this opportunity are handicapped and too easily immerse themselves in the limited life of women and their household.

My father was especially pleased by the recognition of his fellow citizens, because it was only the second time a Jew had been elected as magistrate since the city had its own government. The honor was therefore also a sign of cautious tolerance. My father spent considerable time and love on the practice of his office and found much satisfaction with his colleagues, especially when the present minister, Rudolf von Auerswald, succeeded List in the office of mayor and brought a new energetic spirit to the council.

Our mother, who had few other personal satisfactions and who took pleasure in officialdom and its titles, liked to be called Mrs. Magistrate. Actually, we all benefitted from Father's election in our social position. Matters were going well for us at that time, we did not want for anything, my brothers were maturing, and the old loving family life remained the same. The sons were assured of their futures if they kept on working as they were, the younger daughters promised to become very pretty and were good-natured—indeed, in some cases even talented—girls, of whom one could expect only good things and who had none of those eccentricities that could make a daughter a burden to her family. I felt the power of ordinary life slip over me beneficially again and arrived at a relatively resigned state. I read much, went out often, and lived my inner life alone.

In the fall my youngest brother left us to continue his medical studies in Berlin. He was not yet twenty-one; Father was worried about letting this passionate and daring young man out of his control and the calming influence of his elder brother, which had often protected him and moderated his behavior, because the brothers loved each other very much.

Moritz had involved himself so much in the extravagances and follies of the so-called student life in Königsberg, the quarrels, duels and serious injuries had become so frequent, that he really wanted to go away, especially after this over-emotional boy had become trapped in a love affair with a married woman. His teachers at the university, who had reported very favorably to my father about my brother's great talent and powers of observation, also advised that he be sent away. On one of the last evenings before his departure, he was very worried about one of his patients in the hospital. He came to my room, sat down by me at the window, and spoke seriously about his patient and about his future. Then he suddenly asked me, "What will become of you?"

I was amazed at his question. He had paid little attention to me. He was out of the house often and did not usually know what was going on in the family (although he loved everyone), sometimes complaining that no one confided in him. My siblings teased him because he always entered a door or a conversation with the question, "What?" When it then turned out that he had really not been at home for several evenings, he was sorry; he was angry with himself, wanted to mend his ways, but he lacked the necessary patience to exist in a large family. After he had been very charming and devoted and had listened for a while to all kinds of trivialities, which formed the basis of our satisfaction or our complaints, we could see how uncomfortable he was. With the best intentions of being domestic, he ran away, to find space for himself and his modus vivendi among his friends in the tavern of his student circle.

He had already caused considerable trouble. We had tended him after he had been severely wounded in duels; his patience in suffering and his warmhearted gratitude had been enchanting. We had tried to conceal many of his follies from the strict punishment of our father; we were constantly worried about him because he stormed through life with the kind of audacity only a surplus of intellectual and physical strength produces. Once, in order to defy a customs official, he had spent half the night sitting in water on a balcony in icy fall weather; another time he had made a series of completely senseless and questionable anatomical experiments. If he was asked about these escapades or warned to be reasonable or reminded of his duty to his parents, he was serious for a while. Then the whole brightness of his youthful high spirits beamed again from his broad, goodhearted face like sunshine, and you had to turn away from him if you did not want to show him that he had once more seduced you into laughing about him and with him.

He had the greatest aversion to everything that could be considered family calamities. "I don't understand any of that!" he would say and promptly disappear. He was untiring when tending his patients, however, and he did not seem so young then. I think he was meant to be a doctor and care for the sick.

I was not ready, therefore, for his question, "What is to become of you?" and I asked him what he meant. He really did not know how to answer at first and finally responded, "I think they are planning to marry you off." "Me," I cried, "to whom? Where did you hear that?" "I don't know, but I heard something like that?" "But to whom?" I repeatedly anxiously. "I don't know," he responded.

I begged him to tell me what he had learned and who had said what, but he really did not know anything and had actually only heard my parents discuss it several times.

"You can just imagine that they would say nothing to me about it, and that's the way I prefer it," he retorted. But suddenly, softening his tone, he added tenderly, "Don't do it, if you don't want to. I saw that in N— — (here he named the woman with whom he had had an affair). It's a miserable matter, if a wife does

not care for her husband, and as hateful as life may be as a spinster, it is better than an unwanted marriage!" He then began to
speak of his own future, that he would like to sail the seas as a
ship's doctor and see the world after he had passed his examinations. After we had poured our hearts out to one another for
hours and I was truly afraid of what was planned for me, he was
already occupied with visions of a wonderful life for himself and
cried out, laughing as he had when he was a little boy, "If I can
only live in the jungle and have a great big dog, I'll never get
married!" He always used jokes as a defense against emotion and
melancholy, worries or awkward situations.

I myself was distraught after our conversation. The threatened disaster soon appeared. Moritz had not been gone long
when I came into the dining room one morning and saw my
father sitting by the window over a glass of wine with two other
men, whom I did not recognize. That was not very unusual,
because Father often brought business acquaintances home when
he needed to have longer discussions with them. I made a bow,
therefore, and started heading into the next room, where I had
something to attend to, when my father called me and introduced
me to the gentlemen.

The older one was a merchant from a provincial town, the
other, a man in his middle thirties, a lawyer elected as district
magistrate, who lived in one of the most inhospitable regions of
East Prussia, on Tuchler Heath. We exchanged a few words, I
asked the usual question about how long the gentlemen were
staying in Königsberg, and received the answer that the older, the
uncle, was leaving, but the nephew would stay for a while to
become acquainted with our city. My father invited him to dinner
the next day, a Sunday. That was all in order, but I suddenly had
the idea that he could be the bridegroom picked for me, and I
was not wrong. The following noon I became better acquainted
with him.

None of our regular guests had been invited for Sunday dinner, presumably so that the claimant could assert himself better,
and he proceeded to do this in his own way. He told us of the
pretty honor wreaths in his home town, described his house,

spoke of his important relatives in Berlin and Breslau and of his hopes to be promoted and not always be magistrate in his present district. He threw in remarks about the beautiful species of hyacinths he was raising and lingered lovingly on the pleasures of catching crabs by torchlight. That did not help the situation between us; I disliked him intensely. His short, fat body and expression of smug, arrogant self-satisfaction, a certain assured and provincial manner of speaking, and the presumptuous confidence with which he acted toward me would have made him unpleasant and unsympathetic to me even if I had not the image of another man and a passionate love for him in my heart. I constantly looked at my father, who usually was an uncompromising judge of such airs as my claimant had, to see if he did not find the man as obnoxious as I did. But my father and my mother, who usually saw the comical aspect of such matters, seemed completely blind this time. The magistrate returned several times in the course of the following days. My sisters made jokes about him, my parents praised him, while I was deeply offended and bitter that they could even think of choosing as my husband a man whom they would surely not have admitted to their social circle if he were not thinking of marrying me.

Finally, the chambermaid came to me one afternoon with the request that the master wanted me to come up to my brother's room. I knew what lay ahead for me. With my heart pounding wildly, but certain of what I had to do, I climbed the stairs. I found my father alone and very agitated. He said I undoubtedly knew why he had summoned me. The magistrate had asked for my hand, and Father hoped that I was prepared to acccept his offer. This way of speaking, which was totally alien to my father's usual manner, revealed that he, too, was not really enraptured with my suitor; so I declared quite frankly that I was sorry not to be able to fulfill my father's wishes and hopes.

He was silent for a moment and then remarked, "Think of the situation, my child. You are no longer young. You are twenty-five. I am not in a position to give you a considerable dowry; you know I am not a wealthy man and I have five other daughters. Two of them are already grown, the others will be so in a few years, and six grown daughters will not get along well in one house. The magistrate wants you for yourself; that is something not even many wealthy girls get, and as the wife of a district magistrate, who will certainly advance in his career, you will have an honorable position and a certain income. Don't forget that a woman in a not quite happy marriage is still better off than a spinster."

I asked if my father had learned this from his youngest sister, whose unhappy marriage was a source of distress for all of us. He answered that the magistrate was an educated man who could not be compared with my aunt's husband, and added, "I don't know what wishes and expectations you cherish, but I think they have no basis, and you might later regret having turned down the offer of an honorable man. This magistrate is indeed an honorable man from everything I have heard and found out about him."

The conversation continued in this manner for a while. My father was very tender and calm. The various considerations went through my mind again and again. I wanted to be calm, too, but my heart was beating so fast I could hardly breathe and the blood was pounding in my temples. I felt I had to put an end to this kind of proposal once and for all. I therefore explained to my father that nothing in the world would force me to marry someone I did not want. If he wished to persuade me, if he had the intention of making a cipher of me, as one of the women who sells herself to a man for subsistence, he should not have given me the upbringing he had nor have made me so independent. To me, a prostitute who sold herself for money because she was poor and had no education was not half as despicable as a girl who had learned enough to support herself and sold herself for house and home.

My father interrupted me, because I had become very agitated. "Before you say anything else, I want to remind you of one thing. I know how much you love your Aunt Minna. I did not want to make this decision myself. I wrote to her and asked her what she would do in such a case and if she would not feel justified in forcing her daughters into a marriage, if they rejected it without sufficient reason. Your aunt agreed that I should use all means necessary to exercise such pressure."

He handed me a copy of his letter to my aunt and her reply. I was supposed to read it, but I could hardly comprehend it because of the rage, shame, and insult I felt. I thought that they wanted to break off my relationship with Heinrich by these letters, to take away any hope for his love, and that they believed they would be able to force me. The idea that my father, whom I so adored, could pressure me, could force me into unhappiness (as I thought of it in my outrage) just to get rid of me, made me beside myself.

"You want to force me? How are you going to do that, dear Father?" I asked. "Do you plan to lock me in or let me starve to death? What can you do to make me lower myself so much? Am I a burden to you, dear Father? Just say so and I will go and earn my own living, since you have been generous enough to teach me the means to do so. It would perhaps be best for me and for us all if that happens!"

My poor father's eyes filled with tears. He was obviously not prepared for this and probably thought that I was no longer happy in his house or happy at all. He took me by the hand and spoke to me in that tone of voice I could never resist. "Fanny! Who's thinking of that? But I beg you, your father begs you, to enter this marriage; it would make me and your mother very happy."

I began to cry. To hear my father's request and not to be able to comply broke my heart. "Don't torture me, dear Father," I pleaded. "I can't; I can't marry him."

My father sat on the sofa, I stood before him. He had propped his head on his hand. All at once he stood up. "So this is your final word—no!"

"That is all I can say," I repeated.

"Good, then it's 'no', and I hope you will not regret it later." He kissed me and started to leave; when I wanted to follow him, he gave me a signal to remain behind. "Calm yourself first and wash you face, so that the household cannot see you were crying," he said, and left me after embracing me again.

I remained there to cry out my despair with fervent bitter tears. I have never felt more miserable than I did at that moment. I had many deep griefs in later years. They were very painful, but they did not hurt as much, because they did not come from a father I loved as a veritable god. I have been accused of many unwarranted or unreasonable things, but only by people who did not know me as well as I knew my father did. They could not measure how much they trespassed on my real nature by their demands. The rug had been pulled away from under my feet; I trusted no one any more, not my father, not my aunt. I kept telling myself, "How superfluous I must be in my own home, how little my father must know me, if he wants to drive me out, to force me to be unhappy, only so that he will not have to provide for me anymore!"

It was completely futile to tell myself that most parents would do the same thing, how certain of my acquaintances would have married the good magistrate with great joy, how most people would think that I had turned down a most suitable marriage. I told myself all kinds of generalities to find consolation for the personal element, but it did not work. I was not like everyone else. I cherished a great and strong belief in a noble love, in an ideal marriage, which was something holy to me; I had a feeling for the essential dignity of a human being, a dignity which is violated when a person acts against his own inner convictions. From that hour on, I never ceased feeling all the misery, all the insult, all the furious outrage that the outcry for emancipation has evoked from the hearts of thousands of women, until I achieved what I needed in order to insure myself against the demeaning assumption behind the phrase "What is to become of you?"

These words, which everyone feels justified in addressing to a woman without means, simply and obviously imply this: "What is to become of you if you don't throw yourself into the arms of some man, whether you love him or not, completely, for the price of being supported for the rest of your life."

If you would ask this question of anyone who praises our social arrangements, our current mores, and our family life, as they are now constituted, it would be obvious he does not have much of a sense of true personal pride or feeling of shame, without which neither man nor woman can respect themselves or earn the respect of others.

Even now I cannot think, without shuddering, of what my lot would have been if I had been less certain of myself, less firm in character, and less idealistic in that hour. My otherwise clever and good father would, because of prejudice and shortsightedness, have driven me out to a misery which I could only estimate. When I am happy with myself, am on the heights of life, fully enjoying the sublime, the great, the beautiful aspects it has to offer, I still think of the Tuchler Heath and the unfortunate man my father selected for me. I would have perished in despair, without my strong sense of self-preservation.

11

[In this chapter Lewald outlines many of the ideas she was to present more fully in her 1870 book Für und wider die Frauen (For and Against Women), *which advocates the emancipation of the middle-class woman via education to be able to work outside the home, so that marriage will not be her only option.]*[95]

12

I found myself in a period of dull unhappiness after I had rejected the proposal of marriage. My mother was in a bad mood and worried; yet she and I did not exchange one word about what had occurred. My father was back on his usual track; he very seldom lost his equanimity. He treated me as he had always had; but I could not accept this, as I was constantly reminding myself that he would rather have had me leave and not be forced to have me around any more. My more mature siblings felt sorry for me. They also saw my mother's unhappiness, however, and I told them that my father had actually deigned to plead with me, but that I had still not given in; that hurt them for my father. It was simply incomprehensible to them that I would have been capable of doing that. They were not totally clear about the matter, but generally shared the opinion—those that were old enough to have one—that I should have given in and married. After all, many of my friends had done so under similar circumstances and I was not in a particularly good position as far as an unmarried woman was concerned.

Leopold, who had loved me, had died, and no one knew exactly why we had not seen each other in the years before his death, or if he had not voluntarily withdrawn from his courtship. Heinrich Simon, whom I loved, had only friendship, or at least not the kind of love for me that would have made it necessary to marry me. There was little chance that there would still be many suitors for a woman of twenty-five, one who was so obsessed with thoughts of another man. The family therefore assumed I would become an old maid and I, too, was convinced of that. I had entered society at the age of sixteen and I no longer seemed young to myself or my friends. I had danced at the balls for nine years, and a few generations of girls and young men had passed by me, persons whom I had known as children when I was already considered an adult. My girl friends were largely married; some had been more attractive and richer; others had settled for a marriage of convenience. I had been left behind. I was too serious to fit in with the new younger generation. I had always associated with people older than I. Now I only sought out older men and women and thereby increased the gap between me and the young ones. At twenty-five, I was considered old and thought myself old! The problem lay in the lack of a real career.

The days passed by. The great love that bound us children and our parents helped overcome the unpleasantness of the moment. I took over my month of housekeeping, I tried to be good and useful, to make my presence in the house beneficial. Yet I could not avoid the feeling that I should beg pardon for being there. The sadness aroused by that feeling probably did not make me more gracious. The men in the family, my father and my brothers, soon felt sorry for me and showed me more love than ever before. They could sense what bothered me; my mother and very young sisters obviously lacked this understanding.

I wanted desperately to do something, to undertake something useful, to be convinced that I was accomplishing something for my father and for the family. One day I decided to keep a little book, in which I recorded with painful precision, the number of handkerchiefs I hemmed per day, how many socks I had darned, or what I had accomplished for the family in the way of sewing, tailoring, or music lessons; I calculated the monetary worth of all that at the end of the month. As small as the sums were, they gave me a feeling of satisfaction, but they also demonstrated the aimlessness of my situation then, when I looked at that unhappy little book in later years and saw the long list of hemmed kitchen towels and darned socks calculated by groschen and pennies.

The idea of becoming a writer or earning my living by translating and thus being able to develop myself freely never occurred to me. I do not remember even attempting such work then. My mind was too crippled, and such ideas did not exist in the circle in which I moved; I was once more completely imprisoned by family life and my father's opinions.

[Lewald despairs of ever being able to break out of this deadening circle.]

Sometimes, when I felt particularly useless, I thought about becoming a governess. I could not stay with this idea for long, because I really did not like to teach and because I knew such a plan was impossible for me. My father had an outspoken aversion to any kind of service occupation. He had never been involved in any and would have never allowed one of his daughters to serve strangers without being in dire straits. That was the result of our mores, which measured the wealth of the family by the idleness of its daughters. My father's situation would have appeared in a bad light if he had let me work and earn money.

Now and then I tried to find distraction by helping with the schools for the poor or welfare lotteries and soup kitchens, which were becoming more acceptable. In the mood I was in, I did not feel it was my concern to decide whether they were useful or not. My father opposed all these types of charity and even more the idea that a woman could occupy herself in any way outside her house and family.

"If you want to raise and educate children, we have three girls in this house aged nine to thirteen; that's enough work for you," he said. "If you want to tend the sick, your mother is here. She always needs care and waiting upon, and as far as needlework for the poor and charity organizations is concerned, those luxuries cost the one who does them more money than they earn for charity, to say nothing of the time wasted. Therefore they are impractical and unreasonable."

So I found that my efforts to help myself encountering an insurmountable barrier, because my father's pronounced prejudices stood in my way. The maxim that a woman belonged to her home with her whole being and actions under all circumstances was such an article of faith with him, that I encountered his opposition when, after my return from Breslau, I continued the daily walks to which I had become accustomed and wanted to take my sister along. My father considered it "unseemly" for a young girl to be seen on the street daily; it took two weeks before we received his agreement and permission for this most harmless of pleasures and manifestations of life—to make a tour along the harbor pilings and around the deserted, melancholy Philosopher's Way.

Even that was a favor and a gain for me. I could breathe fresh air and see the clouds pass and the birds fly. We came to the city wall and I could look along the highway, which led to where all my thoughts turned. The walls of the houses, the streets of the city, did not confine me any more; no one observed me to see what I was thinking. It was a form of freedom and at least some physical exercise.

If, in that period, they had assigned me a particularly intellectually stimulating and physically tiring task at one of the desks in my father's office, if they had set me at a lithograph stone and let me work, since I drew fairly well, if they had entrusted me with the supervision of a vocational school or the like, which would have utilized my natural talents for organization and administration, or if a well-taught course of study with a predetermined goal had been open to me, I would have felt blessed and would still have been able to fulfill all my family duties.

To do something I began to learn English, and again, it was my mother who gained permission for me. That touched me deeply. Although it was impossible for me to say to her, "I'm suffering," and equally impossible for her to ask, "What's the matter with you?" her motherly love and the watchful eye she had for each of us children always knew immediately when we needed help. My father obviously doubted during this period whether the education he had given me had really been to my advantage or whether he might not have done better to have me place less value on intellectual matters; he was therefore disinclined to grant me anything. Mother, on the other hand, thought I could not go backwards and that I should be allowed to seek satisfaction where I thought and hoped to find it. Thus I received instruction in English with my oldest brother. Knowledge of this language proved a great advantage to me later.

13

[Lewald finds the letters of Rahel von Varnhagen, who died in 1832, a great comfort when she reads them two years after their publication.⁹⁶]

Through the letters of this woman I gained revelation and comfort. What depresses a person the most is the thought that one is unique in one's suffering. That is true of all people and all kinds of suffering, because man is a social being. What he sees others bear is more easily borne by himself. Terror or loss he shares with others lose to some extent their crippling power and their crushing weight for him. Great periods of universal suffering, like the times of plague, the French Reign of Terror in the previous century, and wars in general, attest to and prove this basic fact.

What had happened to me, what I had to suffer in the way of inconvenience, pain, and suffering, Rahel Levin had already known, had experienced, had overcome with her own innate strength. She had finally reached the position where she found what she sought—the possibility to act according to the inborn demands of her nature. I could empathize with her in everything to the smallest aspects of her being, to the most hidden corners of her soul. I could almost have said, that is flesh of my flesh, that is blood of my blood. In each of the letters of her youth I found it again: the description of a respectable, loving family life, which can become a confining prison and eventually a source of suffering under certain circumstances for the individual, because of its particular institutions and inclinations. She knew them all; humiliation, heartbreak, the pangs of love, the drive to develop herself freely. She lived through them all, surviving and conquering all obstacles by maintaining her identity and the truth.

Just as the motto that my teacher Motherby had written in my autograph book had been in my youth a compass that guided me when I was confused,[97] certain expressions of Rahel's now gave me direction. Many times, when I was unhappy or at odds with the world or in pain, I was helped by these words: "Amidst general suffering I have dedicated myself to one god, and whenever I have been saved, it has been by him—the truth!" When I was beset by the prejudices of the people around me and did not know if I could adapt what my feelings drove me to do to the general rules of propriety, I clung to Rahel's words: "Just so that a bad young woman cannot act stupidly, a good one must be restricted." In short, whenever I needed support, whenever I lacked encouragement, I found them in her. Despite her great capacity for love, there was something masculine, firm, bold, in her personality that appealed to me greatly. She had a constancy and persistence in the maintenance of her convictions for which I had the greatest respect. In her I found the master who preached courage to endure and to act, and persistence in love, in volition, and in self-denial, whenever it could benefit another. Just as a believer opens the Bible to gain counsel and consolation from it, I grasped for Rahel's letters and always found myself and received relative peace and satisfaction when I had immersed myself in the life and being and personality of this remarkable woman. I now regretted deeply that I had never met her personally because of my cowardice.

[Lewald writes of friends of the family, including Ludwig Crelinger,[98] who frequently lives with them and whose acquaintance with the Simon family

in Breslau is a great comfort to her. Carl von Holtei[99] also visits, and his readings from Shakespeare and the German classics renew Lewald's interest in the theater.]

14

The whole epoch was a peaceful one for Prussia. The political movements at the beginning of the 1840s had not particularly affected our country; the striving for constitutional government in South Germany was without direct influence on our homeland for the moment. The relationship of the people to the king was purely personal and very comfortable. We loved the king and depended on him as on the head of a large family. As the folk saying went, we had borne sorrow and joy with him. We remembered his flight to Memel,[100] his stay in Königsberg, his grief over the death of Queen Luise,[101] whose memory we revered and celebrated like that of a saint. We were happy he was now living so amicably with Princess Liegnitz, to whom he had entrusted himself, and that the marriage of the crown prince was a happy one. The relationship of various sons, daughter, and in-laws to the royal father was considered exemplary; even Czar Nicholas[102] was drawn into the family circle of the royal house. The majority of the people were so naive and unselfish that they felt honored by the prosperity and satisfaction of the ruling family and also gratified so some extent. They were happy that the king still enjoyed eating East Prussian gray peas and eels from Lake Narga. They gave him credit for never forgetting the families on whose estates he had lived at the time of his troubles. The clever ideas and witty sayings of the crown prince went from mouth to mouth; many a bold comment which we did not dare to make ourselves—as the old saying goes, to him that has shall be given—was attributed to the brilliant crown prince. In addition, we only found out that which the strict censorship considered wholesome and appropriate and permitted to appear in newspapers and books. The railroad system which would connect people, the rapid, indiscreet telegraph did not yet disturb the peace of the ruler or the placidity of daily life. Travel was still time-consuming and expensive, mail was slow and postage five times as costly as now; all the news we received was relatively old and the events about which we learned had occurred some time ago. The people, individual human beings, were kept separated from one another in this way; their general interest in public affairs was dulled. Everything that happened far away from us was only a historical fact and did not arouse too much real interest.

We did read what happened in the French Chamber or the British Parliament; the names of the party chiefs were recognized by the parties even in Prussia. We were interested in the South German liberals and read the assertions of freedom in German literature with satisfaction, but all that was done in the abstract by most people. We were convinced we had the best government, the best incorruptible officials, the best public school system, and the best source of independence from outsiders in our militia. The alliance with the husband of the king's oldest daughter, Princess Charlotte, the Russian alliance, was the best deterrent against Russian aggression we could have, and we really did not want to govern ourselves, when we thought ourselves so well-governed. We knew we were entitled to demand more freedom, we complained about some repressive measures and occasionally discussed the aborted constitution. But who would have demanded such a document of the good old king, since he did not want to grant one? Once Frederick William III was dead, we thought we could effect changes, for then the circumstances that we always deemed so excellent would surely be different. But we had to wait till then; we wanted to stay satisfied. We could not even admit to our honest self-deception in consoling ourselves with the prospect of the death of our beloved monarch.

At such times of political inactivity, people tend to turn to the theater and the enjoyment of the arts to satisfy their social inclination to act communally. Actors and virtuosos attract attention, people admire their talent and their transitory accomplishments, because the time is not favorable for the development of real characters and the acknowledgment of their power and deeds. I, too, found my greatest peaks and purest pleasures through the theater at that time.

[Lewald discusses the performances of several actresses in Königsberg, most notably those of Wilhelmine Schröder-Devrient, whom she later knew personally and about whom she wrote a lengthy memoir.[103]]

15

For me the encounter with these actresses had quite a special meaning because they presented me with a picture of an independence and personal freedom, for which I longed with all my heart. I could picture to myself for hours, when I was sewing or knitting, what a delight it would be for me to be independent, to have my own profession as these women did.[104] When Mr. Crelinger once jokingly reprimanded his niece, pretty Clara Stich,[105] she retorted laughing, "You can't talk to me that way! I am an actress at the royal theater; I am a royal official."

That was an appropriate answer and everybody laughed. But I envied her. I, who was older, more mature, and more serious than she, envied her because she could say that, because she was somebody in her own right, could make her own living and give herself and others pleasure, without asking anyone else for money or permission. There were other hours when I considered the actresses fortunate because they could show what was within them. It was my love that made this possibility particularly desirable. I imagined it would be the greatest happiness to be able to convey in some way the whole magnitude and passion of the love I bore in my heart to the man I adored, without declaring myself to him in actual words. I thought I could flesh out acting roles with a different spirit, could present them with a far greater warmth than these pretty children. I could picture it for myself in the most glowing colors: how I would feel when I stood on the stage, while my beloved sat in the audience, how I could tell him I was his own, while all the world admired me and applauded and only he knew that I had spoken it all only for him and that I wanted the applause and recognition only so I could lay them at his feet in homage.

On other days I was occupied with Queen Victoria—she seemed the luckiest woman in the world to me! To be young, wear the crown of the largest kingdom in the world, and to be able to give herself, and with herself a royal crown and every conceivable good fortune, to the man whom she loved—that was a thought; that would be such pure happiness that it made me dizzy. I was constantly fantasizing as I carried out the most bourgeois and housewifely duties, but I never thought of shaping my fantasy into something unique that would give my beloved a sign of my love. My feelings were too sacred to me, and too despondent, for me to recognize a talent that made it possible for me to write. Also, my father's constantly reiterated comment that a woman was born only for the home had made such a deep impression on me that I never thought of realizing the dreams to which I constantly abandoned myself.

[The conditions in the Lewald household become more difficult for Fanny, since her mother suffers from an extended "nerve" illness and Lewald's younger sisters do not let her run the house as efficiently as she knows she could by herself. Moritz is also a continuing problem with his duels and injuries. Five years pass.]

16

[The long-maintained sparse correspondence with Heinrich Simon comes to a virtual halt, and she hears rumors from her friends and family about him.]

I had to know what was happening around me, so I sat down one day and wrote to inquire firmly and honestly: What did all the careful feminine whispers and secrets in his sisters' letters mean? What did they want to let me guess or conceal from me? It would only cost me a word, a definite question to find out everything, but I wanted to hear it from Heinrich himself: what had happened with him?

I counted the days until his answer would arrive. At the end of January, there was a small party at our house. Mathilde, whom I was still seeing, even if without the old satisfaction, Mr.

Crelinger, my mother and sisters, and a few other people were gathered in the large living room, when my father came out of his office with a small package in his hand. He greeted everyone and gave it to me, before he sat down in his usual corner of the sofa, with the words, "This is for you, Fanny."

I had already recognized the handwriting from across the room. My blood pressure rose; I knew I was confronted with a major decision, a turning point in my fate. The package burned in my hands; I could not stop looking at it. My whole life depended on its contents, and I could not read—I could not be so conspicuous. I sat down again and maintained my composure with the self-control that everyone learns who has to protect a secret of the heart from painful blows. We talked about—I do not know what; I responded—I do not know how. Finally, when my sister's voice teacher went with her to the piano to perform, and had distracted the others to some extent, I moved to my favorite corner between the stove and the clock and began to break the seal and cut open the strings to undo the double wrappings of the contents. A long letter from Heinrich was on top. I began to read it—I was as if destroyed.

The man to whom my whole heart had turned, who was the object of all my thoughts, wishes, and hopes, the man to whom my whole being was bound, loved another—loved her with the deepest passion but had given her up, in order not to betray his better self.[106]

I was in no condition to hold the letter firmly in my hand; I had a problem in even folding the individual sheets neatly enough to put them in my pocket. I wanted to get up, but my legs failed me; I wanted to speak, but my lips would not move. Indeed, at the moment I wanted nothing; an individual does not retain much will power or deliberation during the Apocalypse, and this was like an apocalypse for me. The ground on which I had stood, in which I had been rooted, from which I had been nourished for seven long, long years, had been pulled away from under my feet. The goal on which I had set my sights, for which I had striven, had disappeared. I had nothing to hold on to, I was dizzy, I did not know what I was doing or what or how I felt.

I arose to leave the room, but went in the wrong direction as if in a dream and stopped confused in the middle of my path. No one but Mr. Crelinger noticed that. He approached me and murmured, "Go up to your room, Miss Fanny. You don't know what you are doing." He accompanied me to the door, walking beside me. I went to my room.

It was dark, the blinds were down; a fire burned in the stove. I threw myself on the sofa with a cry; I thought my heart would burst in my breast, but I could not weep, could not keep lying down. I jumped up, rolled up the blinds, threw open the window, and sat in the opening. The cold was intense, and I was wearing a low-cut dress.

I looked out; the street was empty. Dazzling white snow lay on the ground, on the balconies, on the roofs of the houses across the street. The footprints on the steps in front of the balcony had already been obliterated. The lantern that hung from an iron chain between our house and the opposite corner rocked shrilly in the gusts of wind. I looked at the sky; the stars were shining in the dark firmament with Nordic clarity. I hated their bright light, their thoughtless sparkle. But the icy storm wind, which tossed my curls around and over my eyes, delighted me. I embraced the piercing coldness of the air on my neck and bosom with rapture. As overheated as I was, I was hoping to find sudden death; all I longed for was to die. As it happens, I did not even catch a bad cold! People are protected from any outside harm when they are so unhappy.

What I was thinking? I had no capacity for thought! It was as though I had been struck by a guillotine. I only had some dull feeling inside me, which kept gently intoning, "He is as unhappy as you." I was glad of that, even though it broke my heart.

I do not know how long I spent at the window yearning for death. An exclamation brought me to my feet. "For God's sake, what are you doing?" a voice behind me suddenly said, and a hand drew me away from the window. It was our faithful friend Mr. Crelinger who came to my aid. "We miss you," he added. "Won't you come down?"

I lit the lamp. He obviously saw how upset I was, but I explained that I would follow him immediately. He was satisfied with that and began to leave. But he turned to me at the door and said, "I can imagine what has happened to you. I don't ask that you tell me, but whatever it is, you can survive. Time cures all ills. We'll talk about it one of these days."

[Lewald reads the letter more thoroughly that night, after her sister finally goes to sleep.]

I had put the package under my pillow. Now I lit the lamp and read and read, always the same thing, again and again, and each time I read it, my loss became more palpable, my misery more oppressive, because I was learning for the first time how much this man could really love.

Without defending himself, Heinrich deplored the weakness he had shown in dealing with me. It had made him proud to be loved by a strong honest heart, on whose perseverence he could count, and he had never answered his own question of what would become of it all. He had let life, time, and the circumstances take their own course. He knew how much attached I was to him, had been happy about it, but had wanted to maintain his dominance and freedom simultaneously. He felt and acted as thousands of men do, because they consider themselves and their fate, themselves and their satisfaction, themselves and their future more important and meaningful than the woman and her fate — and his proud heart finally found its nemesis at the hand and the heart of a woman.

His love and devotion gave him an understanding of mine, his deep pain made it clear to him what I was now suffering and with genuine remorse, which looks forward instead of back, he told me, "I can demand nothing, ask nothing of you. If you need to assert your freedom by turning away from me, do it! If you can overcome your feelings, as I had to, stay by me. Let us remain friends and I will always be there for you." And he kept his word until his death.

Only one thing was clear to me. I did not want to be more petty, less generous, than my beloved had thought me. I wanted to, indeed had to, maintain his friendship and confidence at any cost. I wrote him the next day. Now that he was lost to me I was able to indulge myself for the first time and tell him how much I had loved him. As he had asked me for friendship, I offered him mine, and I have kept my word until the end of his life and beyond.

17

[This chapter relates Moritz's continuing problems and Lewald's acceptance of her role in the family.]

18

Moritz left us on the seventeenth of July, and on the third of July, Heinrich Simon went to Paris for the first time. My thoughts were pulled in two directions abroad. I needed that because I was attempting something beyond my strength and was suffering because of it.

I was still writing to my cousin. I forced myself into a calmness I did not feel. I tried to distract him and to deceive him about my own condition. Since I wanted to immerse myself ever more deeply in the virtue of a resignation quite unnatural to me, I began to act in a resigned manner in my domestic life and relations to my family.

I started to change my wardrobe to more subdued colors; I wanted to demonstrate to my siblings and others by my appearance that I no longer considered myself young. I decided to do without dancing; in short, I wanted to accustom myself to being old. Since I, like my father, had already begun to turn gray at twenty-one, I considered the white hairs that increased in my curls as an admonition to resignation—which did not, however, prevent me from trying carefully to conceal them.

The change I was intending to make in myself did not escape my parents. They were not happy with it. My father, who, like my mother, had always laid great value on our appearance and therefore on the way we dressed, remarked that those dull colors did not suit me, that I should not neglect taking care of myself and that every woman had an obligation to appear as young and attractive as she could. I seemed to be out of sorts, but this attitude should be fought because "you should not preserve sadness to keep it fresh as long as possible. Everybody has things in life which they must shake off and forget. The more quickly you do it, the better."

That was all very well and good. I told myself the same things at times, and Mr. Crelinger echoed these notions in slightly different words. It was unfortunate that no one knew what I could do to distract myself, and even worse that I had lost my old power of resistance. The long years of constant mental anguish had not passed without leaving their mark. My health had suffered, and I felt so nervous, so weak and without energy, that I hardly recognized myself. I could have cited Platen's[107] words for my situation: "I was ashamed of my own thoughts, when they flew along the earth like swallows."

There was nothing feigned in the resignation I showed the world, because like all imaginative people, I always had a strong urge to manifest my inner life outwardly. I had always used bright colors, jewelry, and flowers with special pleasure, when I was happy. Now all those were a burden to me, and the lightest ribbons and tendrils pressed on me like lead. I took them off in disgust; I threw them away disdainfully. All my life it has been necessary to me that my outer appearance and my inner feelings be in harmony.

My older siblings were very sympathetic. They often assured me that I was only ill and that I would soon have more eagerness for life than I had at the moment. When I came into contact by chance with some person whose conversation interested me and forced me to think of something besides myself, I did become aware of my own strength again. In the middle of the ashes of lassitude that were heaped over me, Resolution suddenly flamed up brightly and steadily: not to break, not to let myself perish, to keep upright, and—I did not know what to add, but I felt something should and must eventually become of me. Heinrich should see what he had given up in me, what he could have possessed in me. That was and remained the focus of my thoughts and the impetus for all my efforts.

[Lewald tries to write a vignette, but is ashamed of the results.]

It seemed very "silly" to me. I knew the best of our own and English and French literature, and since I respected it, I had a deep aversion to the mediocre and insignificant. To see any talent going beyond the mediocre in myself did not occur to me, and bad women writers had always been an object of scorn for me and their works unreadable. To write novels because of boredom and emptiness of heart also seemed unworthy, and I considered myself too good to entertain stupid women and sleepy personal maids with my deepest emotions and most secret thoughts, as I thought of it then. I estimated the art of writing very highly and the mass of the public very low. I thought little of myself as having talent, especially in my persona as my father's daughter or, even less, as a character in a novel. So I crossed out the three pages with three thick red pencil lines. All writing efforts, which I felt had been prompted solely by boredom, ceased for a considerable period of time.

[Lewald's father brings her a copy of his cousin August Lewald's periodical, Europa, *containing an article by her about the Mucker trial. August Lewald has been using her letters as articles from "our correspondent in Königsberg."]*

I thought about writing again long and intensively when I realized, because of the article in *Europa*, that August Lewald, whose elegant style, whose skilled presentations, had often delighted us and whose experience in literary matters was unchallenged, had found my carelessly written letters suitable for publication. My words and thoughts appeared strange and dignified to me on the white paper with the beautiful black print and in the company of many well-known writers. It seemed as though I were being received graciously, dressed in splendid and becoming clothes, in a magnificent hall by important people. I felt wonderful. But just as I would not admit to myself at that time that I could have any talent for writing, I lacked the courage to ask my cousin for verification.

Meanwhile the idea probably also came to my parents, because of this and certain other little events, that I had something in me worth training and that I had a personality that probably needed to be given more room for development. I was not healthy or happy or satisfied; and my dissatisfaction, which was based solely on internal reasons, could not be appeased by external solutions. The more peacefully family life proceeded (even if Mother was seldom really well) the more uncomfortable the thought must be to everybody that there was a member of this harmonious family who did not fit into the proper and full accord of the group and could not make herself give up what did not agree with the total concept. Heartlessness, coldness, free thinking, and lack of femininity were axioms about my character accepted by all the women of the house, from my mother down to my youngest sister. Although some of my sisters were convinced of my love for them and turned to me trustingly if something oppressed or troubled them, it was nevertheless true that they considered me extravagant and not as good as themselves, particularly since my way of thinking and being had made me unhappier, not happier. They thought they were suffering from my love of power; I thought I was just defending my rights and asserting my individuality. While they complained secretly about my father's partiality and thoughtfulness for me, I did what I did to preserve, by compliance and subservience, the treasure, the anchor I had in my father's love. My closest friends knew I was not happy, but I think even they had no notion of how not only my unreciprocated love for my cousin but the innermost elements of our family life made me miserable. We all suffered, I directly and my family indirectly, from the false morality (which still exists) condemning middle-class daughters past the years of childhood and youth to a useless existence within the bounds of the family, even if they have long outgrown them and are ripe enough in every respect for an independent life and action. As a paid housekeeper for a strange household and family, I would have been very useful, have found peace, and been welcomed and loved during my occasional visits home, as I wanted and earned the right to be. As the oldest of six grown daughters, whose future had to be assured, I was as superfluous and useless as a fifth wheel: I wanted to move independently in my own way—and had to do this, to preserve myself.

Yet I did not want to leave and could not want to, even if I had been willing to admit to my father that I was not happy near him any more. I would never have received permission to go to work, and it was impossible to think of living any place other than home because it would require money that I could not ask of my father, who was still supporting Moritz in Vilna.

It seemed a true blessing to me, therefore, when my parents offered me the possibility of accompanying my father on a trip again. He had been in Germany and beyond numerous times since the first trip we took together and needed to go again in the fall of 1839. He now planned to take me with him as far as Berlin and let me spend the winter there. His desire to help me was obviously linked with concern for my sisters. My sisters could develop more freely and show up better if they were not burdened by such a strong-minded oldest daughter. Even in the forest, you sometimes have to fell an old tree to allow young ones to flourish.

19

[Lewald does not expect as much from Berlin as she did on her first trip, and the uncomfortable quarters she finds at her uncle's do not help the situation.]

I have to laugh when I remember that winter stay at my uncle's house. I had an almost empty room with two windows, which had formerly been yellow, equipped with a small bedstead, a miserable chest, two ordinary tables covered with nailed-down oilcloth, a little mirror, a couple of bad reed chairs, and a framework of boards and unbleached canvas that had been thrown together to serve as a wardrobe. That was my, or rather the chambermaid's, total furnishing, because she had given up her room with great reluctance. My aunt, being in a hurry to make the servant's room into some sort of guest room, had put up white blinds and a sweep of white curtains at the windows and put down a rug in front of the bed, but the contrast between this and my room at home was still immense. I had been accustomed to a very pleasant environment and loved it. Sometimes, when I sat at one of the bad tables and the old Black Forest clock next to the black, constantly smoking, tile stove swung its heavy pendulum; when the sun shone so brightly through the white blinds that the headaches I suffered from in this period really tortured me; when, instead of my ivy wall, my pretty pictures and figurines, which were so pleasing to my eyes and which had often alleviated my bad humor, I saw nothing before me but bare, blotchy walls and the blue-labeled pots in which a colony of loathsome mealworms were breeding—my uncle used them to feed his melancholy black thrush—I wondered what I was doing here. In addition, I did not even have this miserable room to myself. All sorts of household chores, such as ironing and the like, were done there, and since it was the passageway between the kitchen and the living room, there was a constant draft and I was never free from interruptions.

And yet I soon found that I was quite contented in this basically intolerable place, because I had what I longed for most of all. I could think all I wanted, and just as an invalid has no other desire, after a bad attack of fever, than to rest completely, I felt I needed nothing except to be left finally to my own devices.

My father was obviously shocked when, on his return from Hamburg, he found me in the room my uncle had given me. None of us, neither before nor later, had ever had such lodgings, and he asked me with his customary consideration and kindness if I could stand living there, if I were not suffering from it. Since he had always raised me with the thought that you must have wanted the means if they achieve your purpose, and since I also knew that the situation could not be changed, I said I was completely satisfied. After Father had made several visits, had taken me to the theater a few times, and had told me to rent a small piano immediately for my room, so my daily practice would not be interrupted, he returned to Königsberg and I had the prospects of a winter in Berlin ahead of me.

I did not know what I really wanted to do. I wanted to distract myself, to amuse myself. That is easier said than done, because, as I began to think about it, I discovered that to amuse yourself, you had to have certain inclinations, which you would follow, or utilize, and I had no particular inclinations nor certain well-defined abilities or skills, that I would have enjoyed developing.

I knew a number of things, quite a few, and some very well. I had thought long and hard. That was all very nice, but despite that knowledge, I was still a nothing with skills of little practical use to me. Therefore I had to observe, wait, and try. In order to do something, I took group language lessons again from an Englishman, which were presented in French, so we received double practice. I also read much, went out frequently, and soon became friends with a distant relative of my father's, Mrs. Sophie Bloch, whose image brings back many pleasant times to me, since she and her husband gave me much companionship and many rewarding experiences over the years.

Both of them had lived in the best social circles for years and had known the most prominent people of their times. They had been received as good friends by Zelter[108] in Goethe's house and had had members of Goethe's family as guests. They had known Rahel Varnhagen, Professor Gans, Heinrich Heine, Mrs. Milder, Mrs. Sontag, Hegel, the Humboldts,[109] and all the scholars that had made the University of Berlin famous. As an excellent financier, Mr. Bloch had been connected with the then-current statesman of our country and, because of his enterprises, had become acquainted with many of the German princes personally. He and Mrs. Bloch therefore had a store of reminiscences and also the kind of vivacity that enjoys the society of young people and finds it refreshing.

The golden era of Berlin society was already over when I came to Berlin the second time. Everyone spoke of the decade before 1806 and the years that followed the Wars of Liberation with great nostalgia for a beautiful past. Those salons,[110] where all the most important intellectuals of all classes gathered for the sake of conversation and from which the reputation of Berlin society as the leading one in Germany arose, no longer existed. The spirit of the previous century, which proclaimed the rights of man and equality, had produced Berlin society, had brought the bourgeoisie, the nobility, Jews, businessmen, and scholars together to the greatest benefit for each class, and the emergency of the French usurption, the enthusiasm for the liberation of our fatherland, the suffering and sacrifices that each person underwent, had maintained equality, and along with it, the desire for contact and communication for a while longer. As long as Prussian princes shared the concern for army hospitals and the care of invalids with bourgeois ladies, as long as the nobility knew that their wounded sons were safe in the care of the bourgeois homes in the various cities and everyone's situation was fairly equal because the problems were as well, this society, in which the only criterion for membership was education, could survive. Peacetime and the reactionism following it separated the princes from the people, the nobility from the bourgeoisie, and the military from the civilians. The businessman had sought a replacement for the loss of that intellectually liberated social intercourse in the demonstration of his wealth. The scholars and bureaucrats, who did not have this ostentation as an alternative and probably did not like to receive that for which they could not reciprocate, had drawn back into narrower circles. People who are under pressure often come to the unreasonable decision to make others pay for what evil has been done to them; in just such a way, Christian bourgeois society soon allowed itself the pleasure of distancing itself from the Jews the way the nobility and court had distanced themselves from the bourgeoisie.

By the end of the 1830s, there was little left of the Berlin social life so admired in the provinces. What still existed were remnants of a bygone era, and I will return to that later. The different classes were fairly sharply separated; only a few social evenings or homes open to visitors every night still existed in middle-class circles. The aristocrats clustered around the court; the independent bourgeoisie was seldom invited to the soirées of the various ministers.

High-level bureaucrats lived in carefully modest circumstances most of the year in order to give a few anxiously formal parties, provided with a chilly abundance, in those usually unheated chambers, where the walls sweated and servants hired solely for the occasion could not find their way around the rooms. The rich businessmen, both Christians and Jews, had balls, dinners and soirées, which were attended by highly placed officials, intellectuals, and military officers of all levels, who attended them with pleasure but also with a half-ironic air of condescension. As far as I could learn from personal observation and the report of others, who had more opportunity to become acquainted with society in Berlin, matters were not much different than they are today (1861). The year of the revolution in Berlin (1848), which people like to blame for all the vexations from which we now suffer, did not find much left to spoil or ruin in Berlin society. It only made the internal split that had long existed between the various classes more evident and honest. One hopes the epoch will be provided with a new movement to unite the shattered remains of those who belong together into a new society, because intellect needs a center around which to gather and from which, energized by communal current of thought and deed, it can emerge strong, firm, and ready for action.

One of the homes in which the good old way of socializing was maintained as well as possible was the Blochs' house. They lived well, but not ostentatiously. Mr. Bloch was well-acquainted with world affairs and took as great a part in the development of political events as his wife did in literary phenomena. They both read extensively, and, if Mrs. Bloch tended to cite a new work at length with affectionate details, her husband would give a succinct appraisal in one sentence, often with very sharp humor, especially when he was critical, that hit the nail right on the head.

At that time Mr. Bloch lived on the ground floor of Unter den Linden Number 5. The apartment was very spacious for the childless couple, although a young Englishwoman, who served as a companion, and a number of nieces and nephews, who visited almost daily, enlivened the place and there were always many guests. I was a number of years older than the other young visitors, but Mrs. Bloch, who liked to bring people together, and had apparently taken a fancy to me, brought me in with the others, and not a week passed that I did not go there several times.

She and her husband strongly approved my getting away from home. "You are gaining youth, that is, you are winning new life by that," she often tended to say, "and everything you worried about so much at home was just so much foolishness. At home, you think you should call attention to being twenty-eight, because your siblings' becoming older reminds you of it, and you consider it necessary to affirm the lack of demands based on your age immediately. That is very simplistic. No one will accord you esteem because of your age. Youth is much kinder to a young woman. You still look young and attractive—meet the measure of your appearance. Age is a terrible enemy, against which you must defend yourself and not run to meet. Don't always think of home; think about not wrinkling your brow unnecessarily, and above all, hold fast to the thought that the individual helps and is most useful to his family when he is self-sufficient. To further yourself is your next task; hold to this and think about the rest when you finally are something yourself!"

This was encouragement that I needed. Since my benefactress introduced me to the people who visited her in the most positive way, they received me very well and I gained a feeling of youthfulness and with it, a joy for living, and a confidence that I had almost totally forfeited.

[From Mrs. Bloch, Lewald also gains many social graces and an ability to move confidently in more sophisticated social circles.]

20

[Lewald discusses the difference between attitudes toward national issues in Berlin and East Prussia. A new year begins for her.]

A strong desire to save myself, finally to feel light and free awoke in me. I wanted to live again, I wanted to enjoy myself, to be happy, and I felt the capacity to do so if I went along new paths. I had no idea where these were or where I would find light and air and life, but I wanted to look for them, and to do this, I had to break with the past.

In some people, decisions ripen slowly, but their execution is sudden and they never regret that, because their action is the result of long deliberations and struggles. So I sat down that same evening and wrote my beloved what I felt in my heart.

I told him it was still beyond my powers to regard him as a friend and to be one to him. A heart that constantly concealed itself from him in restraint and prevarication could be nothing to him. I also felt he did not need me at the moment. It was pity that now bound him to me, not necessity; I would have to and wanted to find my way without him. I asked him to burn all my letters and, if life brought us together again, to avoid me until I myself told him that I could see him again with a calm heart, in peace and joy. This was the only thing he could do for me, and I begged him to reply to this letter only with the assurance that he would follow my wishes in regard to my letters, which I did not want him to return because I wanted to preserve myself from reading them and thereby reliving them.

After a few days, I received the desired answer, and in the self-imposed emptiness, which suddenly loomed frighteningly before me, I pulled myself up to go forward.

[Lewald works at filling her life with activity and gives a detailed description of the events in Berlin during the last days of Frederick William III.]

21

It had already been decided that I would leave Berlin at the beginning of the spring. I felt obliged to do so, since my absence from home, although my demands were very modest even then, did cause additional expenses, which did not occur when I lived in Königsberg. My friends advised me not to leave. They pointed out that I had recuperated in Berlin in every way and that I would begin suffering from my old problems again at home. The most sympathetic and understanding of them tried to persuade me to take a position as a companion or housekeeper. They gave me the example of Henriette Mendelssohn, the daughter of Moses Mendelssohn, who had once held such a position honorably in the house of General Sebastiani in Paris. Other cases were also cited, and I began considering such a position seriously, because, more than ever, I strongly felt the need to do something with myself. My last inner dependency had been removed when I had to give up my connection with my beloved to preserve myself. I had the right to quote about myself what Goethe writes concerning Ottilie:[111] "A heart that is seeking, feels that it lacks something; a heart that has lost, feels it is deprived. Longing changes into anger and impatience, and a feminine temperament, accustomed to waiting and expectation, would now like to step out of its circle, be active and enterprising and do something for its own happiness."

Stronger than this feeling, nevertheless, was a reluctance to express myself about these matters to my father. If I had received an offer of such a position, I would have probably told him and asked for permission to accept. But to write to him and say I was looking for a job was something I could not venture to do, because it seemed ungrateful and therefore impossible to tell him how difficult life had become for me at home, and how futile, to a large extent, everything he had tried to do for me had been. I therefore decided, as I had done often enough, to deceive myself, to tell myself I did not want to hurt my father unnecessarily, but to look around, wait and see until the opportunity for an actual position arrived. I asked my father in a private letter for what I knew was not right, to let me stay in Berlin, where I was doing well and I liked it.

Naturally I received permission and I wavered back and forth in my tired indecisiveness, losing time and courage, until I received an unexpected order from my father, after the king's burial, to come home, so my ailing mother could move to the country; my presence in the house was very necessary. He wrote that the faster I could come home, the more welcome I would be, and I should hurry home on the express coach as soon as I could, without waiting for someone to accompany me on the trip.

Adolf Stahr (1846), Fanny Lewald's husband. Drawing by Elisabeth Baumann-Jericho. In Fanny Lewald's *Römisches Tagebuch*, 1845–46, ed. by Heinrich Spiero. Leipzig: Klinkhard & Burmann Verlag, 1927.

All my plans, if you can label as such the wavering intentions of an undecided person, were suddenly thrown aside. My thoughts turned toward home. I began to worry that my mother was sicker than they had told me. I returned home immediately.

[Lewald ends the chapter with a description of the festivities in Königsberg, celebrating the coronation of Frederick William IV and pledging him allegiance, and the optimistic —and unrealistic —hopes of the citizens for a more progressive ruler for Prussia.]

22

Two weeks after the departure of the King, I received a letter from August Lewald. He wrote me that he would like to have an exact description of the allegiance festivities for *Europa*, and that I would be doing him a favor if I would do this. I was glad to do it, because I was happy when I had something to write, and the freshness of the impression of the events was obvious in the sketch I sent my cousin. He printed it just as I had written it; and just before Christmas, my father received a letter from Lewald in which the latter expressed his satisfaction with my little offering. He praised the objectivity of the description and its style, making this comment: "Fanny has such a pronounced talent for description that I cannot understand why she has never tried to do more in this line. Without doubt, she was born to be a writer and it would be irresponsible to neglect such a talent and leave a field lie fallow from which she could garner a good harvest for her future."

The blood rose to my face as I read these words; I looked at my father. He could read the happiness in my eyes. That was it; that could help me! For me, it was a glimpse from the desert into the promised land; it was a prospect of freedom, the fulfillment of a dream, that I had never dared admit to myself.

I tried to guess from my father's expression what he thought of Lewald's letter. He understood that. "At first I had misgivings about showing you the letter," he said, "because I think, if you really had a talent for writing, you would have already done it on your own. You are aware, also, that I am against women stepping out of their sphere. On the other hand, you are of an age at which I can't conceal Lewald's opinion from you, and if you want to develop your style in your leisure time, it can only be of benefit to you for the rest of your life. Only don't talk about it, because anybody who speaks about things that he would like to do and may perhaps do some day is a fool."

I felt as if I had grown wings! I could not wait for the moment when I could be at my desk, and when I entered my little room, when I sat down at my desk, my little chamber, as pretty as it had always appeared to me, seemed illuminated and transformed. It was a clear winter day without frost and snow, as is often the case in Königsberg before Christmas after many days of rain. The street was dry, it looked bright outside, when I looked. The noonday sun shone on the pictures that hung over my desk, on the figurine of Joan of Arc, which stood on her little console between them, on my large espaliered ivy plant and my armchair, which still stands at my desk today, thirty years later, and recalls that day clearly to me. I felt as though I were in a fairy tale, as if enchanted, because it was as if I had been given mastery over the world, as if I would only have to take my magic wand, my pen, in my hand and bring forth people, events, and fates from the void for myself and others. A man who had advised and furthered the careers of many talented writers had recognized in me that which my teacher, Mr. von Tippelskirch, had predicted when I was a child, which had often hovered ahead of me, sometimes clearly, sometimes obscurely, and which I had only been prevented from acknowledging because of the great respect I had for the dignity and meaning of the creation of literature. I was supposed to have an ability to write; I was to become a writer. I was unspeakably happy!

With a feeling of shyness, I took my green morocco book out of the drawer in which I saved it. Heinrich Simon had sent it to me from Breslau as a birthday present in 1834. The word "Experiences" was printed on it in gold letters. He had written in as a dedication on March 15, 1834, these words: "What forms a person, but the story of his life? — Surely a rigorous education does! Many experiences also, so that it would take a lifetime to acknowledge them, and after they are perceived, already immediately displaced by others, that likewise disappear without being comprehended. Even the attempt to retain them is worthwhile. Goethe says the highest thing a person can reach is the recognition of his own ideas and thoughts, the knowledge of himself, which gives him the impetus to penetrate the personality of others."

The old book, with its yellowed pages, lay before me at this moment, a witness to the changes in human lives and ideas. Because fourteen years later, under those lines in Heinrich Simon's hand, the man at whose side my life found its purpose and happiness[112] had added: "What forms a person but love, which gives him faith in himself and in humanity? Painful experiences are the sharpened plowshare, which tears open the rich earth of the heart, but love is the seed, which is planted in it and brings forth fruit a thousandfold."

And when all three of us were together years later once again, opened this book, and read these two inscriptions, Heinrich's opinions had changed, and he no longer considered observation and the understanding of the personality of people the most important thing. He also had decided that love was the most important, love for the individual and for humanity, which find its happiness and task in enduring and serving, in helping, advancing, being useful, and acting for the one great goal to which he was dedicated until he died too soon.

I had filled approximately a hundred pages of the octavo volume; now I opened the book. It contained the fairy tales I had begun at times of boredom, but they had never gone beyond the first two pages, because a person who begins writing with a background in and taste for good reading has a difficult task. He lacks the so-called naive originality, which in most cases is nothing but the self-satisfaction of the uneducated—a quality that some writers use all their creative lives for their own convenience if not to the advantage of their readers.

I knew the best, I knew fully how to appreciate it, and I therefore had an ideal before me, which discouraged me instead of making me begin. All my attempts seemed so insignificant to me, so completely futile. I had to laugh about it myself. How could I ever think that an impartial reader would like them? I had accomplished nothing because I was trying too hard. Hardly had I thought of one little fable when another came into my mind, one that I thought was better. If I started to write it down, I said to myself: "How stupid and trivial all this is compared with *Wilhelm Meister*, with *Wahlverwandtschaften*, the novels of Jean Paul and Ernst Wagner, Sand and Balzac, Bulwer[113] and Walter Scott. I did not want to do something silly. I did not want to appear as ridiculous as certain writers, both male and female, seemed to me.

But the temptation, the desire, to write were too great. I did not write a single line that day; nonetheless, the dream of accomplishing something did not leave me. I stood at the window and looked at the ridges, which had formed on the surface of the small frozen puddles between the dry stones. Everything that had moved or devastated me, that I had enjoyed or suffered, swirled around in me, moved by my inner eye like fleeing clouds. I thought, "If you could say, if you could show, what you have learned about yourself or observed about others in the last seven years!" And this concept shaped so clearly for me that I could have placed it outside myself, to observe it quietly and completely objectively, to look at it, to judge it, but I told myself, "That would be a novel!" And a novel seemed like such a tremendous task that I did not think I could accomplish it.

For days my active impulses and lack of self-confidence warred within me. Finally a whole series of personal reasons drove me to try my hand. I imagined how my family members would think about my literary ambitions, if I showed in my writings what inner urges had often made the narrow existence, the daily useless occupations and irritations, so burdensome, so unendurable for me. I took pleasure in the idea of indirectly expressing to Heinrich everything, everything I had suffered from him, and what he had lost in me because he had not recognized or appreciated it properly. Then again—and this was my favorite wish, which I finally realized—I wanted to paint his picture, so honestly and warmly that I would have it before me the rest of my life in all its beauty and so that all who loved him would enjoy it. Finally ambition conquered me. I saw my name recognized and respected by all the best people, I saw my father proud of me, saw all the avenues of life opening for me—the friendship of prominent and famous people, travels, the pleasures of art, and most important, freedom and the right to determine my own life assured once and for all.

After I had dreamed of these rewards and sat down to write, the small bust of Goethe, with its serious eyes and thoughtful lines in the cheeks, which stood on my desk, looked at me so reproachfully, that I quickly came to my senses, i.e., I began to doubt myself again. But on New Year's Day 1840, I could no longer resist the urge to test myself. Since I had always liked the fairy tale I had written earlier, I thought I could surely write another, if nothing else. I took out my green book and wrote a little story, which I called "A Modern Fairy Tale,"[114] the twenty-four pages of which I wrote down without stopping. Its source was a conversation I had had some time earlier. The discussion had concerned the similarity that the upper facial features of some people had with those of animals. We had looked around to see who fit this idea and had then moved on to the concept of the migration of souls. I wondered to myself if the external resemblance to an animal would be reflected in the inside of the person, and how there were probably a considerable number of people whose uncultivated instincts would make them closer to animals than educated human beings. In my story, I had a young woman fall in love with a certain Mr. von Salmon, who was only a fish in human form. The young beauty only escaped the fate of marrying such a half-human because an old clairvoyant aunt, who had been through a similar experience, revealed the secret and saved the girl. A few more such half-humans were around, too; there were some salon scenes inserted. The whole story had a certain epistolary style, although the physical descriptions were fairly sharply drawn. I did not consider letting it be published, because I had written it in the green book, which held all my literary attempts up to then.

I did, however, read it aloud to my father and sisters one evening. My sisters liked it, but my father did not. The moving back and forth between reality and fantasy was not to his taste; he thought a fairy tale should take place in foreign lands or long-ago times, in which people were more likely to take such events at face value. To let miracles happen in his own environment was too unreasonable even for fantasy, and one should not expect people to believe the impossible. He referred me to my favorite fairy tales, those in the *Arabian Nights* and Musäus'[115] folk tales, but forgot that Callot-Hoffmann[116] had depicted the lack of restraint and capriciousness of the fantastic in the actual world around him and that the right to do this to the fairy tale existed from the moment in which you could enliven and disrupt the present with fantastic capriciousness.

We lived very quietly that winter. My mother, who expected great things from her complete rest, had uttered a wish to live completely away from the city and the family in the winter as well. Since my father agreed to this request as he did to all her wishes, she and one of my sisters had remained in our summer residence. My father went out there several times a week, usually with one of us to keep him company on the way. On other days, several of us daughters went to see Mother, so that she would suffer from her removal from the family as little as possible. Although there was a kind of external disturbance of family life, those who remained at home had many quiet days and evenings, because social gatherings were naturally quite restricted under these circumstances.

My intentions and plans therefore occupied me much more extensively, since I could now follow them with less interruption. Since I had not had any luck with my father with the fairy tale, and had myself discovered that I did far better in the depiction of reality, I began to write a short story, "The Deputy,"[117] which was only a few pages long and had as its focus the experiences of a young officer in a garrison town. I enjoyed an entirely new pleasure while I was arranging the material and working out the details; when I went to write the story down, I was as happy as a lark. I could not wait to read it to the others, but the approval I received—and this was fortunate for me—in no way equalled my pleasure in the creation of the story. My father and my older brother, whose opinions were very important to me, did not think I had delineated actual matters clearly enough. My brother actually tore his cravat from his throat in jest during certain long phrases, to indicate to me that he was choking from such long sentences, and his final judgment was thus: "These are common newspaper stories, and if you write them or not, if there are indeed more or less of these is completely immaterial. If you think you are accomplishing something or don't believe us, send them to August Lewald and see what he thinks."

As harsh and even bitter as the rejections were, they acted on me as the few cold days of a very warm spring act on plants. They kept me from hastiness and overestimation; they taught me from my earliest endeavors to temper invention with reason and to stick to reality and truth from the beginning.

I worked on and corrected the little story for quite a while, but then I wanted to know my fate and sent it, with my father's permission, to August Lewald, who was living in Baden-Baden at the time. He soon wrote back that he did not have the time to read the manuscript at the moment, but added, "Your urge to write is very natural. Someone like you, who knows how to depict healthy thoughts in a lovely way, has a calling and should not smother it with purely external considerations." And since I had informed him about all the objections and exceptions my family members had raised against the little work, he wrote me in his second letter of June 24, 1840:

I like your ambition, your spirit, your education, and your independent mind, because you combine feeling and soul. The quiet life in your parents' house, your late development into a bluestocking—if I may say so—has protected you from many of the aspects usually related to that. I am repeating again what I said about your talent: don't let yourself be discouraged by your brother. You can use his criticism positively if you look at it the right way—it can even benefit you, but you don't have to ask him about your vocation. Believe me! Your fairy tale is very beautiful and I like it better than "The Deputy," even though the latter has many advantages again. It really is not an ordinary newspaper story, as your family called it, because to be that, it would have to be more excitingly and attractively complicated, and be more descriptive. But this is better. You can create characters. Your "old deputy" is a truly original figure and the irony with which you color the whole story, shows a degree of artistry for which you are to be congratulated. As I already mentioned, plans and talent—inventiveness, as it is often called—don't always go hand in glove with production. Inventiveness is what you should aim for now.

He urged me to begin a longer work without delay and wrote me that he was publishing "A Modern Fairy Tale" immediately. He was sending me a payment of eight thalers and some groschen—I was totally overwhelmed with happiness.

I read the letter again and again; it seemed as though I was growing and becoming visibly larger. I loved the praise and was not at all averse to ignoring my brother's opinion. I did not realize then how instructive and standard-setting his educated and skillful understanding would later be for my whole style of writing, and my longing for independence was so great!

In the middle of my excitement, my father entered. It was eleven o'clock, time for his second breakfast. It was the middle of the summer and very hot. The large awning had been lowered in front of the windows of the little living room, which looked out on the portico; the room was dimly lit; flowers bought fresh every day in the summer were on the table.

The breakfast table was always set at eleven o'clock, so that Father did not have to wait. Usually there were as many of us in the room as could get away to see him during the quarter-hour he was there, to keep him company and to tell him what had happened. For some reason I was alone with him that morning, and my heart was beating with excitement and joy as I saw him climb the eight steps to the portico. As always, he kissed me when he entered, and then sat down to breakfast, saying, "So, what's new?" as usual.

I said I had received a letter from Stuttgart. He knew that because it had been delivered to his office first. "What did Lewald write you," he asked. I read the letter to him; he smiled. "That sounds very encouraging," he said, "and Lewald probably knows that. But he is wrong when he trusts you to judge your own work. On the contrary, people are usually not competent about what they have done themselves."

I tried to refute that, but Father interrupted me with the question: "You are really thinking of beginning a longer work; do you want to be a writer?"

"Yes, if you have nothing against it, dear Father."

He shrugged his shoulders as he was wont to do, when he was involved with something he did not like. That hurt me.

"Think about it, dear Father," I continued, "and let me mention one fact expressly—I never do anything by halves."

"What does that mean?" he asked briefly and earnestly.

"I mean, when I work, I take off my kid gloves and take hold firmly with my bare hand. If I am to write, I will have to be able to state exactly what I think and touch on every subject that seems appropriate to me. I cannot pay attention to what you want to hear from me, or what you want to let the children (that is what we were referred to as a whole) hear."

"I realize that," he retorted.

We were both equally serious, because, if I entered my new way of life, I did not want my father to have any doubts about what I intended to do. "I can't keep living the way I have permanently," I continued. "If I can obtain the means, I have to see the world and be able to mix more freely with people, with men, who will advance my career, instead of sitting at home at the tea table in your presence, and that of five sisters."

I saw my demands and plans were awkward and undesirable for my father, and I explained that if he was not agreeable to them, I was still willing to give up the fulfillment of my wishes. My father was silent for a moment and was quietly continuing his breakfast throughout the whole discussion. "I can't really see what I can offer you as an equivalent," he said after a while. "You are thirty years old, unmarried, and I can't tell you, 'Here is a fortune which will keep you independent for life.' On the other hand, you have always been reasonable, have never given me cause to be dissatisfied with you, and you say you will be happy exercising your talent. So, do what seems right to you and may God make it for your good. I ask only one thing of you expressly: no one, even Mr. Crelinger or Dr. Kosch (our family doctor) is to know anything of your writing."

"You can count on that," I pledged, "but think, dear Father: all the children know about it."

"I will forbid them to talk about it," he said, with that confidence, that is sure of commanding absolute obedience.

He stood up, took Lewald's letter, and looked at the check that was enclosed. It said "To the bearer," and moving from the serious to the comic, he said, "Since you have begun to earn money, you will want to have it in your hands immediately. I will cash the check and bring you the money."

He went toward the door, turned once more and said, obviously moved, "So, a writer!" Then he raised his beautiful eyebrows a little, an expression that indicated that something unexpected and not quite pleasant had happened to him, and taking my head in both his hands and kissing me tenderly, he said, "May God prosper your work!"

With that, he left, and I was so moved that tears flowed down my face. I felt as great a joy as when I vowed to take my husband for a lifetime. One like the other was the happy assumption of a vocation I had accepted out of the deepest conviction and the innermost necessity, a vocation which I would be happy in pursuing with all my strength and devoting myself to with total love and freedom.

My entrance into the magic gardens of poetry was not made without great self-awareness. I had an enormous respect for the power of the poet on the spirit of his people and for the power of the word on human hearts. Because I sought the truth and valued it above everything, wherever I recognized it I pledged never to deviate from it in line or word. As great or slight as my influence could ever be, I would never use it except in the service of beauty, freedom, and truth—and I have kept that pledge!

BOOK THREE

Liberation and the Wandering Life

1

Trees cannot grow as high as the sky, and serious dramas frequently have a comic intermezzo. Thus a very funny dejection and a ridiculous event followed the happy exaltation of that first hour on the very day when I decided about my future.

Probably to give me pleasure, my father sent the amount of my first payment in actual thaler pieces to me via his apprentice. Instead of making me happy, though, it was very painful to take the money. I had been raised in an environment, in which all the women were accustomed to being taken care of and entertained by their husbands and fathers, and to think themselves of a higher social class the more lavish these benefits were. Although my greatest wish for years had been for independence, I felt suddenly as if degraded, expelled from the caste I had been born into. With these eight thalers, I gained the certainty that I would have to work for my money from this day forward and to earn my own living. I was nearly moved to tears by this realization now that I finally had my way. That did not last long, however, and I was soon thinking about how best to spend the money.

It was certain that it was not to be spent on myself. My oldest brother had set an example for us when he bought my parents a pair of silver napkin rings engraved with the date and the words "The first earnings" with the first money he had earned as a law clerk. It was impossible to buy anything for my father, because he had no personal requirements except his clothes and simple food. He did not smoke; a dressing gown or other luxuries were still completely alien to him in this, his fifty-third year, since he stayed dressed the same from morning until night. To wear jewelry would have seemed ridiculous to him, and until we children jointly gave him a gold watch and chain a few years before his

219

death, his old silver watch was his only possession beyond the minimal, since he had lost his wedding ring.

Therefore, my only possibility was to get a gift for the household, and since our pretty and extensive silver service lacked butter and cheese knives, which my mother had often spoken of acquiring, I decided to give her these.

Mother was still living, as she had for over a year, in our summer apartment. The day, July 4, was extraordinarily hot, but I hurried out to the various goldsmiths' shops in the morning because I could not wait to buy my present. Mr. Krickhahn, at whose shop I found just the right knives, promised to have them engraved with my mother's monogram and the date by four that afternoon. I could not have the words "From my first earnings" added as I wanted, because no stranger was to know about that, but I could hardly wait until four, and when my father came for coffee, I placed the knives on the table before him with great pleasure.

He picked them up with the same happy warmth with which I had presented them. He joked about the fact that his children would soon provide a "state treasury" for him if this kept on. It was understood that I should immediately go to my mother and take her the letter from August Lewald, containing all his good news as well as the two silver knives as the first earnings from my work.

As I stepped out on the portico to leave the house, a sausage seller, who provided us the sausages for tea time every week, came by. She had a type of liverwurst among her wares that my mother particularly liked and that in the summer had to be eaten on the day it was made. To have some fun for myself, I bought the biggest of these still-warm sausages with my money, wrapped them well, and proceeded on my way.

I was a short distance from the house and had just reached the Krämer Bridge, where I had to wait, because it was drawn up. While I was standing in a group of people, a little dog came up to me and was soon followed by a big one. I had been bitten by what was thought to be a mad dog when I was a child; I still had such an unreasonable fear of dogs that stories about my phobia were some of my family's favorite anecdotes. I was seized by real terror with the realization that it was the warm sausage, smelling strongly of marjoram, that was attracting the dogs. I tried to chase the animals away with the folds of my skirt, with my parasol, with fierce glances, but all in vain. The odor of the sausage had a stronger power for them than the so-often praised power of the human gaze. I was at the point of giving the sausage, which had cost me ten groschen—the eight thaler seventeen groschen I had earned made me very money-conscious—to the next deserving poor person I would encounter, when I decided to master my fear so as not to deprive my mother of her treat.

In order to rid myself of the problem, I walked as rapidly as I could up the Steindamm Bridge, along the Steindamm glowing in the sun, calculating in advance and avoiding the side where there was a butcher shop, from which a dog might also possibly emerge. But that did not help me. In my mortal terror, it seemed as if every dog in town had a rendezvous with me. Here a little bird dog wagged his tail at me, there a fat pug—we still had real pugs in those days, fat pugs with black noses and protruding eyes—joined me, and again a mongrel crossed my path and followed me snuffling. I went faster and faster in my fright, holding my sausage as an ensign does his flag in the first rain of bullets, until I finally landed at my mother's apartment, overheated, but with the feeling of having accomplished something very difficult because of love, and with the hope of arousing great pleasure and being greeted and thanked joyfully.

My mother and sisters were having their afternoon tea under the poplars in front of the house. My mother had not slept well during her nap, and had woken up tired and out of sorts. I unwrapped the sausage first, as I recall, to prolong the surprise and laughed while I told them of my adventure. My mother asked if I had not brought some other small item with me that she needed for her little household and that she had requested from us by the landlord's daughter, who had gone to town. I answered no, because the young girl had not come by our house before I left. Mother did not like that, and to assuage her, I, now beaming with joy, took my two knives out, returning to child-

hood as most people do at such moments and thinking my gift
was irresistible.

Unfortunately, I had miscalculated the effect that illness has
on the human personality. "What is that?" my mother asked with
indifference. I said that was the result of my first earnings;
August Lewald was encouraging me most strongly to write and
Father had agreed. In short, I displayed all my pleasures and
concluded by announcing these knives as the sequels to the napkin rings and added that I knew my mother had wanted them for
a long time. She must have completely forgotten this at that
moment, because she, who could exclaim with pleasure on her
good and healthy days about a package of pins somebody had
given her, laid aside the gift, which I had been so happy to bring
her, with the comment that this was a totally useless expenditure
and I should have saved my money.

To be rejected and reprimanded when you have approached
lovingly with an open heart is very painful; such a reception coming from my mother at this moment hurt me even more. My
throat tightened; all my pleasure was gone with one blow. I
thought, "You just never have any luck!" It was good that my sisters guessed how I felt and tried to compensate for my mother's
failure to respond properly with their pleasure and participation.

I was very subdued and repressed by the time my father
arrived in the evening. His presence always made my mother forget her intense suffering and bad moods, and when she saw that
he was suggesting good humoredly that the knives should be
dedicated immediately to give me pleasure, she began to be
happy, too. The siblings were together and very jolly. We went to
eat and were laughing loudly about some funny incident when
Mr. Crelinger came into the room unexpectedly, and, infected by
our laughter, joined it without anyone being able to explain the
cause reasonably, and we returned to town very happy, satisfied
with ourselves and in the best of moods.

On the whole, the plans I had made for my future had a
stronger initial effect on my family than I had expected. I seemed
strange and changed to them for a few days. But the novelty soon
wore off. Everyone looked at the fairy tale in print and asked me

what I would do next, and that was it, except for much well-intended teasing and a series of never-ending contests my sisters and I embarked on dealing with my making a name for myself and achieving great success in the world.

As soon as I had settled in at my mother's, I began to work. I had often thought about what my position would have been if I had been talked into that so-called marriage of convenience and wondered if my sense of duty would have been strong enough to overcome my passion. I had pondered a number of situations, had weighed all the pros and cons, and had considered several solutions, at times a despairing decline, or perhaps a noble and very lofty renunciation of love. Since my personality had always been the kind that focuses on the immediate, I also tried now not to grasp for strange experiences or distant times, or elegant regions, as beginners often do to their disadvantage. I simply wrote about what I knew exactly as far as people, characters, and relationships were concerned, so that I could not gloss over the lack of verisimilitude with the reassuring and euphemistic "it could possibly be that way" or "it is probably so." So I produced the little novel *Clementine*, which I am now re-reading for the first time in years.

I do not have to tell those who have read and remember it that the characters and events of the novel are entirely fictional and that nothing was taken from actual life except the process of my thoughts and the outer appearance of the hero, in whom I tried to capture the image of Heinrich Simon, as he looked at the age of twenty-seven. Difficult as it was for me to present his beloved figure in words, it would be even more difficult to give an idea of the excitement and the passionate happiness that filled me when I was working on the little novel.

The sun shone warmly through the green leaves; the honey-suckle vines swayed back and forth. Here and there a bird flew up from the greenery, and its shadow moved across my paper, while sunbeams flimmered and danced on it—not exactly to the benefit of my eyes. It was magically quiet and beautiful. Even more magical and beautiful seemed the world of the invisible figures that surrounded me. These men and women, of whose existence no one but myself knew, no one was acquainted with but myself alone, who were one and all sympathetic to me with their good qualities and their faults, whom I needed only to beckon to have them appear at my demand, who entrusted me with their joys and sorrows, whom I helped and advised, defended and commanded, whom I supervised and nevertheless placed before me as ideals—I was totally astonished at their existence and yet I had created them all! To the pleasure of observing these characters' lives in the figures was added the ability of saying everything through them that had been on my heart for so many years and to be able to say it without being corrected or contradicted and without having to restrain myself or be careful, or defend my ideas. It is such happiness to be able to express your innermost convictions and to acknowledge your beliefs. If that were not the case, there would not have been nearly so many people becoming martyrs for their faith.

My heart pounded with rapture when I wrote down what I thought about love and marriage. It was like a profession of faith for me. "I do not hate marriage," I let the heroine of *Clementine* write in a letter to her aunt:

I do not hate marriage; quite the contrary. I have such respect for it that I am afraid I would degrade it and myself at the same time, if I joined in such a sacred union without being committed to it. What can be more satisfying than to live your life with your beloved? To take care of him, to share his joys and sorrows, to know that everything that moves my heart, everything that touches me, is shared by my best friend. Both of us would live two lives. I have often thought it would be heavenly bliss, I have wanted it desperately, and even now I still consider marriage the only way that leads human beings to the greatest perfection possible for their individuality. That is why I cannot bear the thought of an indifferent marriage, because it would be an unhappy one for me. I have never been able to understand how anything can join a couple in marriage but their hearts. In its purity, marriage is the most chaste and holy of ties than can be imagined. The wife emerges from the arms of her beloved husband as pure as an angel of light. When Catholics speak of the Madonna as the "pure" Mother of God, it means something completely different to me than the Church intends. Yes, marriage is pure and from the embrace of a loving couple, a divine person, a world savior can emerge. And what has now happened to marriage? A thing, the mention of which makes well-bred girls lower their eyes, poke fun at men, and smile to themselves secretly when they look at women. The marriages I see being entered into daily before my eyes are worse than prostitution. Don't avoid the word, since you want to persuade me to the deed. Isn't this just what a wanton, morally debased girl does when she gives herself to a man for useless frippery or what parents do when they sacrifice their child for so many thousands of thalers? The sales price does not change the transaction. I consider the woman who is carried away by momentary passion and sensual ecstasy a better person than the one who, although having an image of her beloved in her heart, gives herself to someone she does not love for the price of his rank and name.[118]

It seemed to me that I had accomplished something, had endured a battle for freedom, had won a victory that could not be taken from me, when I put words like this on paper and imagined my father reading them as an expression to the public of my convictions. Day and night I thought of nothing but my work; my whole soul was on fire from it. I forgot time and ignored my need for sleep.

[Lewald suffers from certain neurotic ailments — heart palpitations and attacks of weeping. A sensible doctor advises her to exercise more self-control; since she does not want to be a "typical" weak female, she is able to exercise this control.]

After the doctor's warning I bore my heart palpitations and anxiety attacks with growing patience and continued writing my novel with such zeal that I had finished the little book within a month. Now the thorough education and legal precision of my brother, to whom I gave my work for proofreading, was very useful. He examined every sentence the way he would have a legal document. He pointed out every unclear expression and every irregularity in syntax. I did not always like that. It sometimes seemed to me as if he were tugging at my own limbs, when he took apart and logically analyzed the sentences in which I had expressed my loftiest thoughts and most delicate feelings. I could not help thinking of Hoffmann's mechanical doll[119] whose beautiful eyes are removed from her head in the presence of her lover; nevertheless, this training by my brother was very useful.

[Lewald decries the lack of stylistic discipline of both men and women, who think that inspiration is the sole qualification for writing.]

I was very eager—actually, one might say anxious—to have my father's opinion of my book. Since he had a tendency to take his time, I had to wait until I went to Father's office in the city approximately eight days after sending him the manuscript to deliver a request to him from my mother. He was busy; he had a man from Starost and a couple of Polish Jews with him. He listened to the request and promised to come out in the evening if it was not too late. When I wanted to leave, he called me back with a "Listen, Fanny!" and told me quietly, "If you want to take your scribblings with you, they are upstairs in my desk. They read quite well; they're quite nice."

Who was happier than I! I had certainly expected more praise, but also more objections to the trend of my work, criticism of certain views given in it, even of expressions of speech. I could do without the praise if it meant the absence of criticism. I have to give my father credit here thankfully and admiringly for faithfully keeping the promise he made me at the beginning of my literary career. He gave me a totally free rein for everything I wrote, even later, when our opinions diverged considerably. From the moment he granted me the right to fulfill my profession independently and to go my own way, he gave me complete freedom and recognized me as a force, as a person with equal rights which he had to value and respect, even if I was his child. This was the greatest honor that man of my father's character and temperament could accord to a child of his. I have never forgotten. My husband's free and noble character also granted me a similar respect for my personal freedom later. In both cases, obedience and acquiescence, when required by reason, became an easy task and labor of love.

2

The years 1840 and 1841 had brought a whole new dimension to public life in Königsberg. Like Goethe's sorcerer's apprentice, Frederick William IV had summoned forces by his inaugural speech that had long been present, but that had been waiting only for the right moment to come to the fore. He was afraid to ban them, so they grew beyond his control and began to turn against him as he tried to chain them again and suppress them.

[Lewald discusses the political situation in Königsberg with particular emphasis on the role of Johann Jacoby and the periodical, the Hallesche Jahrebücher.*]*

3

[Moritz Lewald continues to be a source of worry for his family, especially his father. Lewald's mother's health deteriorates still further, and everyone realizes she is near death.]

In the fall, when the long evenings came, I still had the joy of reading my finished manuscript aloud to my mother. She listened to me with an air of amazement. She might have felt that way the first time she heard me cry as a baby. What I had written even made an unfamiliar impression on me, when I had to express it aloud in front of my mother and sisters and as the characters I had created appeared in front of me alive and speaking for themselves.

Hardly had I sent away the manuscript of *Clementine* when I began to work on a second novel. I felt a veritable passion for saying everything I had in my heart. Now that I had written my soul free of what had touched me the most personally and deeply, now that I had said what I thought of the axiom that it is a necessity and a fulfillment of duty to marry without loving the man whom you are marrying, now that I had presented my case to my father literarily—now I felt compelled to confront other prejudices, under the burden of which not only I but who knows how many hundred thousand others had had to suffer—the anti-Semitism of the Christians.

The material I had chosen for *Jenny*—that was the title of my second novel—was one that was commonly discussed at the time, because it was obvious: that the government, under the pretext of giving the Jews an independent status, only intended a sharper segregation of them from the Christians. The Jews saw this with great concern. They appealed their case everywhere in speech and writing; and the enlightened members of all denominations were on their side. The emancipation of the Jews on the one side, the suppression of them on the other, were subjects of lively discussions. In writing, as well as in life at that time, I was actually dealing with the same elements.

I was still able to read the first quarter of this novel to my mother from the manuscript and it made a far deeper impression on her than my first work. The theme was closer and therefore more comprehensible to her. The concerns that had driven me to write *Clementine* did not appeal to her; they were beyond her ken, and the passionate tone of the individual characters was surely alien to her.

I was in the middle of my intoxication with work when my mother's illness suddenly became much worse. We saw her weakening every day over three or four weeks; at the beginning of December, we often thought it was her final hour. Her suffering was very great, her patience no less so. Her mind remained clear and bright. For the fourth of December, my eldest sister's birthday, Mother herself had ordered and presented to that sister, her most faithful attendant, a warm robe and some other small gifts, and had ordered that the usual birthday cake be baked. On the evening of December 6, we lost her.

She was only fifty years old.

"Take care of your father," our friend Mr. Crelinger wrote me early on the morning after he had received the news of my mother's death. "Take care of your father. I am afraid that the blow—although expected—will hit him hard. I know his strength and self-control, but they desert us only too easily at the grave of a loved one." But Father, although deeply struck by the loss of our mother as might have been expected, kept his composure and all his strength even in these difficult days.

Weeping quietly, he embraced and kissed us at our mother's death bed, especially his youngest daughters. No sound was heard, no lament uttered. The self-control to which we had always been accustomed came to the aid of us all. We sat for a long time together at my mother's bedside. Around midnight, my father roused himself. "It is late," he said. "Go to sleep, dear children. But first straighten up the room and lay your mother out properly. She would have done it, too. Minna can watch over your mother; I shall sleep on the sofa here. The rest of you should go to bed quietly. Tomorrow morning we will write to your brothers."

4

The Jewish ritual law prescribes the simplest of burial rites. There is only one service for everyone, rich or poor, upper or lower class. The burial of the dead is a community affair, one of the good works it offers. That is an excellent custom, one which the pious Catholic brotherhoods have borrowed from Judaism and which is maintained in Italy to this day.

As soon as a death is reported to the executive board of the Jewish community, old men or old women, according to the sex of the deceased, come to wash the body and to dress it. A long white shroud, a white bonnet for the women, a white cap for the men—that is the total garb. A modest coffin thrown together from bare wood is the only casing that separates the person from the motherly earth, with which they are destined to mingle. Someone from the community keeps watch over the body until it is buried. The burial society, which consists of young men, puts the white wooden coffin in the communal coffin of the hearse and, walking next to it, accompanies it to the grave, while the mourners join the procession as everywhere else; only that women are excluded from the followers, I believe. According to the strict ritual, the mourners tear their upper garments and sit mourning on the ground a few days, and for nine days, prayers are said at home for the dead. However, the enlightenment of the Königsberg Jewish community curtailed all these ceremonies after my father explained that we attached no meaning to them.[120]

After a few older women had dressed my mother, they left us with the body. We could visit it as long as it was still unburied; we could place the flowers in her coffin, the violets that Mathilde and her mother had brought, which truly represented the essence of her being. When the body was removed on the day of the funeral, many young men of our acquaintance had been found to assist in the funeral ceremonies. The silence, the solemnity with which they went about their task was a true charity for us and a really good deed. All ostentation was avoided in the funerals, so that the richest and the poorest would be equal in death. Since this practice relieved the sorrowing family of all responsibilities for external matters, at least for the first few hours and days, it is very well worth imitating by Protestant denominations.

My father had asked his daughters to accompany Mother's body to the door of the house. Neither of his two sons was present, unfortunately, since there were no telegrams or trains then. Although many people had come by to show Mother the final respects, Father followed the coffin alone to the grave from our house, except for the faithful Mr. Crelinger at his side.

Father spent the first days with us in complete retirement. We ate without his employees, he did not go to the office, he did the absolutely essential work in our apartment, and had only one of his clerks come to him early in the morning to give him the necessary instructions and orders. Everything was under complete control at home. Meals were held at the usual times, and my father's excellent constitution was so sound that he had no problem eating or sleeping, despite the heavy blow that had been dealt him. His equanimity and health were not in the least disturbed by what he was suffering. I have never seen a man who was calmer, and therefore all the more moving, in his grief. He pressed his lips firmly together when he wept, and the tears flowed quietly and softly over his handsome face.

On the day after the funeral the old style of life was assumed again immediately. We sat around and went here and there and did this and that, so we would be doing something. The hours came and went; the clock struck, we rushed to do some sort of task out of habit and sat down again, because it was now unnecessary. We looked at each other in amazement; no one really had anything to do. The house seemed as though all its inhabitants had abandoned it, now that Mother was gone, Mother who had been the center of all our concern and our activities as long as we could remember. This desolation, so common after such a loss, is terrible. Thoughts lose their usual direction and a spiritual paralysis sets in. We come gradually to feel the terrible necessity of mortality with all its weight, to think with trembling that nothing of what we possess in the way of people we love is granted to us forever. The first death like this we encounter takes the certainty of existence away from us forever. If you have seen a beloved one die, you see the sign of death imprinted on the face of everyone dear to you and treasure each day of life and togetherness with them as a favor that must be earned by active love.

My father had always expressed a great indifference to the external manifestations of mourning for the dead and to the details of where he should be buried and by whom, but Mother had laid great value on these things. Father now decided we should wear mourning for her a full year and, as though he had changed his mind about these details because of his wife's death, when he put up the tombstone for her, had the markers of his parents and grandparents, his brother, and the two little boys who had died in infancy redone. A whole row of generations could be seen in the cemetery, where he would one day be laid to rest next to our mother.

My father did not believe in leaving anything to chance that could be regulated by organization, so he set up new household rules at the beginning of 1842. According to his axiom that all his children were equal before him and therefore were equal in their general position and in life—an axiom that is incorrect, cannot be carried out in actual practice, and cannot be maintained—we four oldest sisters should take equal turns in running the house independently. My mother had never known exactly what it cost to run the household. She had received what she considered necessary in her thrifty spending of money and had asked and received any extra needed from my father, so that he was the only one who could supervise exactly what was being spent. My mother had always felt uncomfortable with this arrangement, while my father had wanted to keep her in uncertainty, so she would not worry about the size of her expenditures and not come upon the idea of limiting them by beginning with personal items for herself. Now Father met with us and we set an exact budget, which contained certain sums for the household, for acquisitions for the house, for parties, for lessons, luxuries, etc., and which should not be exceeded under any circumstances. Various daughters received money for clothes, and each month the housekeeping one received the total sum for household expenditures; every month the bills had to be reconciled. We all learned how to manage a household this way, if we did not know it already, and we reached an agreement that we would lay aside reserve money and supplies every month so that the machine would not come to a halt and the housekeeper at the time encounter difficulties. Our household had become considerably smaller anyway. Mother was gone and my brothers were abroad. A housemaid could be dismissed, and the whole middle floor rented out again. When my second sister went to Berlin in the middle of the year, to be a companion to a distant relative who had been left alone in her home by a series of closely ensuing deaths, we thought our household was very small, because it had shrunk from eighteen to thirteen persons.

We became more and more intimate with our father. He had become gentler than ever and showed a still-greater tenderness toward his younger daughters, as if compensating them for the love of their mother, lost to them at an age earlier than the older siblings. His strictness abated; he let us lavish more care on him and did not prevent us from rearranging his bedroom more comfortably. We now centered all the attention formerly given our mother on him. Since we now had a good idea of what our expenses were and could allocate the means offered us where we wanted, we found ourselves in the position of accomplishing more in the way of comfort and elegance at home and even doing more for the well being of the individual than had been previously possible.

My work had come to a virtual standstill because of my mother's death. The many changes we had to make, the correspondence required by a death in the family, and my own bad health had made writing impossible for me. I had few good days at that time. I was ill in various ways and could not control myself, no matter how hard I tried. I knew that I was exaggerating the significance, if not the complaints and ailments themselves, like a hypochondriac, but at the moment that they seized me, they were so painful and frightening that I thought I would die, even if I had mocked this fear five minutes earlier and damned its return during each new attack as a weakness in reason. It is an ill wind that blows no good; my constant thoughts of death had the benefit of making me put my small affairs in order every night and keeping all my dealings so unequivocal and clear that they could easily be turned over to someone else and be looked at by the eyes of others. I have been aware of the imminence of death all my life and have become accustomed to be ready to depart at any moment with my various activities and affairs and external matters up to date, even though I cling to life with all my heart and love and the desire to stay on this earth is very strong and certain in me.

At the beginning of the spring, when I had begun to work on my novel again, August Lewald sent me a letter from Brockhaus, who had inquired if the writer of *Clementine* could not deliver another manuscript to him for the next year's offerings of the paperback series of Urania Press, which was still publishing books then. That made me very happy, because it was proof of the success of my first work. I had no novella to submit, but, encouraged by the inquiry, offered the editor my new novel, which he accepted at once and under very good financial terms.

I then worked on steadily, as much as permitted by my health, which became still more delicate. If it was my month to keep house, I had to stop my work and could only write in brief moments, e.g., in the evening, between five and seven, between coffee time and the time when I had to make preparations for supper, but I conscientiously maintained that schedule. Warm and excited, I would then come down to the living room, in which my father and sisters were already waiting, each one usually occupied in reading. I had spent several hours by myself and wanted to talk; the others, who had been conversing and wanted to read, because Father was reading, naturally told me not to bother them. It was impossible for me to pick up a book; all the characters I was creating swarmed around me, and my thoughts, still not completely defined, strove for clarity. I sometimes found myself continuing to work silently in my mind without being able to stop, even when I went to bed. I was robbed of my sleep; my thoughts raced from my works back into the past. Memories that I had been able to suppress forcibly during the day came back. When I arose in the morning, I had advanced my work considerably and defined my thoughts, made a number of good resolutions and developed a series of plans for my writing and my life, but I had not slept. The effects of this became more obvious and visible in me all the time, because I came to look so ill that my father looked at me with great concern. I, too, was amazed at how my clothes, my bracelets, my rings, hung on me loosely and how much I had aged in a year. I suffered from that more than I could say; it really hurt me to see this premature decline and to have to tell myself that my youth was gone. I envied the trees, who shed their leaves in the fall and deck themselves with fresh greenery in the spring, in contrast to human beings, who must witness their own decay. That we also can gain a new and enduring youth with a renewed spiritual life and faith, rejuvenated ambition and hope, was an experience that I had not found among the people I knew and was still to encounter myself.

In the middle of the summer, the first that the family had spent in the city for a number of years, I finished my second novel and at the beginning of August, my brother came to visit us from Russia. He did not return as the old carefree boy he had left.

[Lewald continues the saga of the prodigal Moritz in further detail.]

5

*[Mr. Crelinger encounters problems from his political activities in Königs-
berg, from which Fanny Lewald eventually extricates him with a tactful
letter to the Minister of Justice.]*

At the beginning of 1842, my older brother in Berlin, who was
kind enough to act as the go-between between me and the book
dealer in Berlin, sent me a copy of my first printed book, and I
still remember the strange effect seeing it had on me. I could not
tire of opening it or looking at the cover. I read the epigram on
the frontispiece: "Woman's love! How strong in its weakness,
how beautiful in its guilt!"[121] although it did not fit into the novel
at all, in which no sin was committed and only pure renunciation
was exercised. I opened the book here and there, not to read it—
I knew it by heart from beginning to end, because I had recopied
it myself—but to enjoy the beautiful paper, the elegant black letters and the splendid, copious print. I took a great deal more
pleasure and seemed far more important to myself with this
example of my production than hitherto with the society sections
of *Europa*. I felt so close to the little printed book, which had naturally appeared anonymously, that I was frightened when our
friend Crelinger found it lying in my room once and took it home
with him to read, as he often did with other books. I thought he
would recognize my views and my way of expressing myself and
would guess the secret of the authorship against my father's
wishes. That did not happen, however. He spoke with me about
the book quite unsuspectingly, and I thereby had the first taste of
the comedy I would have to play often in the next several years,
when I had to discuss my books with someone as if I were a third
party, affording me the opportunity of hearing the most honest
criticisms.

The book was a success. I was greatly amused to find it
ascribed—I do not know by whom initially—to the aged author
of *Agnes von Lilien*, old Mrs. von Wolzogen.[122] This idea, that people were considering me an old lady, gave me the notion of writing several letters from a great-aunt to her great-niece about edu-

cating children as well as an essay about the situation of women servants, which was lamentable and totally hopeless in Prussia at that time.[123] Submitted by my brother, both pieces were published in the *East Prussian Provincial Paper*.

I had sent the manuscript of *Jenny* to my brother in Berlin after completing it, and he had returned it with a whole notebook filled with comments, questions, and advice, so I was revising this novel accordingly with far greater thoroughness than I had the first. The considerable success of *Clementine* had fired my ambition. I was driven to work even more seriously by a lively sensitivity for the great and the beautiful, for an ideal, by my respect for human beings, instilled in me by my whole environment. I wanted to offer them my writings; I actually asked them to participate in them with me. And finally I felt that simple bourgeois sense of duty that does not permit delivery of shoddy merchandise for good money. Just as Heinrich Simon had once written me that his judicial duties gave him a sense of worthiness which he had never experienced before in the exercise of his legal profession, so I became aware as a writer, I was in a position to teach and advise people and to encourage them to educate themselves. I wanted to bring myself and my work into accord; I did not want to teach anything that I could not validate in my own life and under all circumstances.

[Lewald's deteriorating health and the fact that she is not really needed at home make her decide to take a trip to Berlin. With her earnings from Jenny *and her clothing allowance from her father, she has enough money to maintain herself there for a year. She finds that Berlin has become far more cosmopolitan during the reign of Frederick William IV. Upon an invitation from one of Heinrich Simon's sisters, she visits the family in Breslau, since he fortunately is not there. Minna Simon asks Fanny if she liked* Clementine.*]*

By now I was accustomed to the question, but it had a completely different impact coming from my aunt's lips. With the heart palpitations that attacked me with the slightest stress, I answered affirmatively. She stopped, seemed to want to tell me something, then reconsidered and kept walking with me. She was apparently waiting for some revelation from me. I could not oblige her, though, because of the promise I had made my father. We strolled up and down for a while, speaking of this and that, when she suddenly said, "If you have any special reason for concealing the fact that you wrote *Clementine* from me, I won't force you or ask you about it, just as I have spoken to no one in my family of it"—she emphasized this strongly. "Because," she added with a quiet smile, "talking too much is not my shortcoming; but I am sure you wrote the book."

"Were you satisfied?" I asked, instead of answering her. "Yes. Completely satisfied!" she replied, and we walked up and down some more, and each knew what the other was thinking. There is great happiness in such a chaste, silent understanding.

After a while she wanted to know what had made me have the novel published anonymously. I told her of my father's wishes. She did not agree with my decision to comply with those wishes, but understood my position and promised complete discretion. I saw, though, that she had something else on her mind. She finally started again after thinking it over. She said, "It is good that you have finally decided where your talent lies and have learned to use it, my daughter"—she called me this occasionally when she was particularly affectionate—"but your father certainly wanted another way of life for you. He wrote me about it once. Why didn't you marry? The man presented to you seemed good and kind, and you can live very peacefully and very honorably in a marriage without being passionately in love with your mate."

I wanted to walk away. These words, especially from my aunt, hit too close to the mark. I pulled myself together, though, and replied, "I have put everything that can be said in support of Father's and your views in the mouth of the aunt in my novel, dear Aunt! So you see I understand that point of view, but you should realize, on the other hand, that I cannot subscribe to it, though it might be possible for some others." She sighed, laid her hand on mine and said very gently and sadly, "Just because I do realize it, I fervently wish that it were otherwise. You have changed very much, Fanny. You are no longer healthy. It would be reassuring to me, to know you were really happy—and it would be a comfort not only to me!" she added with great fervor.

I asked her not to worry about me, assured her of the approximate truth—that I felt much better now than I had in some time. She wanted to believe me. When the rest of the family came in and we were interrupted, she repeated once more, "Think about it, daughter! The day when I see you really satisfied and happy will remove a tremendous burden from my heart, and not only mine."

As perspicacious as my aunt was, she could not realize what a gift she had given me with this simple conversation. The same words have a different impact in different circumstances; the right words and the right moment must coincide to have the proper effect. My siblings and my friends had often told me that my cousin's behavior toward me had not been irreproachable, and I had often felt that myself; he had accused himself of that at times. Yet I also knew what a large part of my own predisposing fantasy had played in my pain and suffering. Every criticism by a third party of the man I so dearly loved seemed an injustice to him and annoyed me. The person who has created an ideal in the one who loves would rather blame himself than his beloved. All the long years during which I had not seen him, during which I had only been with him in spirit, had distanced me from real life and had allowed me to regard him as my own and bound to me, although I knew he did not belong to me. Just at the time when, prompted by an instinct for self-preservation, I had renounced all contact with him completely my thoughts of the ideal I had made of him only increased. When I returned to Breslau, to the home of his parents, it was very difficult for me at first to hear his family speak of him and judge him with great love, but also with the cool objectivity of sound reason.

After Aunt Minna, Heinrich's mother, spoke to me, I was free and returned to myself in every way. I felt like a new woman. I had to forgive him. And yet he did not need much forgiveness. He was a man who had admitted that his weakness in not forcing the truth of our relationship upon me earlier—a weakness of

which almost everyone in his situation would have been guilty—
was a deeply regretted mistake. For the first time I saw the possibility of a new future and a new healthy relationship with my
cousin. I could speak of him freely and could think of him even
more freely. I began to feel calm and cheerful in the room where
I was staying—Heinrich's room!

I went around in it and picked up objects he used. I sat and
wrote at his desk; I stood and looked at his books. Many of his
works were among them. At the end of the 1830s, Heinrich
Simon had begun to write about the Prussian laws and their significance, in addition to working as a practicing lawyer. He had
published a series of works, some by himself and some in association with friends of the same mindset, that dealt with criticism,
explanation, and clarification of the Prussian legal code. When I
saw this series of books standing in his room and read their title
on the spines of the volumes, an image of the entire occupation of
this man of many vocations arose before my eyes. I picked up
some of the legal books and leafed through them. I took pleasure
in the clear analyses and the single striking words and sentences
I happened upon.

It was primarily the laws about the Jews that caught my
attention. I felt a deep happiness that we were both, without
knowing it, dealing with the same subject and had worked for the
same good cause. While Simon was trying to prove the right of
the Jews to recognition by the state and to civic equality, as well
as the injustice perpetrated on them by jurisprudence, I was
doing the same in the area of literature. Although I had decided
definitely not to see Heinrich again yet, I could not prevent
myself from giving him a sign from afar.

Just before I left Berlin, I had received the last pages of
Jenny for revision. Only the title page remained to be printed,
and I had reserved the right to chose a motto for it. I had been
looking for the appropriate one for some time, had chosen first
this one, then that one, and had finally decided on a saying by
Börne, when I accidentally picked up a work of Simon's one day,
about the condition of Jews in Prussia, and found the following
quotation: "A race from which the Savior, the Madonna, and the

apostles sprang, which has remained true to the beliefs and customs of its fathers after millenia of persecution, and still produces outstanding results in science and art after millenia of oppression, must be equal in birth to every other."

These are the words I had been seeking, and now I had found them. And with this motto, my second novel went out into the world, anonymously again—the motto as a marker and recognition sign for my friend from behind the mask of anonymity.

6

[Lewald returns to Berlin, before Heinrich Simon returns to Breslau.]

With the firm determination to begin a new life, I saw my old friends in Berlin again. I knew myself and the human heart well enough to realize how much it is within our own power to control ourselves and our circumstances if we view them objectively, how differently a fate can be seen according to one's point of view. For years I had lived in the belief that I was an old maid, and therefore without any expectations of happiness and good fortune. Now I began to tell myself that I was a young writer, that I had a father who was fairly affluent and good siblings, that I possessed loyal friends and a talent I enjoyed using, which promised to provide me with a certain independence, and I had a goal before me I was pursuing with enthusiasm and ambition. The more often I repeated this to myself, the firmer my belief in my blessings grew and my belief not only made me happy, it made me strong.

I became eager to use my good fortune and to enjoy the things at my disposal—to take such pleasure in living as I had not felt for a long time. Pleasure in life is a balloon lifting us up and letting us regard what we previously considered unscalable heights as mere molehills.

I now liked Berlin even better than before. My returning strength, my sense of freedom, my independence, of which I became more and more aware, let me view everything in a friendly light. Every pair of gloves I bought myself, every glass of lemonade for which I paid, pleased me and tasted better because I had bought them and paid for them with my own self-earned money. Spending, saving, giving were all a pleasure to me. I thought that I could have everything, or rather, the whole world now belonged to me, because I could call about five hundred thalers my own. It was foolish, but there was something youthful about that. At home, where we had spent, as I knew, thousands of thalers a year, five hundred would not have seemed a great sum to me; I could calculate very well and knew we could not get fat on that. But in Berlin, where I was responsible only to myself, where I realized how modest my personal requirements were and how easily I could do without a number of luxuries to which I had become accustomed at home, and which I had even considered important, here in Berlin, it made me feel younger to be forced to adhere to a strict budget.

Even more than in the various galas and state functions, I was interested in the life of the people. My entire upbringing had imbued me with a desire to participate in everything to do with the activities of business and the relationship between management and the so-called working classes; this desire had been heightened by the direction of contemporary literature.

[Lewald recounts a meeting with a blind beggar woman, who plays a harp, and who tells the author all about her method of supporting herself.]

With similar questions and answers I gathered many details from the lives of the people around me in those days of tedious waiting and observing, partly through deliberate questions, and partly through chance. This practice of mine served me well later and saved my works from certain misconceptions. I was made aware of how different the concepts of justice and injustice, of honor and dishonor, are according to the individuals' differing levels of education and of how wrong it is to transfer the feelings of one class to another without modifying them.

I sauntered through life in this period like a strolling botanist who is walking along without any specific purpose, but still cannot avoid looking around observantly and collecting whatever he finds interesting for his herbarium. I spent the Indian summer and early fall in this spiritual strolling around. In October I was able to send a copy of *Jenny* home to my father. I had put many of my own experiences into this novel, especially the relationship of Jenny to Christianity. I had depicted the problems of the race to which I belonged to the best of my ability and had embodied some traits of my dear father in the character of old Mr. Meier (Jenny's father). Heinrich Simon's beautiful motto was on the title page. I had the firm conviction that my father would enjoy the novel, the public reception of which I was nervously awaiting.

Immediately after receiving the novel, my father wrote me:

My dear Fanny!

My most profound and heartiest thanks for the copy of *Jenny* you sent me, dear daughter! May your Jenny bring you as much joy as you, my good daughter, have always tried to give me since you were old enough to distinguish right from wrong. May God keep you and may everything go well for you; take special care for your health. How is the matter of anonymity going? I should like it maintained as much as possible. But write me what you think and what you are doing, so we proceed the same way. By the way, you sent the letter with postage paid. Are you that rich already, my child?

Love, your Father

It was the tone of soft tenderness with which he usually addressed me when he wanted to encourage me in my new career and aspirations. My best reward was when my father demonstrated pleasure in me and my works. As much as my mind was set on independence and a worldly life, I was still so attached to my father and my home that everything I accomplished only gained its true value from the effect it would make on my father. Everything good that we enjoy only becomes true happiness when it finds a resonance in the heart of someone we love.

[Lewald is introducted to members of Berlin society and finally meets Henriette Herz, who, with Rahel Varnhagen, was one of the premier hostesses of the brilliant and eclectic Berlin salons of the previous generation.]

Mrs. Herz was the daughter of a Jewish physician, a Dr. Lemos, and was born in Berlin in 1764. She had been married off to a prominent older man, Dr. Markus Herz, when she was still almost a child, at the age of fifteen. Dr. Herz was a famous physician and was greatly respected and consulted as such, as well as for his personality and outstanding education. As the wife of this man, of whose originality and sometimes very drastic cures I had heard many stories based in personal experience in my own paternal family, she had lived in great style until her husband died at the beginning of the century. Her financial situation was not very good at his death, but sufficient for her needs, even permitting her the trip to Italy, which she had long desired fervently. Upon her return, when she discovered that her means were even more restricted, this worthy lady had known how to cope with the limitations placed upon her by dignified resignation. She had participated as much as previously in social as well as personal matters, full of helpfulness for everyone whom she could assist, and remaining the center of a large and significant circle of people.

It was fairly late in the day, already twilight, when I visited her for the first time. Mrs. Herz, whom I had always heard referred to as one of the beautiful women of her time, was then already in her middle seventies, and she was sitting, having just recovered from an illness, dressed in a white robe and a rather large white cap, in an old, low armchair near the window.

She received me very graciously, although I had no real claim on her of any sort, repeated the friendly words about me that the lady presenting me had said, and then asked me a series of that type of question with which well-meaning, confident peopled bridge the gap for the newcomer into a social situation and make his first few minutes comfortable.

This gave me an opportunity to observe her and note the perfect regularity of her head, clearly evident despite her age and wrinkles. The beautiful broad forehead, the prominent brow, and the noble shape of her nose were still unmistakable, although her mouth had sunk in and the chin therefore protruded. Her eyes still regarded the world in a friendly and intelligent way. Most of all, her voice was still very pleasant and her whole manner extremely benevolent.

Since she had been told that I was a native of Königsberg, she spoke of the fact that she used to have many dear friends in East Prussia. She asked me about this one and that one still living, and then arose from her armchair with a slowness necessitated by her physical condition. Since I had seen her seated at first, I was surprised at her height; it seemed almost unnatural to me, although she was bent by age. Her tales of days gone by, of a time very distant to me, which she related with an air of immediacy, had already seemed somewhat mythical to me. Now the tall, gaunt figure that rose higher and higher in its white robe in the fading light had a ghostlike appearance, and I would not have been surprised if she had veiled herself in a mist, dissolved, and disappeared from my view. It was an impression that will remain with me forever.

Later, when I knew her better and was permitted to visit her frequently, I noticed that the upper part of her body was very short in relation to her height, so that she seemed to be just the size of an ordinary woman while seated, while she was said to have been much taller than the average and a truly majestic woman in her prime.

When I became acquainted with her, she lived on Markgrafenstrasse on the first floor of an old and fairly run-down house. By way of a dark staircase and an equally dark hall, one came through a small sparsely furnished room into a simply arranged living room with two windows. None of the modern furnishings we now considered almost indispensable was evident: no armchairs, no fancy sofas, no large mirror, nor knickknacks. A pale paper covered the walls and a dark carpet the floors. There were a sofa and chairs available for those who wanted to sit, a round table where one gathered, and an old mirror over the chest of drawers. None of the furniture required for the bare necessities was missing, but there was nothing extraneous. Yet you did not miss anything, but felt comfortable from the moment you stepped through the door. You were completely accustomed to this room already, because there was nothing special to look at or admire or about which to be amazed. Even the bust of her friend Schleiermacher,[124] which stood on the desk, and the portraits hanging on the walls did not seem unfamiliar. You had seen them so often, these pictures of the two Humboldts and their great contemporaries, but you saw them anew now; this woman had known these men, admired from a distance as the great men of our country, in the days of their youth, and they had been her companions and close friends!

There was only one picture in her room that could make a pretense of being a work of art. It was a portrait of herself at the age of thirteen, and, as was the custom in the eighteenth century, she was attired as a goddess or muse. The painting was by Anna Dorothea Therbusch,[125] Lessing's friend, and so extraordinarily beautiful that you would not have believed it accurate if the picture by the renowned portraitist Graff[126] of her, painted at the beginning of this century, had not been even more perfect in its regular beauty and more radiant in its expression of nobility and goodness.

Although no one would have been better suited to elegant, beautifully decorated rooms than Mrs. Herz, the undecorated simplicity of her room, in her case, becomingly framed the elegant dignity of her person. When you saw her in the plainest clothing, surrounded by the most modest furnishings in her narrow room, and remembered that the beauty of this woman had been renowned throughout Europe; that for sixty years there had scarcely been a famous man who had not known and honored her, that Mendelssohn and Mirabeau, Schiller and Goethe, Jean Paul, the Schlegels, Fichte, the Humboldts, Schleiermacher and Börne, the most prominent artists, both men and women, of every country, the intellectuals among the princes and rulers of our time, had acknowledged the beauty and the spirit of this woman—the great friendliness that she accorded even the most humble was something magical and touching.

Even when we became better acquainted and familiarity had eased the surprise of the first impression, a feeling of reflective solemnity, the kind you feel in the presence of the ruins of great structures of the past, always came over me. Involuntarily, you saw a procession of the spirits of those to whom this woman had once turned eagerly and supportively; involuntarily, you thought you saw the reflection of bygone days on the face of this old woman. "I knew everybody!" she said once in jest, when I asked if she remembered a certain, not particularly important person from my home town. Everyone certainly seemed to know her! Just as she had been the friend of our intellectual heroes, she had gradually become a spiritual symbol of Berlin to later generations. Those who saw and knew her still surely remember her with love.

It was a pleasure to talk to her and hear her tell her stories. On such occasions all her attributes of grace and charm would be on full display. She never tried to be the center of attention, or to focus the conversation on herself, yet she always participated. She enjoyed talking, as one enjoys practicing an art that one has mastered. Everything she said bore witness to a clear mind; nothing was done precipitously, no comment was tossed in at random or without due consideration. Yet nothing seemed premeditated or self-conscious; her long training in society was such that she only needed to proceed naturally to have a noble and beneficial effect on every person, with a sense of nobility and beauty.

When I think of her and her circle, I sometimes ask myself what distinguishes the type of socializing of which she used to speak, so longed for now, from today's society, about which we all complain more or less and which we tend to blame on the change of the spirit in our century. I think, however, that this so-called change in the spirit of the times is just as convenient an abstraction as the spirit of the history of the world, where everything is placed in historical context, so that human beings bear no responsibility. Each one of us helps to form society; each one of us therefore is partly responsible for its ills.

We always think of this "society," which became such a tremendous influence on the cultural history of our country at the end of the eighteenth and at the beginning of this century, only as a circle of heroes, and tend to forget that these heroes did not spring into this world as complete as Minerva, but had been young, developing, erring, striving, and unfolding persons for a long time. We hear the names Humboldt, Rahel Levin, Schleiermacher, Varnhagen, and Schlegel and think about what they became. We forget that the Humboldts were just two young noblemen of their age, that Rahel Levin was a lively Jewish girl, Schleiermacher an unknown clergyman, Varnhagen a young physician, the Schlegels a pair of rather frivolous young journalists. We forget that we have similar young people among us today, who, even if not necessarily geniuses of the first rank, still have an excellent education, much talent, and a great ambition. Most of us do not want to sow, however, or to tend a crop, but just to reap, and especially in a way that is more often directed toward impressing another than in satisfying ourselves.

[Lewald also meets another famous Berlin Jewish hostess, Sara Levy.]

She was a year older than Mrs. Herz, and also born a Jew. While Mrs. Herz had converted to Christianity when she was middle-aged, Mrs. Levy had remained faithful to the law of Moses and had made it a personal mission to be its representative whenever it was attacked and to support every step of its adherents toward intellectual progress. She was just as rich as Mrs. Herz was poor, as ugly as the latter was beautiful. The two women had been friends since childhood and were completely alike in the goodness of their hearts and their charity. It was only that everything Mrs. Herz did bore a stamp of her feminine grace, while Mrs. Levy displayed a rather unbecoming masculine aspect. She was the daughter of a much-mentioned and very rich merchant of the period of Frederick the Great, who had given his children an excellent education and whose beautiful daughters, the Baroness von Arnstein and the Baroness von Eskeles, had played a prominent role in society at the time of the Congress of Vienna. Unfortunately, Mrs. Levy had none of the features of these sisters. She was of average size and very thin but carried herself very straight in spite of her seventy-six years and moved with an energy and strength quite remarkable for her age. She had an obvious squint and was nearsighted. Her voice was very deep, her manner of speaking very curt and imperious, unless she was involved in a longer conversation. It therefore sometimes sounded comical when she uttered friendly and polite remarks in a tone of command. Once, when I was praising her to my broth-er, he retorted, "I know all that and respect the lady as much as you, but she is too belligerent for me."

That comment made us all laugh, and there was some justice in it, but not entirely. She was not belligerent, just a brave woman; this bravery was something she had recently demonstrated, if not for a particularly good reason, as far as I was concerned. Mrs. Levy owned and lived in the large building, still standing, that extends behind the Packhof to the new museum of today. She had lived in the house forever and had moved into it, as she told me, when it was still surrounded by open fields. It was a doubly beau-tiful site, with its large, lovingly tended garden, shaded by magni-cient trees, because such wide expanses of land and magnificent gardens had become very rare in the heavily populated capital. When Frederick William IV undertook the building of the new museum, it was determined that in order to build it properly, he would have to confiscate not only a corner of Mrs. Levy's garden but also tear down a wing of the house and, what was worse, the wing in which she herself lived. She was therefore offered a sales contract with the most generous provisions. Mrs. Levy did not have the kind of personality that sacrifices the comfort of the indi-vidual for the good of the whole without any objections. She was willing to give up a part of her garden, although reluctantly, but she absolutely refused to give up her apartment. "After my death, they can have the whole property and I will see that they get it inexpensively. As long as I live, however, what is mine remains mine. Since the king likes to live like his ancestor, Frederick the Great, I will be the miller of Sans Souci, who gives him an oppor-tunity to show anew how to respect property." The architect com-plained vigorously, and the king also wanted to build the museum as he had originally planned. But he, being very original and arbi-trary himself, gave in to unusual arbitrariness and originality when he encountered them. He thus found himself amused by the intransigence of the old lady and finally asked Alexander von Humboldt to intercede in the matter. The latter was also quite old and knew how much the home to which they are accustomed means to old people. So an agreement was reached that Mrs. Levy would keep her house untouched, and that only a small part of her garden that was absolutely necessary for the construction would be taken. This compromise made it necessary to place one wing of the musuem at an angle.

7

I had come to Berlin with the firm resolve of maintaining my literary anonymity. My father's wishes had strengthened me in this resolve. But my cousin, August Lewald, who had formerly supported this idea, had changed his mind, probably because of the favorable reception my novels had received. In the fall, when acquaintances returned from Baden-Baden, they brought me the news that August Lewald had inquired about me closely and that they had had to tell him of my appearance and the way I acted. For his part, he had told them that I had considerable talent for writing and that he liked my second novel, which had just appeared, even better than the first.

The acquaintances then asked me what I had written, but I fended off their questions jokingly to be true to my promise. One day, however, Mrs. Bloch, who had continued to show great kindness to me, witnessed such a conversation and told me my silence was foolish.

"You once confided in me," she said, "that you earned the money for your stay in Berlin yourself. I thought that was very decent and naturally assumed you earned it by literary activity. Since you obviously did not want to divulge the details, I did not want to force you and still do not know what you have written. It is clear that you do not only want to become world famous by your writing, but also to make a new life for yourself; it is therefore unreasonable to forego advantages which would certainly be to your benefit, just to preserve your anonymity. If you want to confide your secret to me, I will endeavor to talk it over with you. I think it would be very useful to you."

Mrs. Bloch could be so charming in such half-joking, half-serious conversations, and her reasons were so indisputably right, that I gave in to them and brought her the novels on that very day. She and her husband really enjoyed them and me. "You will be somebody," he told me, "because you know what you want. Few people do. Most want all sorts of things and would like to find these things already prepared for them. That's why they usually don't accomplish anything. Somebody who really wants something and has the means that lead to his goal will eventually reach it."

My relationship to this fine couple changed and I was only too happy for their advice, namely, to acknowledge my authorship of *Clementine* and *Jenny*. My father also soon saw the good sense of this step. Only the sisters still living at home wrote me, advising against it with naive arrogance. They adjured me to keep my anonymity, if I still could; they were following some obscure drive that I did not understand and whose reasons were probably just as unclear to them as their letters to me made me. Some were too young and all were too inexperienced for their opinions and thoughts to bear any weight with me if they went beyond their own personal wishes and desires. None of them had been able to tell me what they were afraid would happen if I were known as the author of *Clementine* and *Jenny*; but they all agreed that it would be unpleasant for them if someone spoke of the books in their presence. It would also be disagreeable that I would be mentioned and criticized in the newspapers and that I was working for money. They thought I should seriously consider the fact that I was our father's daughter and act accordingly.

I would not even mention the foolish letters and the inappropriate advice if they were not a proof of how a number of vague impressions change into unclear thoughts and even a type of obnoxious familial intolerance in the minds of women who lived in a tightly closed family atmosphere, which can be very harmful and for which even life with its bitter experiences is sometimes unable to provide a cure. From this familial arrogance eventually emerges that concept of family solidarity, which can cripple an individual in certain cases, and from which I had to suffer my good measure. Although we demand equality before the law for all classes, most families maintain a sort of caste prejudice that is more appropriate to the ancient laws of the Hindus than the concepts of the nineteenth century. Even I had initially considered it a humiliation to earn money, and although I had escaped from this Brahmin-like family spirit much earlier and forever, unjustified and uncomprehending opinions and advice still ruined many a happy hour for me—and our life is made up of hours.

Now a new and good time began for me in Berlin. I was like a ship that had long lain complete its blocks and was finally prepared for sailing, for sliding down into the bright fresh current, the waves of which would lift and carry it. I experienced for myself what an advantage it is to be like those who are born with a famous and well-known name. A name is like a pedestal. It lifts a person out of the masses, it distinguishes him and reflects what its bearer does in the way of good and praiseworthy actions. It gains him more favorable notice and is soon at his service. The person whose deeds demonstrate a sorry contrast to his name arouses more attention with his lack of accomplishments, his weaknesses and flaws. There is something seductive about fame, and I suddenly realized that we have to defend ourselves against this temptation. How had I actually changed, I often asked myself, with a secret contempt for the people who suddenly began to greet me in a more friendly way after they knew I had written a few novels? I was older than three years ago, but the young men, who had earlier left me to sit as an old maid at the balls earlier, now sought me out; I had a choice of the best dancers, if I wanted to dance. I appeared no healthier; in October they had found me faded; in January they found me interesting. I was not more intelligent, cleverer, more educated than previously, but what I did and said was suddenly interpreted in the most favorable light. People who had formerly left me to sit in the corner like a pedestal table now tried to be introduced to me and could find no end to their interest in me.

I would be untruthful if I said that all this did not give me considerable pleasure and that my vanity did not find occasional satisfaction in it. But a strong sense of my own identity preserved me from the type of vanity that is permanently satisfied by such small triumphs. The attention paid me actually made me more reserved than I had previously been, and rather than liking more the people who suddenly approached me, I only considered their changed attitude a measure of the lack of independence in their opinions.

[Lewald meets several contemporary writers in Berlin, notably the novelists Wilibald Alexis and Henriette Jeanette Paalzow, who are little known today.[127]*]*

8

Almost every day that winter brought me new experiences, new impressions, and new pleasure. Fortunately, I had enough time to abandon myself to them, since I could not and was not supposed to work all the time. My freedom, my independent situation gave me renewed satisfaction every day and I often repeated to myself Goethe's words, "What you wish for in your youth, you receive fully when you are old," to refer these to my own case, because I now had far more than I had ever expected to accomplish for myself.

At that time Berlin was very entertaining in itself. Frederick William IV's predilection for the arts, as well as his fondness for an intellectual society, drew many foreigners to Berlin. We saw him and the Queen many times in public during that period. He seldom missed the lectures delivered on Sunday afternoons by the Berlin academics in the music academy; he came often to the symphony concerts. People spoke of him whenever there was a cultural event. He participated in his own lively manner in everything personally and intervened wherever he participated. The results were not always appropriate and sometimes caused considerable dissatisfaction but there was always something to discuss, and the spirit of society was kept in a constant state of agitation.

One day we spoke of the founding of the fairy tale-like Order of the Swans; the next day, we saw how the King shook with laughter in his box at the theater when Mr. Alfred Neumont used the phrase, in a lecture about Italian literature, "They are writing

enthusiastic freedom songs under the supervision of the police!"
Another day we learned that Felix Mendelssohn, who directed
the cathedral choir on important occasions, had been instructed
by the King to compose a psalm with accompaniment by harps
and trumpets for the choir at Easter. The Bible said that King
David had his psalms accompanied this way, a fact that was to be
checked with the Rabbinical Council! There was also talk of the
presentation of Tieck's *Bluebeard* and daily discussion of the new
laws concerning Jews, divorce and the changes the King meant
to introduce into the Protestant church service, because of his
reputed fondness for the Anglican Church.

Everybody had a vague feeling that these circumstances
would not continue as they were, that "something would happen." We hovered between fear and hope, because we did not
know what to expect from the King with his changeable spirit
and his stubborn determination. The mood of the day was *carpe
diem*; the good old traditions of Berlin society seemed to want to
revive. The tavern life of the men was not as common as now.

There were still some women in whose rooms a mixed society
of all classes could gather, and the most prominent of these was
the oldest sister of Felix Mendelssohn, Fanny, who was married
to the painter William Hensel. She was small and rather ugly,
except for her large soulful eyes; but she was extremely intelligent, very well educated, very determined, and equal to her
brother as a musician.[128] Her younger sister, Rebekka, the wife of
the famous mathematician Lejeune Dirichlet and the younger
brother, the banker Paul Mendelssohn, were very musical. The
matinees, which Mrs. Hensel held in the large quiet rooms of her
garden apartment, were extremely interesting. She lived in the
garden wing of her parents' home, where the Reichsrat[129] now
meets, and from the French windows of this attached wing,
which consisted only of a ground floor, from its rooms decorated
with works of art, you could look out on the great trees of a large
garden while enjoying the most wonderful musical performances
by professionals and talented amateurs playing together.

It was at such a matinee that I saw and heard Felix
Mendelssohn for the first time. Among the listeners were Henrik

Steffens, Friedrich von Raumer, the artists Wach and Tieck, a Princess von Dessau, Prince Radziwill with his family, the English ambassador Lord Westmoreland, two of Bettina's daughters, a daughter of Prince Karl of Prussia with her governess, Schönlein,[130] and a number of other people whose names were important, or which later became so. One such name was that of the musician Joseph Joachim,[131] then only a boy, who performed brilliant variations of *David* accompanied by Mendelssohn.

While these two were playing, all eyes suddenly turned toward the door and a happy smile crossed everyone's face, as a young man appeared at the entrance to the room. He was a slender, active figure. He entered noiselessly, his head held high and eyes sparkling, gleaming; his presence had something surprising, even overpowering. It was Franz Liszt.

I had already seen him once before, at the home of a friend of mine. I had stood by quietly as a naive woman, who considered herself an intellect, had found it appropriate to ask him about George Sand and her way and manner.[132]

"Does George Sand dress like a man?"

"That's what they say."

"You know George Sand very well?"

"Oh yes! For many years."

"Does she smoke?"

"Yes, she smokes," answered the poor man, with despairing patience, since he could not escape from his tormenter, a very important and influential lady in Königsberg.

"Is George Sand beautiful?"

"She is very attractive."

"How old is she? Is she young?"

"You are always young if you know how to please," he replied. He bowed to the woman, who was no longer young, and rescued himself from her boring indiscretions, by generously throwing her a compliment—generous in light of the torture she had inflicted on him. She, of course, did not hesitate to apply the compliment to herself and boasted about it long thereafter.

I had never spoken to him personally and never heard him play, because we could not afford tickets to his concerts. I really was more interested in Liszt as a man than as a muscian. The man must have a mighty soul, and a strong desire for truth, which had first led him, because of his longing for an ideal, from an enthusiasm for Pietism to fraternization with the St. Simonists, from which he then later also separated himself. I had great pleasure in seeing him from a distance on that morning and observing the wonderful head, from which the hair springs over the proud forehead like the locks of Jupiter Otricoli. I wanted to meet Liszt very much at that time and never thought it would happen, that one day I would be able to love and appreciate him as a friend of my husband and of myself as well.

The music that morning began with a quartet by Weber, which Mrs. Hensel played and which the Gans brothers and Felix Mendelssohn accompanied. Then Mrs. Hensel and her brother performed variations of the piece for four hands. Pauline von Schaetzel, then already the wife of the printer of the court journal, Decker, sang an aria with a chorus from *The Creation*, and later, with an excellent singer — I think his name was Baer — performed several long scenes from *The Templar and the Jewess*. Felix Mendelssohn accompanied the singing on the grand piano and finally played the previously mentioned variations with the young Joachim.

It was a pleasure to watch Mendelssohn when he played. He was quite small, and his delicate, rather pale face bore the mark of his people; it distinctly reminded me of Moses Mendelssohn. Everyone who met him would have found his head attractive, but as soon as he began to play, his features almost seemed to gain new dimensions and a much deeper significance. He became a different person when he stood in front of an orchestra, as I saw and heard in symphony concerts when he conducted his overture to *A Midsummer Night's Dream* and another time when he presented his overture to *The Hebrides*. It seemed as though he were rising upward with the fullness of the tones, that sounded under his leadership, the tones he had created and which now surrounded him with their waves of sound. He grew in strength with them, his head rose proudly, his eyes shone with a beautiful light, his face expressed his earnest joy; you were then completely amazed when he laid down his baton after the last measure, he stepped down from the podium to be on the same level as other people, and the same gently mobile, delicate, and sensitive face that you had observed before the performance reappeared.

I had been greeted in a very friendly fashion by the two sisters of the composer when we met for the first time at a party at Miss Solmar's.[133] They were Jews, too, although married to Christians, and had that decided partiality for their derivation which is always a sign of culture and a characterful independence among the Jews. The semi-educated Jew, who lacks this sense of self-reliance, has always, in previous times as well as now, considered the prejudice directed against his people—by non-Jews with insufficent education—as a humiliation, which he tries to avoid by concealing his derivation or by not mentioning it, so he can make others forget it; he endeavors in every way to join those who want to avoid him. That was and is dishonorable behavior, and since bad things are usually also stupid, this rejection of your own identity was and is also folly. The prejudiced individual and the prejudiced mass of people in Germany and England do not forget and forgive the Jew for being a Jew, even today, and they have a right to scorn him as long as he does not have the self-confidence to assert his human dignity to them as equal to theirs, as long as he is ashamed of his origin to some extent. We cannot expect another to respect in us what we do not value in ourselves. There is more to achieving self-respect than fine carriages, dinners, and beautifully papered rooms, than the furs, diamonds, and gallant passions with which our nouveau-riche Jews try to convince their opponents of their right to equality these days. We need to return to that level of education achieved by the Jews at the time of Lessing and demonstrated by Moses Mendelssohn, to that education which was in step with the best of their age, and which, though striving for knowledge and acquiring it, never forgot that education of the character is the most important of all.

In a repressed nationality, still not emancipated in the spirit of the German people by any means, each member increases the positive attitude toward the whole group by his own achievement in education. Whatever Moses Mendelssohn, his children and grandchildren, whatever Mrs. Herz, Rahel and her friends, Mrs. Levy and her sisters, whatever David Veit, David Friedländer,[134] and men or women of their kind achieved in their age in the way of education and character and made work for themselves, is the foundation of the capital from which the social conditions of today's Jews draw interest. It is appropriate and necessary that they increase this spiritual capital in themselves. Although there are many honorable exceptions, there are a great number of them that have become very materialistic. The marriages, almost rubber-stamped in style and manner, of rich Jewish bankers' daughters to poor members of the aristocracy, are certainly not the right way to promote social equality and respect for the culture and character of the Jews—quite the contrary!

It was a very healthy side of Felix Mendelssohn and his two sisters that they had an affinity for the race to which they belonged. I remember with enjoyment how valuable they considered the reminiscences connected with their family's past. Soon after I had met Mrs. Dirichlet, I noticed one day that an extensive collection of ugly porcelain monkeys stood in a large cabinet in the dining room of her otherwise very tastefully decorated apartment. Their effect was doubly appalling because of the good quality of the rest of her furnishings. I could not help but ask what had moved her to use these nasty figurines as decorations. "Oh," she replied, "these are not decorations, but heirlooms and historical documents. At the time that my grandfather, Moses Mendelssohn, settled in Berlin, every Jew who had married had to buy a certain number of pieces from the Royal Porcelain Works, which Frederick the Great wished to promote in this manner. It was not enough that this was a real financial hardship at times, but the Jews had no right to select their own figurines and had to take what was given to them by the factory. In this way, my grandparents acquired a whole menagerie of monkeys, which their children later divided as memorabilia and which we in turn inherited from our parents. We keep them as a remembrance of the good old times."

[Lewald begins working on her third novel, A Vital Question, *in which, inspired by the proposed new divorce laws in Prussia, she examines the*

question of whether divorce is better than a failed marriage. She is also
writing a novella, The Third Estate, *for an annual "calendar" published*
by Reimarus under the auspices of the Royal Calendar Commission. Mr.
Reimarus had not read her previous works before then, and after doing so,
is very nervous about the controversy she might arouse. He tries to censor
her work somewhat, but she resists.]

Now he was a delicate, well-educated man, who did not want
to hurt my feelings. I was quite willing to meet his demands, but
the scene was too funny when he came to his purpose. At that
juncture he spoke more quickly than usual, praised me lavishly,
and commented (rubbing his hands quickly in embarrassment):
"Now, my dear young lady, since we are going to be finished
soon, let us go through your lovely work and if we find something that seems questionable, we'll easily remove or change it."
He got up, gave me his hand and made to leave. I also arose, and
holding on to his hand, said, "Excuse me, Mr. Reimarus. There's
one thing I have to tell you. Since I have written the novella and
not both of us, I will also revise it myself, and you will print what
I have written verbatim. I can hardly recognize your censorship,
when government censorship is already such a burden on our
creations. I will try not to provoke this censorship; but on the
whole, I stand behind what I write. In the worst case, you can
plead your blind trust in the recommendation of Mr. Tieck. I am
a child of my times. You should have known that. I don't think,
though, you'll have any problems because of me."

We parted on friendly terms, and I worked busily on my
novella, being happy each day that I could do something I
enjoyed and could work and live as I pleased. I thought with
increasing love of my sisters at home, I steadily purchased ribbons, collars, fabric for dresses, and God knows what else for
them, although it was burdensome for me and they could have
bought them equally well at home. When you are happy, you
enjoy giving others happiness. It did not yet bother me that I still
had no amenities in Berlin.

Since I had returned from Breslau in the fall of 1843, I had
been living at my aunt's; and she had other boarders besides

myself. Since these were more profitable than I, with my limited means, I had to be satisfied with the worst situated room. Even though I did not have to do without the most necessary furniture as earlier, I had to suffer all the more from music and a continuous passage through my room. On one side of it, my very musical aunt made music, whenever she had spare time; on the other, an English-language teacher, whose musical talents were truly English, played on peacefully, fortified with all her English pride, even when my aunt was playing one room removed. So I sat at my old desk, wedged in between two musical fires in an oppressively small space, and the cook and maids, and every other visitor to my aunt—elegant dresses, brooms, or washtubs—everything passed by me. It was lucky for me that I had learned as a child to work in the living room at the family table and to hold on to my thoughts and put them down on paper no matter what went on around me. Without such early toughening, I would not have been able to write one word in these surroundings.

The most intolerable part was that I was not mistress in my own room. You can get used to the most wretched quarters, and make yourself and others comfortable in them if you have the freedom to suit yourself. A cellar room or a peasant's hut can bear the marks of a cultured person, but a "decently furnished rented room" is far more difficult to obtain. I paced up and down at times in the room and thought, "What are you doing here?" I looked at the porcelain vases with their dried flowers, which faded stiffly under their glass domes. I looked at the poorly drawn family portraits of people I did not know on the walls. I stood in front of the pier glass, which bore no relationship to the room or the other furniture, and wondered, "How did we both get here?" I seemed as alien to my environment as if I went around in the faded clothes from an old costume wardrobe. It was even worse when I had to fetch my purchases from craftsmen myself, carry my own packages for the family to the post office, and to go out on the street unaccompanied in the evenings.

It had been a standing rule at home that none of the daughters went to a laundress, seamstress or milliner at a strange place, if the shop was not open to the public, and so we had never been out on the street after dark without being accompanied by one of the maids or the porter. Since we had enough servants, this was never a problem; there was always someone available. This was also the case in the families we knew, so I had never thought it could be otherwise. When I spent my first winter in Berlin, the first arrangement my father made for me was to engage a servant to accompany me if I went out in the evenings by foot or coach, because my father was afraid that even riding, I could encounter some unpleasant situations. I had to do without things I wanted to maintain this arrangement, which was quite expensive, but I did not want to overspend the monthly allowance my father had allowed me and misuse his caring for me.

Now that I had decided to live from my own earnings, this companion servant was the first luxury I did without and had to do without. I did my errands myself, I went out alone after dark, and I was not afraid, but I felt a certain discomfort; I felt humiliated. I seemed humbled, and even so lonesome and abandoned at times that one evening, when I was wading in cape and hood through the wet snow in the street during slushy weather, tears came to my eyes. It was the same arrogance that had raised its head when I received the first money I had earned, and I was no sooner aware of the source of my depression than I became heartily ashamed of it. With all my strength and reason, I began to fight the conceit in me that wanted to obtain the advantages of the self-supporting man, of the worker, without having the courage to submit to the conditions of such independence honestly and joyfully, if it became necessary.

I had often discussed the working classes, both in writing and in conversation, had uttered beautiful and elevated statements about them and had spoken my whole life long of the equal rights and emancipation of women with great forcefulness. Now I found, to my great astonishment, that I was playing "the lady" in the worst sense of the word, that I thought my better self was affected by taking money for my work, that I was doing some injury to my position, or presumed I was offending my sense of propriety, when I went peacefully on my way as thousands of poor decent working girls do every evening. This caused a complete revolution in me, and I suddenly seemed so beneath my true worth with my "parlor decency" and my ladylike formality that I immersed myself emotionally in the thought of becoming only a good working woman for the rest of my life, wherever fate would lead me or whatever work was required of me, as long as I could keep my honest independence. You have gained something when you stop judging a person exclusively by the kind of work they do, instead of how they perform it, and when you realize that those who work with their hands are not the only ones who belong to the working classes. You then at least cease to evaluate the worthiness and the rank of women solely according to their economic status and to feel humiliated and abandoned because you do not have enough money to pay for unnecessary taxicabs and the services of a footman.

9

[Lewald's father, after repeated invitations and plans, reluctantly consents to visit her and her older brother in Berlin. Afterwards, she travels to Breslau to stay with her uncle Lewald and his second wife. After many years, she finally meets Heinrich Simon again.]

For eleven years, I had tried to imagine this moment in many different moods and circumstances, had pictured it with the longing of burning passion and with the contrition and despair of utter hopelessness. Now it was close at hand and I scarcely recognized myself in the calmness and peace that reigned in my soul. I wanted to be happy about this state, but I could not; involuntarily there came to mind a sentence from a letter by Prince Louis Ferdinand to his beloved, Pauline Wiesel,[135] which I had heard quoted during the winter. It was: "Where are the beautiful days, when we were so unhappy?" That sentence had already moved and touched me very much, when I heard it. Now I found myself in the position of saying it about myself with deep emotion. Where were the beautiful days, when I was so unhappy?

I continually had me and my life before my eyes, as if in a

magic mirror. I saw myself, as I sat in the snow flurries of that March night and drove away from Breslau with my father, my heart full of despair, my soul darkened, my mind without any prospects; young, fairly healthy, fairly carefree, but without hope. Now I was thirty-three, old for an unmarried woman; my youth lay behind me. I was not healthy, I had had no luck in love, which could have been a consolation; but I felt rich, I felt young. My soul was full of hope; I loved life, because I had a wonderful goal in mind. I hoped to accomplish good and wonderful things. I had work that made me happy; I had independence; I had freedom! I no longer felt that attachment that I had always felt before in the presence of the man I loved.

I looked forward to our reunion with quiet pleasure. I did not only wonder, "What will he think of you?" but also asked myself, "How will he have changed?" And the feeling of being equal to him made him even more valuable to me. The evening I left Berlin I had written him that I was coming to Breslau and that I would be very happy to see him again in peace and with a free heart after so many years.

It was almost nighttime when I arrived in Breslau. My uncle Lewald picked me up at the coach station. I felt very much at home with him and Breslau. In my room lay a welcoming note from Heinrich. A temporary political disagreement with my uncle had prevented him from coming personally.

On the next day we met again in the presence of his family. We were both very touched, but calm; the others seemed more emotional than he and I. Eleven years is a long time! Eleven years change a person greatly, but this is no cause to complain if the years have improved us.

[Lewald describes the positive changes in Simon as a person and as a jurist.]

When I knew my cousin in our youth, he still had strong prejudices and was therefore very dependent on the opinion of others. Because people despised the Jews, he had carefully avoided being reminded of his Jewish background. That is probably why he had chosen the career of a civil servant and directed his ambition toward rapid progress in a career in government service. Now all that had changed. Far from not wanting to remember his Jewish heritage, he had found a calling to battle all prejudice. Since a serious person does not initiate something without examining his soul about it, Heinrich Simon had finally found and recognized the true nucleus and content of his own nature: the urge and necessity to stand up for justice where it is obscured or threatened. The jurist, the legal scholar, had become a man of justice, a representative of justice.

My aunt Lewald had planned for us to leave for her spa a few days after I arrived in Breslau. But many obstacles kept us from leaving, I saw my cousin daily, and we enjoyed each other's company. My cheerfulness and zest for life made us similar, but he noticed that I was still clinging to habits to which I felt bound, to complete large amounts of handwork because it had earlier been my task to do so to prevent any unnecessary expenditures. He made fun of me when he found me sewing and altering my clothes. He made fun of me when I imagined I could not go somewhere alone, to a museum or the theater, or make a trip without being accompanied, if it was a case of more than just not having transportation from one place to another. While I was careful to deviate from the habits and the precepts of home as little as possible and, more accustomed to dependence and subordination than I realized, still regarded my literary activity as a privilege that might be withdrawn at any time, he cried out to me almost daily: "Take your stand once and for all! Don't sew; read and learn! Go where you want to go; live the way you like. Represent the spiritual independence you defend above all in your own person. Simplify your life and your requirements as much as you can, because women are enslaved by the thousands of trivialities which shape their existence. Rely on yourself for advice about what to do and not to do. Take the freedom to be as free as you are."

One evening we spent in his brother's house. Almost all the younger members of the family were present. Heinrich and I stood at an open window and looked out over the broad surface of the railroad station, because my youngest cousin, an employee of the Upper Silesian Railroad, lived in one of the buildings belonging to it. I made the remark that it was most difficult for the imagination to feel comfortable in a place you remember as being open land, but which you now find crossed by streets, changed by new paths and robbed of its trees—in other words, completely changed, like the area in front of the Schweidnitz Gate had changed since I first saw it.

"It seems to me," I said, "when we came out of the Schweidnitz Gate before, we had to go past the little church, to come to the garden where your parents used to live; even the garden looks completely different to me than it did then. I hardly recognized it when I came a year ago, and now all the paths and roads out here are completely strange to me."

"And we walked on them for many a happy hour," he replied quite naturally. But it often happened that our simply uttered words held a meaning that we did not mean to imply, and that surprised us ourselves, because they laid bare our innermost thoughts to each of us quite unintentionally. That's how it probably seemed to Heinrich, because he repeated, as if sunk in reflection, "Many a happy hour!"

He had taken hold of my hand and we stood quietly at the window next to each other. "Come!" he cried, after a while. "We really haven't had a chance to talk to each other, and eleven years are half an eternity. We haven't changed as much as the paths and roads and must get things settled once and for all. Let's go downstairs."

"Alone? Only we two, away from all the others?" I asked with my customary cautiousness.

"Child!" he cried half in jest, but he turned to the others and made the suggestion to go for a walk outside in such nice weather. Everybody agreed. No preparations needed to be made; the area was isolated and it was late. Couples and groups soon formed, and I went with Heinrich. For a while, we all stayed together; then the varying pace separated the groups and Heinrich and I found ourselves alone.

It was a beautiful night at the end of May; there was not a

cloud in the sky. The moon hung full over the horizon and hovered in the air light and free. It was quiet on the ramparts; the promenade stretched peacefully toward the city canal. The scent of lilacs wafted from the shrubbery, from the gardens, the nightingales sang in all the bushes and through the branches of the trees, the full moon spread its golden beams over our path. Here and there we saw a brightly lit garden house with its white walls; here and there we met a few people or music from some room came to our ears. Finally even that ceased. The windows in the houses became dark, the music stopped and we met no one any more. The sky and the moon, the scent of flowers and the coolness of the night, the song of the nightingale and the moonlight on the water, were there now only for us, belonged to us alone.

And we walked and walked and sat down and walked again and told each other the content of long, long years, for hours; and with the dew, which began to fall through the air refreshingly, many tears of memory flowed down our cheeks, and under the bright moonlight, everything, everything brightened that had been dark between us, and as the moon sank down, the whole past with its sorrows and its misunderstandings, with its guilts and its sufferings, sank into the night, once and forever. A bright day of mutual liking and firm trust arose from it, which bound us forever in friendship and illuminated not only me and the beloved of my youth, but all those who were ours in later life, with undimmed clarity until the hour when we all lost that wonderful man.

Day was already breaking when Heinrich left me at the door of my house.

"When are you leaving?" he asked me.

"We are going the day after tomorrow."

"Are you staying in Bad Teplitz long?"

"Four to six weeks."

"I have time," he said. "Do you want me to come visit and stay with you a while?"

"No, don't do that," I told him. "We'll meet one of these days without that. But start writing to me again, and write soon!"

"That goes without saying," he replied. We shook hands. We could never lose each other now.

"Count on me as I'll count on you for anything," he said once more, "and if you need me, call me, and I'll be there!"

"I know that," I assured him—and so we parted.

10

On June 2, 1844, we left Breslau for Bad Teplitz. Only my aunt Pauline Lewald and I went. My uncle had bought a beautiful new travel coach for this trip, the baggage was comfortably stowed, the maid sat on the coachbox, and in the completely open carriage, we were as cozy as on a drive around the town.

It was five o'clock in the morning when the coachman blew his horn; when the whip cracked, the other members of the household waved their handkerchiefs and we left behind the court of the railroad station, of which my uncle was a director. There was still dew on the bushes and trees of the promenade, the sun was shining brightly, unobscured by any fog, the birds sang everywhere, and here and there a few butterflies, the kind children call "lemon birds" and cherish greatly, fluttered over our heads playfully, as if they wanted to accompany us, or go along on the journey. It is lovely to drive out into the springtime like that! You always have a feeling of ownership. Actually, you *are* taking possession with your mind of that piece of earth which imprints its image on your imagination. It is there only for you; it is there forever.

I was very happy that morning. Since the day I had first left Königsberg with my father for the first time, I had never made a trip again, on which I was heading toward the strange and unexpected. The suspense that makes the beginning of such a journey so exciting lies right there, in the expectation, the uncertainty, the hope for the fortunate happenstance. For eleven years I had really not been completely happy, but on that day I was as merry and carefree as a child. I had seen my father again, healthy and strong, knew I was loved and respected by those who were dearest to me, as I loved and respected them, and was therefore completely satisfied and filled with courage for the future.

I perceived everything good that I had received throughout my life as a great whole; I remembered with deep emotion all the kindness I had already enjoyed. I thought of my father, who was now sleeping after his day's work, of my sisters, who had no concept of the glories I had perceived; I thought of my brothers and their different ways of life and I also thought of all the loved ones I had left in Breslau. I was very attached to all these people; I would not have wanted to live without knowing that they were living with me, that they loved me. But I was happy to be alone; I was living for myself. I was, as I was, because of my own strength, my own talents, myself—and I was free! Free! The nightbird, which passed by over our heads, did not seem freer to me than I.

It was an indescribably blissful feeling with which I looked down from the quiet height over the broad dark landscape. And just as I had taken spiritual possession of the beautiful world around me when we left Breslau, I now took possession of myself.

The time of my bondage was over; the time of my freedom was dawning for me. I was in control of what I would do with my future.

11

[In Bad Teplitz, Lewald becomes good friends with her new aunt—her uncle's second wife—and meets a middle-aged widow of a Prussian government official, an avid reader who is much impressed by Lewald's books.]

Turning to me, she said, "I am very happy to be alone with you at last. I have wanted to tell you something that has been in my heart for along time. I have you to thank for the best gift one person can give another. You have healed my heart of a great mistake and my reason of a terrible error. She pressed my hand, but I still did not know what her words meant. "I'm sure you are aware of the strong prejudice Christians have against the Jews," she continued. "I shared this prejudice, this aversion, yes, hatred toward the Jews completely, and was rather proud of it, until I read your novel, *Jenny*, last year. Day and night I thought afterwards, about how many people I had arrogantly sinned against, and I was thoroughly ashamed of my harshness and blindness. I had a strong desire to meet you and to tell you how you had changed me." She laid her hands on my shoulders and looked at me tearfully in a friendly way. "May God bring you happiness," she added in an emotional voice, as she embraced me. "Someone who speaks up so fervently against prejudice and for humanity will do well in the world. May God bring you happiness, much happiness, my dear child."

I was already far happier at that moment than she could realize. I kissed her hand, which she had put on me as if blessing me, we remained standing by one another for a while, and I promised myself in my heart to remember this hour if I should ever be tempted to be untrue to myself or my convictions. I have preserved this moment so firmly in memory that the self-admonition has never been necessary.

[Lewald's further travel plans are interrupted when she has to take her ailing sister, Elisabeth, to Franzensbad for a cure. She finds out that despite her precautions, the censor has found a scene in her novella, The Third Estate, *objectionable and will not allow publication of the whole calendar until she changes it.]*

The editor of the calendar, not knowing what to do, had gone to my brother, who had turned to the Higher Censorship Office. We now had to wait to see what would happen.

[Lewald quotes the censored passage—one in which a major character inveighs against the plight of the poor and the apathy of the rich.]

In my character's honestly intended, if not completely accurate assertions, and especially in his accusations at the end, far more valid then than now, the censor had seen an incitement of the lower classes against the upper, the poor against the rich. I received a letter from the publisher of the calendar with a request to revise the chapter containing the above conversation; otherwise he would find it necessary to print new covers and take out the censored material—that is, if he could not succeed in preventing the confiscation of the calendar as it was, an act that my brother was also trying to prevent.

I realized, naturally, that I would have to make such a change, if it were unavoidable, but I did not know exactly where to start. It is a miserable matter to be forced to alter your work, which you have conceived as a whole and written as a single work of art, for outside considerations.

In this particular case, it was a matter of taking a conversation that is structured to rise to a climax and removing this climax. While I was working on my revision, I constantly had in mind the image of a runner accelerating into a tremendous sprint that ends with a careful step over a threshold. It seemed impossible to me to have two figures, which I had imbued with much warmth, a lively eloquence, and a certain pathos, break off a conversation so characteristic of their whole personalities with an apathetic anticlimatic comment; I constantly felt that the characters themselves were struggling against it.

Since I had begun to write, I had acknowledged only a relative and limited power over the figures created by me. In this regard I had always thought of Goethe's "Sorcerer's Apprentice" as the symbol of the relationship of the writer to his creations. The writer has the power to call forth his beings out of the void; he can conjure them up, assign them to a certain place, give them an appropriate activity; but once they exist, have their own shape, have established activities and relationships to others, the master who created them becomes their servant. If they are really capable of life, they become independent and free because of their inner necessity. The writer then has to let them do what they like and to prepare and set the scenes for the situations in which the characters he has created can develop their individuality. Because of their inner necessity, they then become co-creators and promoters of events.

I was saved from having to change the dialogue according to the censor's demands, but the explanation of how this came about was almost as disagreeable to me as the alteration would have been.

After considerable negotiations, the publication of the calendar had been permitted, with the comment that the censor would not pursue the matter further because the novella was written "by a woman." This news, delivered to me from Berlin with great satisfaction, made me furious, as welcome as it was as regards the calendar. It touched upon a question, on which I had thought considerably since the beginning of my literary career, a question I discussed with many of my friends and one which I still ponder, after many years of experience, just as I did long ago.

With a work of art, we should consider what has been created, not its creator. When something good or bad is written or painted, its quality is not affected by the accidental personal position or life of the artist. The criticism of a work of art should be an absolute, not a relative matter; it should deliver a judgment of the work and not a report card for its creator or author. Now, a student presenting a completed assignment to his teacher or master must and can accept the fact that the latter will consider him in connection with the work. It means much to him if the teacher consoles him by saying that the work might not have been finished, but could be said to have succeeded because of the amount of effort the author put into it. "Good according to your ability" is a grade with which quiet, diligent souls can turn from their work very satisfied to the enjoyment of life, or just as satisfied, go to their eternal rest.

It is different with a work that is offered to the public. It is a step by which everyone who takes it, puts himself in the position of being independent and, to some degree, teacher and master in the area in which he performs. Whether this more or less successful work is done by a man or a woman, whether a man or a woman utters a fallacy or pronounces a truth seems completely immaterial to me. The public and the critics are dealing with the work itself. No matter who produced them, the fallacy is just as reprehensible, the truth just as worthy of consideration, the beauty and nobility just as elevating, and the ugly and mean just as damnable.

The national spirit in England, France, and Italy recognizes this fact by language usage. The creator of an intellectual work is called the author, no matter what his sex. In Germany it is different. German literary criticism lags behind even the national spirit of our country. While the people have become accustomed to counting those German women who produce worthwhile work as "writers,"[136] the critics treat the women writers in the majority with a polite condescension or with gallantry—both equally insulting to my mind. These attitudes embody within them the automatic tendency to think that what women have accomplished is good enough considering their limited capacities or insignificance so that their failures are excusable.

They say quite accurately: "The best is no better than the right thing." I have had the impression all my life that there would be nothing better for women writers than to be judged abstractly and to lay upon them, as is done for every other writer, the complete, difficult responsibility for their work and its effect. The development of a human being can only become complete within a total system of equality with those striving for the same goal. If you raise someone above the general public, you damage her development as much as if you try to keep her below the norm. That is why princes and women share a number of bad qualities; they are both kept remote from the bottom of the public, handled and judged according to certain conventional rules and evaluated by special standards. Therefore, they finally become accustomed not to make demands upon themselves, not to face those simple, serious, and difficult challenges, without facing which no person ever achieves anything worthwhile in life.

As long as I can remember, it has made me angry to hear that this or that achievement was good enough if you considered it came from a woman. When I sent my first work to my cousin Lewald, I therefore signed it with a man's name. I wanted to have my "rights," no more no less. My father supported this, and Lewald had nothing against it. My first novel, *Clementine*, appeared completely anonymously, the second, *Jenny*, as a novel by the (woman) writer of *Clementine*. I was amused because, after the appearance of *Jenny*, people strangely enough wanted to think that this pseudonym concealed the identity of a [male] writer. It was with mixed emotions that I read in Heinrich Laube's[137] paper his admission that, after he had finally learned the true identity of the author of *Jenny*, he was happy to recognize that he had underestimated the ability of women. I had just as mixed emotions when the censor decided to ignore an ordinarily unpublishable opinion because a woman had written it.

Once you remove a sense of responsibility, you also remove a sense of its importance. If you explain from the beginning, as the critics are only too wont to do, that you see in women writers just a very relative and limited ability, you take the proper joyous seriousness of effort away from them. You direct them to trivialities, which are then held against them. All I want for women writers is that they be treated without special consideration, but also without prejudice, that they be judged by their production and not by their sex. In other words, men and women writers should be equally responsible and therefore entitled to the same rights, something that is by no means the situation here today. So I return to my demand for that emancipation for women, which I have stated many times for us in these pages—emancipation to do meaningful work, have significant responsibilities, and be able to gain that equality of legal and social rights to which serious work by serious workers entitle the individual.

13

[Moritz Lewald continues to cause great concern for his family. Political problems are occurring in Prussia and Bohemia.]

Some of our Prussian compatriots were appalled and frightened by the assassination attempt that Mayor Tschech had just made against the King, while the Bohemians and Austrians had even greater worries in their countries. We received constant oral and written communications about the riots in Prague, which apparently had been going on for weeks and the cause of which was difficult to determine from our information. There was not much about these disturbances in the newspapers, which reported minor unlawful assemblies, dispersed by the police without any problems. What we learned from eyewitnesses was quite different.

While we were still in Teplitz, some families were arriving there, having fled Prague. They bore frightening news of the death of a child, shot in the arms of his nurse in the middle of a room; of heavy street fighting and the loss of many lives. Some of them spoke of the severe need among the working classes; others, of Panslavic plots and general dissatisfaction with the Austrian government. Still others asserted that anti-Semitism or even resentment of the Protestants had caused the first disturbances and that these were disrupting the general peace, even if in less violent form.

If you heard these tales and simultaneously saw the boundless poverty of the women in Bohemian villages, the hordes of beggars and cripples surrounding our coach when we passed through them, and then met with people from Viennese society or with Catholic clergymen who found everything was wonderful in the country—you became aware of such a mixture of opinions and views, such pronounced hatred between the opposing nationalities, religions, and political parties, that you thought you had been transported back to a previous age. I had to admit happily to myself, that the spirit of Protestantism in Prussia and North Germany had had an enlightening and humanizing effect that encouraged tolerance. As lively as the conflict between the Catholic bishops and the Prussian government was at that period,[138] it was able to excite the various denominations only upon the rarest occasions. I believe there never was an actual demonstration of hostility because of religious differences in the larger cities.

14

[Lewald travels to Prague despite the disquieting rumors and has a good time. Then she returns to Berlin via Dresden. She meets Karoline von Woltmann, a minor writer, who has known Rahel Varnhagen and tells

Lewald about some of the flaws in her idol.[139] *Lewald also finds that some people want to make her into a believing Christian.]*

Strangely enough, it was those who themselves had converted from Judaism to Christianity, both men and women, who undertook this mission. These well-meaning people complained that my talent (I use their words) should be spent in the service of falsehood. Since in my second novel I had dealt with, among other things, the relationship of a young Jewish woman toward Christianity, they had the idea that I had depicted my own heartfelt experiences in my presentation. I made no secret of the fact that I considered the conversion of a Jew to Christian dogma as puzzling as my inability to believe this dogma no doubt seemed to those who wanted to convert me. Since they often asked me very penetrating questions, I declared to them candidly that I considered it an impossibility for a person born a Jew and raised among Jews, if he had a clear understanding, to accept a miraculous faith of any kind. I therefore had to consider Jews who really believed in Christianity as excused by self-delusion if I did not want to think even worse of them.

My most ardent proselytizers were two elderly gentlemen, whose position in life and in the civil service was very important, whose characters were impeccable, and who had far more consideration for me than I had patience. While I believed them to be guilty of an intentionally cherished self-deceit, they reproached me for a spiritual arrogance, which, according to them, complacently rejected the effort of meditation and the humility necessary for a proper conversion. As often and as much as I tried to convince them of the contrary, we could find no common ground.

"How is it possible, not to believe?" they asked me. "How is it possible for you to believe?" I would reply. "Where do you find comfort and support or a refuge in the hours of suffering, distress, and temptation?" they cried to me, and I had no response other than, "I bear what life gives me to bear, I reassure myself with the view of the conditions of human existence and the view of what cannot be changed. When I feel tempted to do something wrong, I would have no restraint, to be sure, other than the feeling of what is right in my heart and the conviction, gained by experience, that every wrong committed carries within it the seed of its own punishment."

They were not satisfied with this, of course. They thought I had taken up strange ideas; my convictions did not belong to me; I was too young for such self-reliance. They forgot that I was thirty-three and accustomed to serious thinking from childhood on.

The most immediate results of these continuing conversations was that I began to think more deeply about the great ethical ideas, like the Christian dogma, and to clarify for myself how it was possible for these mature men to accept a myth as a matter of conviction. They had, after all, become accustomed to rigid proofs and analyses in their intellectual studies and work. I wondered why it was impossible for me, who lacked both their formal education and philosophical knowledge, and also the power of discrimination trained by exercise of the reasoning faculty in legal practice, to believe something that was not rational. I mulled over this but did not arrive at any conclusions or gain any faith in the depth of conviction among the converted, just as they were not firmly convinced of the seriousness of my thoughts. Both sides neglected one factor in our concepts—the epoch in which they had converted and the time at which they demanded a change in my convictions.

All those people, men as well as women, had converted to Christianity at the end of the previous and the beginning of this century, a time when, if one can say so, sentimentality reigned in the world, when feeling was given priority over thinking in many circles. Tired of excessive sensuality, of easy cynicism about the serious and the sublime—fashionable attitudes that had spread from France throughout the world—they had longed for a refuge from themselves, for a focal point where they could find peace and contemplation and, most of all, themselves.

The inexorability of the French Revolution caused the same kind of break in the licentiousness of their lives as was made by Christianity in Roman society at the time of Caesar. Only the later break was far more sudden and powerful; the ideas of the equality of man, which Christianity had brought to the world as a precept of love, were transferred from the hereafter to the present with the return to this precept. The doctrine of the equality and brotherhood of all people before God was converted into the doctrine of equality before justice and the law. In the first powerful excitement, the Revolution tried to express its idea of love with the guillotine.

Shuddering at the insanity of this bloody means of proof, soft hearts, seeing before their eyes the powerful reversal of fortune and the transitoriness of earthly life, turned away from the theory of equality transplanted to earth, to look for its spiritual equivalent. Frightened by the sudden social upheaval they had witnessed, they sought something intangible and eternal. The same reasons that had made hearts in the time of the Caesars turn to the teachings of a life in the hereafter, a hopeful and self-sacrificing love, in this later age caused the conversion of many Jews to Christianity, the turning of Protestants to the Catholic Church, and a willingness to believe in miracles. Because people felt forced to hope for redemptive miracles, imaginative persons immersed themselves in mysticism. The more lyrically disposed souls were inclined to look for the unanimity of feeling, strength for living, and ability in situations furthest removed from education and culture. The predilection for a romantically created "life of the common people," romanticism, and the inclination toward the popular national elements in the past arose from a revulsion against the common people before one's eyes. So many terrible things had happened under the reign of the Goddess of Reason that one willingly gave up one's investigative reason. The arrogance and selfishness of the aristocracy that had been overthrown were so great and so terrible for the aristocracy in its consequences that humility and self-abnegation had to seem like means of salvation.

It is different today. An observant, unprejudiced person must admit that, since the days of the French Revolution, the true spirit of Christianity has become more deeply rooted in the hearts of people and that it is more effective and a greater influence on standards than ever before. The brotherhood of man has become a matter of incontrovertible conviction for every reasonable human being.

It is quite different with the dogma of Christianity. Alexander von Humboldt wrote in a letter to Varnhagen von Ense: "All religions are composed of three completely separate parts: ethical teachings, which are basically the same for all of them and very pure; a geological dream; and a legend or historical novel. The most emphasis is always laid on the last." My Christian proselytizers forgot that Strauss and Feuerbach[140] had lived, written, and been influential, that the history of the origin of the earth has been traced back to geological bases in all the scientific books, and that there is no reason for us to reject the exercise of reason or the test of understanding any more.

15

[Lewald finally meets Varnhagen von Ense and relates details of him and his friends in Berlin.]

16

Rich in a number of new impressions and experiences and filled with longing to see my father again, I returned to Königsberg in the middle of September, after an absence of fifteen months. The feeling of being at home enfolded me gently and warmingly like a spring breeze after the days of cold. To know in the morning that my father was there, to be able to wait for him during the day, to feel that he was happy with me, that my stories entertained him well, to sit at his table, to eat his bread, to receive everything I wanted and enjoyed from his hands, which gave these gifts so lovingly, to sit at his bedside at night and to be able to say "Good night" to him, in a word, to be a child of the house again, his child—all that made me very happy. It was sometimes almost strange to me that I was spending no money, that I only had to ask to receive not only the essentials but what I wanted or what was superfluous. I did not have to calculate anxiously whether I could do this or that, I did not have to think constantly whether my expenditures were in line with my income. The lack of responsibility let me rest easy for a while; the closeness of my father really refreshed me. But after a few days, I could not conceal from myself, no matter how hard I tried, that I no longer felt this place was my home. Nothing was as it had been, but I could not really say what had changed in the time I had been gone.

I became quite sad, without knowing why, when I found myself alone in one of the rooms, although much in them was prettier and more elegant than previously. My father's circumstances had evened out more and more during the last few years. We now needed far less for the daily necessities so that more could be spent on the amenities and for the decoration of the house, which was maintained by my sisters with the same care and cleanliness my mother had exercised. But everything was so quiet! So quiet in the living room, so quiet in the corner room, so quiet in all the halls and stairwells!

If the family had appeared small the previous year, it seemed even smaller to me now. Instead of the eight children who had gathered with their parents around the dining table, there were only four at home. My sister Elise had not returned with me, because she was to try a new cure next summer and we did not want to expose her to the rigors of winter in Königsberg. The large living room, where fourteen people had usually sat at the table, had become too large for us; a smaller room had been recently furnished for this purpose. My brothers' rooms had been empty for years; the floor on which my mother had lived toward the end had been rented to a strange old lady. My little room was empty also and I — I could not deceive myself about this and was quite sad about it — I myself was only a guest at home, was looked upon as a guest, albeit a very welcome one.

My whole family was happy about my return. In my absence they had discovered that when I was not there, the invigorating element was lost. Just as I had often spread cheerfulness in earlier days with my tales and inventions, there was usually no lack of laughter now, when I began to relate what I had seen and heard.

My father sat there, visibly amused and chuckling quietly to him-self on one of the corner sofas, joking about the grateful audience I had in my family. It surprised me, however, that he remained with us so long and sat on that sofa. It was so strange to me that he sought out the warmth of the stove and complained about the coldness of the room. He had never been susceptible to cold before. Whenever we complained about it, he would hold out his warm loving hands to us and say, laughing, "Why am I never cold?" Now he often had cold hands and praised and loved the warmth of the rooms.

It struck me how much he had aged since I had seen him five months earlier in Berlin. I mentioned it to my sisters, and they shared my concern but thought that the change had occurred earlier and he had only seemed better in Berlin. I asked our fami-ly doctor. He also found Father changed, but consoled me by saying that old age manifests itself earlier in some than in others, without necessitating a cause for concern. When I turned to Father himself with an urgent request for information, he made fun of me. "Now that you are no longer hypochondriacal about yourself, you have become so about me," he said teasingly. "Leave me alone! Nothing is wrong with me but the lack of severe worries. I have had them all my life. Now that I am rid of them and have less work, I don't know what to do with myself much of the time and I get tired of reading so much."

There was much truth in this, but his explanation did not really satisfy me. Father basically had no financial problems any more. He sometimes spoke with us very cheerfully about how we would sell his real estate holdings one day, receive his estate, and move to Berlin. But he worried that none of the daughters were married,[141] and even good news received from Moritz did not make him happy for long. He had obviously lost his old vigor and zest for living.

My sisters did what they could for him. All the care that had formerly been spent on Mother was focused on him alone now. Everything centered on him and yet I often wished Mother could return for him. I even occasionally thought it would have been good for him to have married again. Daughters do not replace a man's wife. The man who is used to a satisfying marriage, the love of a wife, the devotion of someone who has no future but him, undoubtedly misses these things again and again. I had no illusions about that and remained inwardly sad despite my father's pleasure in me. I continually thought of his death although I realized how foolish a concern this was. But I had lost the quiet confidence that I had always placed in him and my home, as their being like the enduring of the earth or something that had and would always exist for me.

My relationship to my home had heretofore been like that of the fledgling to his old nest. I had wandered here and there and had always relied on the fact that the good old oak tree would stand firmly rooted in its place and would preserve my nest home in its protective arms whenever I was driven to seek peace and refuge under its secure roof. Now I often realized that the tree could be felled; I could find empty the place where it had stood and spread its sheltering branches over me. Because this thought frightened me, I asked myself, "Why him? Why my father, who still stands so tall and has not reached the fullness of his years yet?"

Meanwhile, the longer I remained at home the more I felt the fears I had initially felt were ungrounded or at least exaggerated. My father seemed much better, was recuperating again, I thought, and I occasionally said jokingly, "I am like a spa bath for Father and all of you; I make you more lively." I immersed myself deeply and with pleasure in my novel, the plot and characters of which became dearer and dearer to me. It concerned the moral justification of divorce, when a marriage has ceased to be a marriage in the true sense of the word, that is, the union of two people bound together by mutual love and respect for the same values.

In *Clementine* I had tried to depict that a marriage based on mutual respect should not be sacrificed to the reawakening of an earlier legitimate love. In my new novel, *A Vital Question*, I wanted to prove that a great number of marriages entered upon without inner necessity frequently carry within them the seed of an unwholesome development, and how the cohabitation of man and wife based solely upon habit and the permission of the church becomes immoral, when this relationship lacks love. It is not my purpose to give a summary of my earlier works or to demonstrate their good qualities and excuse the bad. They are complete, they exist; the critics have judged them, and the public has become acquainted with them. The critics and the public have helped me, because they have always made me consider matters more deeply and clarified and determined my convictions. I certainly did not, as is probably thought and asserted against me, fight for "house and home" in *A Vital Question*; I did not work according any portrait or model, I tried to keep as an objective an attitude toward my material as possible, and I was perfectly satisfied because, contrary to my expectations, my father really approved of the work.

I had been afraid that he would neither like the material itself or that I expressed this idea, but then my father had always maintained his old philosophy of completing matters and doing nothing halfway. It made me happy and touched me greatly to see that he completely gave up his authority over me when it came to my work, that he kept his word and let me find and chose my way without dissuasion or inducement.

When I had finished some chapters, I would read them to my father in the evening after his office hours, something which had never occurred earlier. Once he asked me to read an excerpt from my novel to an old friend of his, a very cultured businessman, who had known me since I was a child, when he visited us one evening, to "give him a treat." I had to choose several scenes for this reading, which featured the actress Sophie Harcourt and in which "much happened," because Father was basically only interested in the plot of a novel. He did not think much of the finished figures, of "ideal characters." They were never his taste; and in this I shared and still share his inclination. It has never been the so-called ideal persons that I most enjoyed creating and developing, because they usually have no counterpart in the real world. Those characters representing absolute evil or absolute virtue had already seemed just as unreal as they were boring, when I dragged myself, with laboriously maintained patience, through the twelve thick volumes and tidy gravel paths of *Sir Charles Grandison*.[142]

Those utterly virtuous heroines, those idealized women, so-called misunderstood souls, which were being introduced into our

novels from French models at the time I began writing, were just
as false and no less boring than Grandison. After I had naively
admired them for a while, I soon felt a real revulsion toward them.
There was something surprising, something powerful in the auda-
cious and fiery passion expressed by George Sand, the premier
living French writer, in her women characters. Their great hearts
were not appreciated by men; they could never achieve peace or
happiness because no man existed who was capable of honoring
and deserving such a heart. Of course, I myself went around in
those days believing that I and my heart would never be understood or honored, because the man I loved did not happen to love
me in return as I wanted. As long as I was still confused and
absorbed enough in my passion to blame my state on him rather
than my own self-deception, I raved just like all the others about
the poor misunderstood souls and found great satisfaction in
counting myself among them, to raise myself to heaven with them,
and to condemn the men who misunderstood us.

It was infinitely more poetic to place oneself in the category of
suffering nobility, to join the community of silent saints, than to be
a girl who has unfortunately remained unmarried! My enthusiasm
for these women characters, for these great feminine hearts in
George Sand's novels, for the women who loved undaunted again
and again in *Lélia* and *Leo Leoni*, even when they were trampled
on, was so immense that I ignored the true meaning or did not
really appreciate what George Sand can do when she finds herself
on a foundation of truth and reality. Only much later, when I fully
understood her errors, did I honor her great significance in the
proper spirit. Yet so often, people who must not know her works
and mine very well, have compared us and have liked to call me
her imitator, although I have never been this and could not be so;
the backgrounds we came from were too different and our talents
and religious and social attitudes too diverse. As much as I
acknowledge her mastery, I have the right to call my knowledge
and my mistakes, my successes and my failures my own.[143]

My blind veneration of George Sand lasted for some time.
The foreign writer has an advantage, because he can not as readily be imitated or controlled, so that he is more easily believed.

That which I found acceptable in George Sand for a long time, I could not believe in the works of the Countess Hahn-Hahn when they first appeared among us. I was a few years older, had become calmer and more mature, had recognized my mistakes and how to cope with myself. Even if the noble hearts in Hahn-Hahn novels still impressed me, it was basically not only by the ideal perfection of these countesses, but also partially by certain external charms.

[Lewald delineates the differences between the works of George Sand and Ida von Hahn-Hahn. Her aversion to the works of the latter—and possibly the fact that Hahn-Hahn was the woman who had won the love of Heinrich Simon—finally led her to write, as her next novel in 1847, a scathing and very funny parody of Hahn-Hahn's works in Diogena *under the pseudonym of "Iduna von H."]*

17

My work proceeded apace in the quiet atmosphere at home. However, I could not conceal the fact from myself that the intellectual freedom permitted by my father was of little use to me. The longer I remained at home, the more clearly I realized that, in my writing, I was always thinking about whether my father would be satisfied with it—if it would please him and not be counter to his opinions.

Although I feared no man when it came to presenting my convictions through the press, I always felt like a child around my father, because his displeasure or approval were what I most feared and longed for. On the one hand, this constant concern about my father was sometimes an advantage, making me write more deliberately and carefully. If you want to create freely, though, you must stick to the matter at hand and not worry about the judgment that will follow. The longer I remained at home, the more I lost the ease, freshness, and confidence which I had felt away from home. I often felt spiritually hemmed in by the bounds of home, although I would have been unable to say why. I was also the only woman writer in my whole home town, and therefore had no one around who was doing anything like or similar to my work. I grew weary of my efforts to stay cheerful and to keep up my spirits, and I became melancholy and elegiac, which did not really suit me.

This was particularly the case on Christmas Eve. We were usually not together so much any more. We looked at each other shyly, as if to ask whether this was still our room, our house, if we were still ourselves, standing here across from one another. While the lights burned brightly as usual, I thought back to the times when, although the gifts had been simple and restricted to the necessities, there had been scarcely place for all of us in the large living room. I remember how we had once celebrated Christmas Eve with Leopold, how much laughter and joking and high spirits there had been on that evening and how happy my parents had been about our pleasure. Now everything had changed.

Father was alone with us; it was no longer difficult to provide gifts for us—but there were no children, only grown-up daughters in the house, and no one rejoiced any more. The time of immeasurable childhood joy was past. We had all suffered, learned to know separation and the mortality of human beings. Our thoughts did not dwell exclusively on the Christmas tree. They ranged far away, in the past, in the future; home was no longer our whole world, the moment did not exert its power over us as it had in the past; it no longer captured us.

[Lewald decides home no longer holds any real attraction for her. Her father encourages her to travel. At first both of them decide on a journey to France, but upon the advice of Heinrich Simon she chooses Italy, first stopping in Berlin to make preparations. She never sees her father again; he dies suddenly while she is abroad.]

18

In Berlin, I first had to find an apartment. That was not particularly difficult, because my means were very limited. I had to save my money for the trip and knew I must watch my expenditures. If I could just have an apartment to myself and was certain I did not have to live with my aunt any more, where I had to cope with occasional half-educated English and American boarders, whom I frequently found unbearable, the rest did not matter that much. At any rate, I was determined to do without all sorts of things if I did not have to show consideration for people whose hollow insolence constantly hurt me without my being able to reject them as they deserved.

While I was looking for an apartment, I found a notice for one in the paper. Two rooms, one with one window, the other with two, a small bedroom, one flight up on the Markgrafenstrasse near the Gendarme Market—that really sounded too grand for me! But I still went to see it and found there what I wanted: the house (long since demolished) was run-down, the stairs narrow and dark, the rooms unattractive, and the deteriorated walls bare. It was impossible to ask a high rent for such quarters. The landlord and I soon agreed on a price. I tried to cope with these rooms as best I could. I was already used to bad accommodations and to doing without many comforts; a woman can make almost any place habitable.

I moved the worst furniture into the one-window room and turned it into an entry hall, put the two worm-riddled wardrobes into the dark corner that had been advertised as a small bedroom—to sleep there would have been a subtle form of suicide—and lived mainly in the middle room, in which I placed a sleeping sofa, a desk, and some other pieces that I had gradually acquired on earlier stays in Berlin. I finally achieved something close to a very modest sitting room. A young sculptor I knew gave me a haut-relief copy of Schlüter's head of the Great Elector[144] and fastened this small work to the wall himself. It was the first work of art I had ever owned and I have faithfully preserved it as such and as a memento of those days. My sister gave me some flowering pot plants, which I placed in the window. Thus I started my first own household.

Each day at noon, my dinner was brought to my room. The landlady, a modest, uneducated woman, the widow of the mayor of some little border town, had undertaken to feed me. Thinking of the burden that strange table companions, not chosen by myself, had always been to me, I had made up my mind to eat alone; so I sat down for the first time quite alone at my table. Everything was very bad: the linens, the dishes, and the meal. It was different at home, but I decided that things would be quite different also, when I had my own house. I was so firm in this resolve, so determined to reach this goal, that I almost enjoyed encountering so many discomforts on the way; I paid no attention, therefore, to the means and the sacrifices that were to bring me to this end.

However, in the evenings, when my brother who had been there left, when I closed the door behind him and had to go to bed in the three empty, lonely rooms, I became afraid, because the apartment was not directly connected to that of the landlady and I suddenly felt very alone. I tried the door once more, because I thought of thieves. Paradoxically, when I found it securely locked, I worried about how cut off I was from all help if something should happen to me! My depression increased after I turned off my lamp and only the reddish glow of my nightlight brightened the walls. The stained pale blue wall was such a ghastly color that my sofa, covered with green and white cotton, and my green blinds looked terrible against it. There stood the chest of drawers, there in the bedroom, the wardrobe. They were all in the world I owned with the exception of my books and the few bits of furniture in my little room in Königsberg. It was not very much.

I started to calculate my ready cash and the money owed me by my publisher; it did not take long. A year ago, I had felt like Croesus with my few hundred thalers. Now I seemed quite poor with a large sum; I was certainly far from rich. To be sure, many other women my age did not have more, but they did not have to support themselves as I did. A despondency I had never known before overcame me. Everything I was doing and working on seemed completely worthless and ill-considered; my plans for the future looked like whims. I could not imagine how I had come upon the idea of wanting to become independent and even less, how my wise, provident and loving father could have believed that I would be able to support myself at all.

There was the fact that I had written three novels just as they had come to my mind. They had gained me friends and earned me money. But did that prove anything for the future? The axiom "What has happened can happen again" only presupposed a possibility, a hope, but nothing more than the expectancy of a certain something. The more I thought about it, the more anxious I became. Finally I seemed like a sleepwalker to myself, arriving at a height by instinct, an instinct upon which he cannot rely when awakening and a place from which he dare not climb down, even if he wished to. I was seized by a strong feeling of vertigo, as if I were actually standing on a cliff. I could not endure the fear. I finally lit the bedside lamp again, and the worst specters of my fears fled with the brightness around me. But my heart remained heavy, because I kept brooding over matters that bothered me at other times, too, and that I had tried to keep far away, but which could no longer be avoided.

I have never known any other escape from the depression that I felt that night, and that has sometimes come over me in the different turns and changes of my life, than to withdraw into myself and treat myself objectively. There is also no consolation nor relief whatsoever in blaming what we endure on external conditions. We usually only realize we have acted foolishly, and that is neither encouraging nor liberating. So I told myself that night very firmly and with determination: "This is the way you wanted it! You have what you wanted." And with all my uneasiness and worrying I suddenly felt a certain defiant pleasure in the realization that I had gotten my way. That was something positive that I could cling to; because I had succeeded in this, I could succeed in other matters! My hopes rose with the dawn. The bright morning sun shining into my room returned to me my cheerful confidence along with my lost courage.

Now I had some happy months, which I still like to remember. From day to day that carefree life began which only the young know and which only seem happy when one is young. As if Fate wanted to strengthen me in my good humor and my self-

confidence, I received a request from the publishing firm of
Brockhaus to write a novella for the periodical *Urania*. My latest
novel was finished and sent off to the printer. An uncritical
beginner is never at a loss for new material for a novella; and the
thought of beginning a new work here in my own apartment, a
work I could leave open on my desk without any curious person
coming by being able to read it, was invigorating for me. Without
undue consideration, I accepted the offer. Now I sat alone
through the livelong bright beautiful mornings and began to
select my ideas and thoughts and to sort, construct, and arrange
them, and I became more and more contented. A room in which
you have heard a loving word, in which you have thought good
and useful thoughts, is not a strange place any more, but becomes
home. After I had begun to work in my new apartment, it
became as familiar to me as a good, old comfortable piece of
clothing, which has nothing that irritates or presses on us, with
which we are as at one as with our own house.

Gradually all my friends, men as well as women, came to see
how I had settled down and how I was doing. The women
praised the cleanliness of my room and were amazed at what I
had done with the apartment, but I noticed they were all rather
concerned about me. Finally those who knew something about
our house in Königsberg patted me and looked at me with such
compassion that I could have very easily let myself be pitied or
admired, were I inclined to take these effusions seriously. Some
of them found it very strange that Father had already given me
permission to live alone. I told them I would soon be thirty-four.
They maintained I looked much younger. "Does that affect my
sound reasoning ability? Does that make me irresponsible?" I
asked. I believe I became an object of admiration for some.

"If you only had a maid!" another lady sighed, although she
knew quite well that I did not have the hundred thalers to spare,
which maid service for a year would have cost me. "What would
I do with a maid?" I asked. "Is she supposed to wait on me? I can
do without that, and I don't need a maid to protect or watch over
me." "It would be more decent," she replied in a well-meaning
way.

What kind of decency, what kind of virtue was it, the appearance of which could be maintained by the presence of a poor maidservant, by one of those young creatures of whose morals the ladies who were speaking generally felt justified in thinking the worst!

"Are you going to receive men, also?" someone asked carefully.

"Yes, why not?" I responded.

"I guess you can. You are a writer, after all," an unmarried lady mused, who still let herself be watched over, although the endangered and dangerous days of her youth lay far behind her.

When this company finally left me, I patted myself on the back and said triumphantly: "Thank God, I'm not like that woman!" And I was struck by a horror of the hypocrisy of social mores, the bases of which are an immorality and an immoderation that can scarcely be imagined. I sometimes found them obnoxious, these mothers and these daughters with their fixed friendly expressions, their tightly buttoned gloves and their spellbound eyes that were not permitted to stray left or right, if the mothers had not previously looked at the place where the daughters could turn their eyes. They were ridiculous and pitiable to me in their lack of freedom and their puppetlike restrictions. I thought with admiration of my milliner, who is now my good friend, who already lived at that time completely alone in a small attic room on a remote street, advised by no one, protected by no one but herself and her own sense of honor. But it would have not occurred to anyone to reproach that stout young worker because she had no attendant, or to consider it praiseworthy that she knew how to protect herself so well.

It has surely happened to everyone at some time or other, that after regarding an object from the same point of view for a long time, he suddenly becomes convinced that he had not stood in the right place and that he has not seen correctly. You are always very surprised at yourself when this occurs. You cannot understand how you mistook what is a wretched tree trunk for a figure, how what you considered a mountain range suddenly dissolved into clouds before your eyes. That happens to people on an intellectual level, too; that is what happened to me quite early on with the so-called good morals and decency of the equally so-called good society.

When a mother tells me, "I don't let my daughter go alone to a ball at a girl friend's house," I involuntarily add in my mind, "She is going to find bad society there from which my presence is necessary to protect her." If I hear, "I don't let my daughter go out on the street unattended," I add, "because I don't trust her to find her way, and she is so naive and frivolous that I have to have her supervised wherever she goes." "My daughters receive no visitors in my absence" really means "The men who visit my house are so coarse and immoral that I must expect them to disregard even the most elementary courtesies!" I would always ask (silently) how men could have the slightest desire to have anything to do with those young women whose worth their own mothers judged so deprecatingly; or why men would want to visit a home in which they were trusted less than the male servant who was supposed to become the protector of the daughters. According to the opinion of high society, we have progressed greatly in morality; but actually, with all its Christianity and culture of which it is so proud, society has not gone far beyond the culture of the Oriental harem. There is no morality without personal freedom, as indeed there is no virtue whatsoever without the freedom to choose to live virtuously. Our mores give the man a virgin for his wife; to give him a truly virtuous, moral wife, our social circumstances would have to be different, girls would have to be raised with greater freedom to be more self-reliant, and our culture would have to be more than just a hedge of preventive measures behind which we fence ourselves off from a coarseness and immorality luckily are exceptions in our society. To wall up all windows because a careless child has fallen from one now and then or a mentally ill person has thrown himself from one would certainly be a very foolish measure.

19

The spring that brought me the pleasure of my own household also brought me a friendship that was to be a constant joy to me until the death of my friend. Her memory will be dear to me as long as I live.

One day I received an invitation to the home of Professor Theodor Mundt. I looked forward to the evening because I always had a good time at his house. Theodor and Clara Mundt[145] had been married and living in Berlin for a number of years when I first met them. The expression of complete serenity common to both of them would have had something attractive about it even if their names had not been so well-known as to create interest.

(I have not dealt with the works or literary significance of my friends in these pages, only with our mutual relationships and the impression their personality made on me or the consequences for me of meeting them. It seems to me that memoirs have to restrict themselves to that or they will stray into the realm of criticism and literary history. That would change their purpose, and I have tried to avoid this. With this presupposition, I continue my story.)

Theodor Mundt was slightly taller than average, sturdy and strong, without actually being too stout. His features were fine, his dark eyes calm. With his full head of brown hair and good posture, you could certainly call him a handsome man. His movements were somewhat deliberate; his speech and his manner of expression by no means fluent. He was very reserved in larger gatherings and it was in one such that I first heard him speak. He seemed to me more suited for a conversation *à deux* than for a general address, as is common in people who have learned early on to confide their thoughts to a silent piece of paper. His earnestess and calm were the first things I noticed about him. As much as one tried to draw him into the discussion and demanded his opinion, he did not let himself be lured into taking an active part in the general conversation of the group, which was composed of the most varied types of people. He listened, and later, sitting beside me at the dinner table, gave his opinion of the topics previously discussed, which he had by then slowly assimilated and tried to form into a unified concept. He seemed to want to understand matters and then be finished with them.

His wife was a complete opposite, full of liveliness and quick openness. I could say that I have never met anyone who possessed greater joie de vivre and vivacity than Luise Mühlbach. She thought quickly and determinedly, expressed what she thought in the same manner, and uttered many fortunate words the candor of which was startling. She received me with the same candid cordiality. She said it was irresponsible that people who knew of one another as we did, did not just get together without much ceremony, and she asked me to spend one of the next evenings with them, an invitation I accepted gratefully.

At that time they lived on the Marienstrasse and always had much company. So it was all the more amazing to me that Luise Mühlbach could find time to accomplish everything she did. She wrote a great deal, was always current on what was appearing in English and French literature, followed German literature even in the journals, played music, learned Russian and another foreign language, and had painted a whole china service, which was displayed. There were actually books around that she herself had bound. You could tell that ceaseless activity was a necessity of life for this woman. As long as I have known her, I have never seen her exhausted or even weary. Her true strength, however, was shown by the love with which she gazed up at her husband. You gained the unmistakable conviction that you were seeing a truly happy couple.

That made the whole social atmosphere at their house as cheerful as it was intellectually stimulating. We played music, performed dramatic scenes, and just generally entertained ourselves. When I was invited to the Mundts in the spring, after I had arranged my apartment, I found a large number of people there again. They were standing grouped around a table in the middle of the room. As soon as I entered, I was struck by the appearance of a woman sitting across from the door. Her head was slightly bowed, because they were all looking at an etching. The light of the lamp fell on her shining and abundant dark brown hair, gleamed on her lovely bare shoulders, and was reflected by the large diamond clasp on the string of pearls she wore around her neck.

When I approached the table, the stranger looked up and I saw one of the most appealing faces I had ever seen. Everything in her features was lovable goodness, enchanting friendliness: even the slight squinting of the eyes, which nearsighted people use to sharpen their vision, and which I immediately noticed as one of her features, became charming in her, because it made her seem delicate and, at the same time, helpless in a certain way.

"Mrs. von Bacheracht!" said Professor Mundt, introducing us formally.

"Oh, call her 'Therese'," cried Mrs. Mundt, and gave Mrs. von Bacheracht her hand. "At our house she is Therese!"

"How grateful to you I am for that!" replied the stranger and the voice with which she uttered these words, the expression with which she pressed our hostess's right hand, were as soft and sweet as her look.

I was introduced to her. She rose to give me her hand, and I could look at her more closely. She was of average height, but bore herself splendidly, and since she had a long and slender torso and a very lovely bosom, there was something imposing about her figure despite her gracefulness. The shape of her head was not exactly beautiful; it was not oval enough. Her face was too flat and her neck too short and thick, but there was a certain regularity in the cut of her forehead, nose, and mouth, and in the definition of her eyebrows and the curvature of her eyelids, that was quite unusual and pleasing to the eye. You had only to keep looking at these regular shapes continually, to rest your eyes on them involuntarily, to continue enjoying them from then on. It was not a classical head, but an unusually fascinating, attractive face. What gave it its greatest charm was the velvety soft skin, with its warm satisfying color, and the inexpressibly sweet expression of the gentle brown eyes. The eyes and the lovely soft tone of her voice held something irresistible—and not only for me.

Therese von Bacheracht was then almost forty, but she looked considerably younger, and must have seemed like a beauty at first to anyone meeting her unexpectedly. She was very aware of this advantage and had enough imagination and good taste to enhance it by her carefully selected and lavish manner of

Therese von Bacheracht.
Fanny Lewald's *Meine Lebensgeschichte* ed. by Ulrike Helmer.
Frankfurt/Main: Ulrike Helmer Verlag.

dress. A heavy violet moirè dress emphasized the shape and gleam of her neck and shoulders; large cockades of pale pink ribbon made her hair look even darker without diminishing the freshness of her complexion. I was very sensitive to beauty and could not get tired of the pleasure of looking at her loveliness.

It had been a few years since she published her first book, *Letters from the South*,[146] and these travel memoirs—because you could hardly call those notes a travelogue—had been very well received. The strangely pedantic introduction, with which an older friend introduces the pages from the journal of the anonymous author, had served as a peculiar background for the warm overflowing sensibility that characterized the whole work. Just as Therese gained the affection of people because of her grace and goodness, so the very individual nature, the strangely devised spiritual direction of the journal won over many hearts. The secretiveness with which the author surrounded herself contributed to raising interest in her and her work.

The book was supposed to be by a noblewoman who knew elegant society and had seen, experienced, and felt all kinds of things, and who, as one was wont to say, thought with her heart. Raised in the views of the class into which she had been born, she had nevertheless educated herself as an individual, as her environment apparently did not give her the right atmosphere for her spiritual development. This withdrawal into herself had taken from her an understanding and feeling for the commonplace in many respects. She was only rarely capable of an objective observation; she saw everything from her point of view and judged everything solely in accordance with the standard of her own feelings. But these feelings were acute; even if you did not always agree with the views of the traveler, you still liked her and wanted to become acquainted with her, to learn more about her than she had expressed in the letters. So much was revealed in the journal: Therese was married, had borne and lost a child, was surfeited and yearning, high-spirited and without faith in life, religious without having any real belief or support in religion. She betrayed a certain vanity and coquetry, which went strangely with a great rectitude and an almost childlike naiveté. Everywhere that you might have thought the events and impressions of the trip might have caused her to think, instead her feelings came to the fore; and the expression of these drew the reader involuntarily into the reveries to which the lady loved to surrender herself.

It was a gentle charming book, these *Letters from the South*, and you only had to look at Therese to recognize how completely she had given herself over to her own nature in these letters without at all considering the impression on the reader. She had written two novels after this book, which had found a favorable audience, especially among women. I felt very pleased in every way to meet her.

She sat down by me. We chatted about this and that, but were not able to converse seriously, as the party was very large and lively. There was all sorts of teasing among the guests, who were old friends. We joked about our various works in the best of humor. Theodor Mügge[147] bore the brunt of the teasing because of one of his novellas, which he, as the others reproached him, was supposed to have given a totally unexpected and almost impossible conclusion out of sheer good nature. He accepted this criticism as cheerfully and innocently as it was given, but he did defend himself against the accusation by insisting, quite rightly, that, where it was possible, the writer must think of relieving the reader's heart at the end. The art of literature existed to brighten and beautify life, so it would have to maintain the beautiful and the friendly. If it left the reader with a heavy heart, with a dissonance, a feeling of dissatisfaction, or even with strong regrets and an accusation against fate, without the direst necessity, the writer had made a mistake.

[Lewald ends the chapter with a sad comment that half of that happy group around the tea table—Therese von Bacheracht, Theodor Mundt, and Theodor Mügge—is now dead.]

20

The night had been beautiful when we left the Mundts' house. The next morning, it was pouring. I sat at my desk, but I was unable to work, because I was worrying about a faux pas I had committed the previous evening that I did not know how to remedy. Therese had been very gracious, very friendly to me. She had asked me if I knew Hamburg; when I said no, she had encouraged me to visit it and her soon—she would put herself completely at my disposal. I let her tell me that and thanked her, without once asking her to visit me here in Berlin. I was ashamed of this carelessness, which must have seemed very discourteous. I regretted it even more on my own account: I had really liked

Therese, I wanted very much to see her again, and I did not even know in what hotel she was staying.

While, completely dissatisfied with myself, I was still debating whether to write Clara Mundt or someone else to obtain Therese's address, there was a knock at my door. I went to open it, and there stood Therese, soaked to the skin.

"You didn't invite me to visit you," she said in her sweet voice, "but I am sure that you don't exactly mind my coming, and I wanted to speak with you again before I left."

I told her I had just been thinking of her, and, interrupting me, she said, "I am very superstitious and you'll probably laugh at me. I immediately felt a strong attraction to you yesterday, dreamed about you all night, and you were doing nice things for me in my dream. I am particularly happy that you were thinking of me, too, just as I was on my way to you, and thinking of me with a bad conscience at that."

"Why is that?" I asked.

"Haven't you discovered that we always love those toward whom we have acted unjustly, a little for it?"

She looked quite enchanting while saying that; but I could not give in to my pleasure at her charm, because I noticed that she had suffered even more from the rain than I had thought at first. Her shawl, her hat, her shoes, and her dress were all completely soaked through. I pointed this out to her, but she considered it unimportant.

"I have an iron constitution," she said, "and have become accustomed to all those things like rain and cold and heat, and if you want, hunger and thirst, on my many trips. But one question: do you have time? Can I stay with you?"

I assured her that I could think of nothing better, and she now laid aside her wet shawl, let me fetch her another pair of shoes and commented, "I arranged with Bacheracht to wait outside for me for five or ten minutes. If I did not return by then, I would remain here. By now he will have left and I am staying."

The morning passed as in a dream. We spoke about books, of our work, of the conditions of our life, of our past, as you do at the beginning of such relationships. It happened that we had opposite ideas about almost everything, that our opinions, our experiences, the course of our lives had deviated even more than you might expect from our different positions in life. Nevertheless, we became closer and closer, we still felt a strong attraction for one another. How could that happen? Her life with its broad horizons engaged my imagination; her charm, her unmistakable goodness won my heart. She found the simplicity of my past touching; my seriousness and openness gave her confidence in me.

It was three o'clock before she left. She told me that she planned to make a trip to the Tyrol with Karl Gutzkow at the beginning of the summer and to go on to Interlaken alone later on. She would write me from there if the Sonderbund War[148] in any way hampered traveling or remaining in Switzerland. If she did not write me, nothing had happened, and in this case, I promised her I would arrange my schedule to meet her in Interlaken at the beginning of August.

The next day she left Berlin. I had visited her at her apartment in the Hotel du Nord, but had barely spoken to her. She had been dressed very grandly, adorned with diamonds and flowers, ready to go to a party, and various men, who had come to pay her a visit, took up her time. The scene was dazzling for me. Therese looked so beautiful; the opulence that surrounded her, the homage paid her, the carefreeness I sensed in her, seemed the best of fortunes. I almost envied her because she was able to paint and describe thousands of things from actual life that I had to construct from my imagination or hearsay. She was completely the great lady in her magnificent attire, in the confident posture, in the friendly condescension she showed toward the men. In the middle of her conversation with them, she suddenly turned to me, pressed my hand, and said softly and quickly, "I wish I were sitting with you on your sofa and this party were behind me! I am completely exhausted today."

I was surprised. "What happened to you?" I asked.

"The bottom dropped out from under my feet again and years of work have been destroyed!" She broke off suddenly with a sigh.

She was told that her carriage was waiting and left, giving her maid an order to call Mr. von Bacheracht. I did not stop thinking about her. I wanted to know if she was truly happy, if there was serious pain hiding behind this cheerful, gentle countenance. And because I could hope to see Therese again on the trip, the prospect of it became more and more inviting to me from then on. Therese's visit to Berlin had engaged the whole circle, in which I had met her. Without asking any direct questions, I heard people speaking of her frequently in the next few weeks. I learned the story of her life, at least what you could see and know of it superficially.

Therese had been born a von Struve, the daughter of a Russian diplomat, who had been assigned to the courts of Oldenburg and Mecklenburg, and to the Hanseatic League; the family lived in Hamburg. She had been married at an early age to a legation secretary, von Bacheracht, who was a city councillor and the Russian consul general in Hamburg in 1845. They had been at the court in St. Petersburg for a short time and traveled extensively. Their marriage was not a happy one. If people spoke of Therese then, they seemed to think that she was not at all suited for the calmness of a peaceful marriage. They spoke of unhappy love affairs that she was supposed to have had and especially of a long-standing passionate relationship with a German writer that had apparently made her completely unhappy.

People who knew her fairly well spoke of her with great sympathy. Mrs. Paalzow belonged to those who discussed her most affectionately. "Always think the best of her," she told me one evening, when we were speaking of Therese and I was describing the pleasant impression she had made on me, "and you will only be doing her justice. Therese's inestimable good qualities are all her own; her faults are partly due to her circumstances. If you can say of someone that she only has the faults that come from her virtues, that is certainly the case with Therese." This opinion made me very happy, and I realized how fond I had already become of Therese. I loved Mrs. Paalzow for the warmth with which she had spoken of Therese. (I have seldom seen her show such affection for anyone else.)

At the time I had no news of my new friend and I did not really miss her, because I was very busy. I had to prepare for my Italian trip, had begun to learn Italian, was working hard on my novella for *Urania*, was wasting much of my time looking for a suitable travel companion, and was also going to many parties. My old friends were happy about my progress, and I was making many new acquaintances. I was independent and self-reliant enough not to require anybody's help to make my way around, but not so old or set in my ways that I could not accept the protection of older or important people willingly.

[Lewald does eventually tire of this protection and the unwanted advice accompanying it. She states that society should accept the woman who is making her own living as it does a man in the same situation and give her the same respect and responsibility for her own actions.]

I am not a person who finds it necessary to depend on others; yet I have still felt the misfortune our training to be dependent places on us. As long as I can remember, I have always been fairly certain of what I wanted and not lost sight of the goal toward which I was striving. I had wanted to be independent; now I was. I saw, however, that a large number of my acquaintances wondered about that and some of them disapproved of the decision I had made. Instead of leaving them to their opinions and going my own way, which no one could prevent me from doing, I felt compelled to convince each and every one of them of the correctness and the necessity of my course. If possible, I wanted to win the agreement and approval for every single action of mine from people who were of no importance to me and with whom I had very little connection, except for what I occasionally had been told they had thought or said of me. I was like a sailor who is sanguine in the middle of the actual dangers of a storm and is afraid of sea monsters when the sea is calm. If you are inclined to see monsters, however, and are forever looking for them, you will peer into the darkness until your imagination provides your own fantastic images. In this state you can be frightened by anyone who can look confidently into that emptiness. Few people are able to resist the temptation to frighten a fearful person or to alarm a timid one. It was perceived immediately that I was weak enough to be quiet when given good advice, and I was soon bombarded with such advice and well-meant admonitions from all parts.

I had not done the least thing that might have occasioned this outpouring or given people cause for criticism. I associated exclusively with members of my family circle. The few young men who visited me occasionally were men of honor whom my family had known for years; or else some stranger, some writer, who came only once. Their relationship was no different to me than that of young men to a girl in her own family home. None of them had a real love or passion for me, none of them were seriously courting me; I never even had a close male friend around. But that did not matter.

I frequently could not escape all the well-intended warnings and good advice. If I had received as much help and encouragement as admonition, I would have much to be envied for and my life would have been considerably easier. Fortunately the excessive advice did not confuse me. It did not divert me from what I knew was necessary and proper for me. It did, however, put me in a bad mood, and far worse, it made me angry and provoked me into a stubborn defiance that caused me to make inconsiderate remarks. These went far beyond what I intended, and I usually regretted them when I reconsidered them later, realizing how little those people who had evoked my vehemence had been worth such an expenditure of my strength. Such an outburst primarily hurt me.

I fought windmills with such heavy weapons that I risked dislocating my arm; and only because I had been raised to be submissive and could not be content with my own good conscience. I constantly listened to the judgment of others, because I lacked that self-confidence which let men far less significant than I pursue their goals unhurriedly and peacefully and choose the means to do this without second thoughts.

Much has changed since the time of which I am speaking; the position of women has become more liberated in many ways in the last decades. There is hardly a reasonable person today who would be shocked if a sensible thirty-four-year-old unmarried woman with a good reputation had her own household, went around in public alone, or undertook a long journey by herself. Things were different in those days. I have helped break a path for many a young woman who proceeds unopposed on her way now, though I underwent experiences that were not always pleasant for me and had to make many exhausting strokes with my ax.

Fortunately, I had a very firm trust in the moral element in mankind, a trust in myself, and, along with it, the unalterable belief that a woman like me should be able to assert and advance herself in her own way among good and moral people. I was convinced that it would be possible to tread the straight path without being a hypocrite, to gain recognition for myself, and to win a share of freedom for others also, with the freedom and recognition I gained for myself. That is the truly beautiful and encouraging aspect of freedom; no one struggles for it just for himself. Its faintest beam shines like the sun for everyone in its area, wherever it breaks through the darkness.

I learned one particular lesson from that period of time, one that has probably stood me in good stead in my dealings with others; this lesson: it is an arrogant presumption to give unsought advice, if you are not ready to provide, with all the means at your disposal, the assistance necessary to follow that advice. People who give advice and who are not honest and steadfast helpers at the same time should be avoided, because they usually are or will become enemies, whether we take their advice or not, and whether our compliance or resistance brings us success or failure.

21

[Lewald meets Berthold Auerbach,[149] of whom she has long been an admirer and they become good friends. From him, she gains a deeper understanding and appreciation of nature. She discusses Spinoza with him and his friend, Doctor Julius Waldeck, and finds a key to her own ideas about religion.]

I asked Doctor Waldeck once what he considered the basic premise of Spinozism and how this could be formulated most concisely.

Fanny Lewald (1846) as she looked at the end of the autobiography. Painting by Elisabeth Baumann-Jericho. In Fanny Lewald's *Römisches Tagebuch,* 1845–46, ed. by Heinrich Spiero. Leipzig: Klinkhard & Burmann Verlag, 1927.

"Everything that exists, is God," he answered casually; now, all at once, I had what I needed. Now I had the basis for the rest of my life, the regulator for my thinking, loving, and actions, and simultaneously, the reminder of that subordination of the individual will to the universal, which no one can achieve as long as he considers human beings and their welfare the only purpose of the Creation. To be sure, it is placing a heavy demand on arrogance and selfishness to consider yourself only as a cog in the wheel rather than the lord and ruler you previously thought yourself, but you gain tenfold in increasing love for what you sacrifice in the way of consciousness of your own power and importance. Monarchs and aristocrats will probably never find their reckoning in Spinozism, and it could never become a state religion in anything but the most humane of republics. It is a wonderful means for the education and happiness of the individual and for his peace and resignation. Like all great and incontrovertible truths, Spinozism penetrates the consciousness of a person and the activities of life in the unlikeliest manner and by the most remote ways, even against the will of those who generally find it advantageous not to recognize this truth. Spinozism pushes the old ideas it replaces farther and farther back; it wins control over minds without their being able to say this was sought or how it was achieved.

Since this epiphany I have become calm and resigned to the grim necessity of our own personal extinction in the moment of death. As painful as it is for us to depart from our laughing lives, from the sunny world, from the hearts that belong to us, in which we live a second life, as puzzling and as incomprehensible as this extinction seems to us—while we still exist and act, there is a strongly moving power in the consciousness of our own mortality. Hesitation, procrastination, vain promises, all become impossible with the realization that what I do not do here, I shall never do; what I do not enjoy here, and grace through love, do not recompense or atone for, remains forever lost for me and for others. The certainty that I am participating in the perfection of the universal with every honest striving for all time and eternity is much more satisfying for me than to be rewarded for it in a mysterious hereafter. And is there not a gentle enchantment in the concept of a further existence in the metabolism of the All?

22

[Lewald tells of a meeting with Countess Elise von Ahlefeld, widow of General von Lützow, legendary folk-song hero, and long-time close friend of Karl Immermann.[150]]

23

In the middle of June the time I had set for my departure approached. After a long selection process, after many consultations with my father, I had chosen a traveling companion who would be compatible with my plans and intentions. She was a Berliner, fifty years old, unmarried, the daughter of a prosperous artisan, who had received a fairly good education, and seemed to have a very good personality. She was as cheerful and full of life as a young girl, undemanding and steadfast as a young man. She had already been abroad and made several longer and shorter trips. I could hope not to be abandoned by her, if I should have some sort of accident on the journey; conversely, she could promise herself some small amenities and advantages traveling with me that would have been otherwise unavailable to her. My father was satisfied because he knew I had an older woman as a companion and was therefore not completely on my own. We got along very well together in the eight months that this lady was with me—until an amusing intermezzo separated us.

I felt quite strange when I saw my passport from the Ministry of the Interior with its visas for the different countries—Italy still consisted of so many countries then!—lying on the table before me. I looked over the letters of introduction with which my friends had equipped me, the money for the journey, and the letters of credit that I planned to take with me. I had a great sense of satisfaction about them, but I could not say that I was actually happy.

I had achieved what I could with my own ability; I had reached that goal. While many of my woman acquaintances considered me fortunate because of my successes and independence, I knew with certainty that everything that I could gain by way of outer or inner striving could be no substitute in the long run for that love which joins two human beings together exclusively and which I now cherished no more hope of finding.

I did still have my precious father, whom I loved as one can only love a father; I had my siblings, to whom I was very attached, and friends who were dear to me. I had the affection and trust of all these people. Yet these gifts which I treasured at their true value, and the independence and recognition I now enjoyed, were nothing but a consolation to me, a refreshment and a strengthening that sustained me in my resignation. Despite all the freedom for which some envied me (and which would only have been torment for the majority of women, who claimed to long for it—the sensible usage of such a great freedom demands a firm purpose), I was reminded of a frequently cited expression of Goethe's, which hovered before me like the fiery pillar in front of the Jews wandering in the wilderness: "And if the future ever becomes the present, everything will be as it was before, and the heart will still long for the comfort it is seeking."

In a half-happy, half-elegiac mood, I buckled my suitcase on the eve of my journey; I was also somewhat depressed the next morning. I felt like an invalid who has made several futile attempts to regain his health and finally prepares for a trip to a spa, a cure, which he has been promised will heal him. I told myself that I was traveling to see the world and to educate myself, and my conscience added silently: "You are going to try to see once and for all if you can learn to be enough satisfaction for yourself." As I dressed, as my aunt offered me friendly help and my brother and sisters stayed lovingly close, it suddenly seemed completely foolish, yes, almost incomprehensible, that I should want to travel out into the wide world, which held nothing I really wanted. This world seemed so large to me, so empty, so strange! I had a moment in which I was completely terrified of my trip and of foreign lands.

I had asked myself numerous times if it were possible for me, now that I had overcome my love for Heinrich, now that I was thirty-four years old and my heart was free, to make a so-called marriage of convenience. Would it be possible for me to feel at ease in a relationship based on mutual respect and to give myself to a man, without the greatest passion making this surrender a pleasure and a necessity? And I had always finally answered this question from the depth of my convictions with a firm "No!"

But on that morning, if a man I really respected had given me his hand and asked me to be his wife, I would have taken up his offer. I found this lonely departure so painful, and I held it to be so impossible that I could still find true love, that this moment was almost overpowering. Now for the first time, I understood Eugenie's actions in *The Natural Daughter*.

My family accompanied me to the train station; we parted tearfully. But although the moment had a depressing effect, it was also stimulating, and the beautiful bright summer morning and the happy face of my traveling companion finally drove away the melancholy, which, unbeknownst to my loved ones, had burdened me for days. It would have been impossible for me to show anyone how afraid I felt confronted with my own decision, my long-desired goal. And it is surely good if you become accustomed to keeping such emotions, justifiable though they may be, to yourself and dealing with them alone. No matter how honest we are with ourselves, there are still hours in which we delude ourselves with some sort of rationalization, hours in which it seems some other person has taken us over, on whom we can blame our problems, despondence, or cowardice. And as in thousands of relationships, where a handful of might is worth a sackful of right, a small helpful self-deception is often a far greater blessing for honest and truthful natures than the loftiest but disheartening admission caused by the pure love of truth.

After I was a few hours distant from Berlin, I had already rationalized my situation very nicely. I tried to forget about what bothered me; I philosophized away what I lacked. Just as one erects a beautiful facade in front of a house that is crumbling, I set up all my happy expectations in a row in front of me and soon found considerable comfort and great satisfaction in the picture I had created.

[In Baden-Baden, Lewald finally meets her cousin August Lewald, who actually started her on her literary career. She stays with him for several days. With him she discusses his predilections for Romanticism and Catholicism.]

Since I wanted to go to Italy, it was natural that our conversation frequently turned to Catholicism. Lewald admitted to me that he did not agree with my religious, or, as he unjustly called it, my "irreligious" attitude. He thought that the spiritual life of human beings, and particularly of women, could not exist without a vision of something infinite, mighty, and omniscient, if it were not to be an unhappy or impoverished life. He consoled himself with the fact that the sight of works of art created in Italy during the Middle Ages, at the height of faith, would reveal to me what was now distant and incomprehensible.

I promised my cousin that I would heed his advice and let the paintings and art, and the poetry of Catholicism work on me without resistance in Italy. I did in fact do that; and I have gained great happiness and benefit from my progressively loving involvement with art. But a seed does not produce the same fruit in every soil. Italy did not make me Romantic or Catholic, even though I learned to understand Romanticism and to recognize that for certain types of people Catholicism is the proper element. And since human nature does not change, basically—since there will always be people who cannot be at peace with themselves and with the predetermined conditions of existence, either because of lack of self-control, excessive demands, fantastic longings, or unrestrained sensitivity—it would be difficult for the world to do without a religion responding to such organisms. Whatever outer form the new Italy will have to give the Papacy, Catholicism or a similar cult religion will long remain a necessity for a great number of people. It sometimes seems to me that the world will one day be divided between believers and free thinkers, between Catholics and philosophers. Ultimately, since each religion imprints its adherents with its political beliefs, the political future of the world will eventually only be able to move between the two forms corresponding to the two "religions." Those who think for themselves must restrain and rule themselves. If you let others designate your path to inner satisfaction, they will set the conditions of your life and impose a master—and where possible, an absolute master—upon you. Intermediate positions can still be maintained for centuries, but reason has a consistent necessity that is irresistible in the long run. Just as freedom in religious matters inescapably creates freedom in all areas, the belief in authority with its self-deception also has its own inner necessity. So I cannot help thinking that the world will someday be divided between free thinking Republicans and Catholic despots.

24

[This chapter is devoted to a description of Lewald's reunion with Therese von Bacheracht in Interlaken and their long-lasting friendship until the death of the latter.]

25

[On a two-week stay in Vevay, Lewald reads Rosseau's Nouvelle Heloise *and* Contrat Social *for the first time and is much impressed. She begins work on an epistolary novel of her own,* A Prisoner's Love Letters, *the subject of which was the Polish uprising of 1846 and its consequences. She stays in Switzerland until the weather is cooler and then resumes her journey.]*

With each day I became more cheerful. I could hardly remember the dejection which I had felt while leaving Berlin; even the calm attitude that had followed began to diminish with my happiness. I counted the days remaining before my departure. I wandered a little farther along the Simplon road every evening and looked over at the snow-covered mountain peaks and tried to find the pass through them on which we would travel.

Finally the day came when we left the steamer in Ville Neuve to catch the post-coach that would take us over the Simplon Pass into Italy. My heart was pounding with joy. It was no longer the nervous happiness I had felt a year earlier when I had made my first self-financed trip alone through Bohemia nor the inner jubilation over the freedom I had gained, a jubilation that still concealed the painful memory of slavery. The rush, the excitement of the upstart, had left me; I no longer had to call upon that energy which is needed for every purposeful assertion of a definite position. I had become master of my freedom, my situation, myself; only now was I able to use and enjoy them properly.

It took two whole days to go over the Simplon, but this passage is the loveliest I know. It alone would be worth the trip, even if you had to turn around at the end and not see Italy. On the evening of the second day we arrived at the foot of the Simplon, in Domo D'Ossola. We were to spend the night there, but I could not resist the desire to set foot on Italian soil right then. A light one-horse open carriage was soon found. Our suitcases were loaded in it. We climbed in, and in the sinking rays of the sun, we drove into the valley.

Mulberry trees, fields of corn, vineyards, and fields of blooming hemp surrounded us on all sides. The air was full of an aroma strange to me. When the coachman made a momentary halt and we climbed out, I picked a handful of plants—thyme, bindweed—and clover, which grew along the roadside. They smelled different here, stronger, sweeter, than at home, and the unaccustomed full aroma touched my heart. Women passed by carrying grape vines and corn leaves in large baskets or bundles on their heads to feed their animals at home; a Capuchin monk rode through the countryside on a donkey; on a garden wall sat a parish priest surrounded by several women and children. When darkness came, the Ave Maria bells rang from various points through the valley.

I was in Italy!

Clouds gathered with the sunset, the air became humid, the way longer than we had expected. The coachman seemed to us to drive more slowly, and it became totally dark while we were still on the road. Threatening clouds hung over our heads, and lightning flashed here and there. We caught brief glimpses of Lake Maggiore, which quickly disappeared from sight into the darkness again.

It was late when we finally arrived in Baveno. We climbed the stone steps of the house. I was taken to my room; the floor was of red tile covered with a straw mat. The arrangement of the room was strange to me. Two doors led out to a balcony. The bellboy opened them; it was very dark outside. Only the quiet murmur of the lake could be heard, and that strange wonderful aroma streamed into the room again through the open doors. I stepped out onto the balcony; I could recognize none of the area. In silent contemplation I looked through the night. "What will the year I plan to spend on this soil bring me?" I asked myself involuntarily. Whatever I might have imagined, I could not dream, I could not hope, that it would bring me the happiness of my life.

Large, heavy drops fell one by one from the sky, and the wind increased. A thunderstorm erupted; bolts of lightning split the darkness and thunder rolled across the water. The lake competed with the storm in sound; rain made the lake sizzle at the same time it pounded the earth. The tempest lasted for an hour and more. Then it was quiet; tired, and subtly moved, I lay down to sleep.

In the morning the lake shone for me, Italy with its dazzling, intoxicating splendor shone for me. Involuntarily I thought of the words with which Fouqué begins his *Magic Ring*,[151] which had always held a great mysterious charm for me since childhood:

> From night you go into the sun,
> From horror into rapture pass,
> From death into a life renewed.

These words held something prophetic, something symbolic for me at that hour.

Italy surrounded me; Italy took me into its magic ring, and like those knightly pilgrims who sought the Holy Sepulcher, I was to go from night into the sun, from suffering into rapture and from death to a new life of happiness!

Endnotes

1. Johannes Ebel (1784–1861), a preacher and teacher of religion, history and Hebrew, founded a Pietism-based charismatic sect in Königsberg derisively called the "Muckers" (religious hypocrites or bigots), similarly to the manner in which the members of the Society of Friends were nicknamed "Quakers." In 1835, Ebel and his sect were the principals in a trial that shocked all of East Prussia, in which the Muckers were accused of unspecified sexual practices. Ebel lost his civil-service posts and was actually imprisoned for a while.

This trial and its consequences play an important role in Lewald's novel *Wandlungen* (1853).

2. Ludwig Börne (1778–1837), Jewish critic, journalist and writer, who eventually converted and moved to Paris after 1830. He was a leading figure in the "Young Germany" movement. Because of the number of liberal Germans who settled in Texas after the 1848 Revolution, Boerne, Texas, was named in his honor.

3. On May 27, 1832, a gathering of 25,000 met at Hambach Castle and demanded a republic and German unity. It resolved to adopt armed revolt as well as peaceful means to ensure freedom of the press and the right of assembly. Metternich answered the demands by having the German Confederation adopt six extremely restrictive articles in June, and other measures followed promptly in July.

4. August Lewald (1792–1871), editor (1835–1846) of the periodical *Europa*, was to be the man who started Lewald on her professional writing career.

5. In a unprinted letter to Lewald quoted by Rudolf Göhler in his introduction to Lewald's correspondence with Grand Duke Carl Alexander of Saxe-Weimar-Eisenach, Ebner-Eschenbach wrote, "I have known and admired you since my youth and have faithfully followed your shining path; your example always hovered in the distance before me...," etc. Göhler also cites Paul Heyse's adulatory correspondence with Lewald (XXVI). Kenneth Bruce Beaton documents Lewald's influence on Fontane in his article on *Irrungen, Wirrungen*.

6. Although Lewald was influenced by Goethe, it was frequently his style and general literary philosophy she emulated. She heartily disagreed with his ideas of marriage and divorce in her early-1845 novel *Eine Lebensfrage* (A Vital Question).

7. Orthodox Jewish women are not supposed to show their hair to anyone but their husbands after their marriage. In the last two centuries, this has often involved wearing of a wig or "sheytel" (Yiddish, from the German word *Scheitel,* meaning "crown of the head" or "part in the hair") over very short hair.

8. The famous philosopher Immanuel Kant (1724–1804) spent his whole life in his native Königsberg, where he taught at the university. His daily walk was so regular as to its time and place that housewives were said to be able to set their clocks by his passage. The route became known as the "Philosophenweg," the philosopher's path.

9. Rosa Maria von Varnhagen (1783–1840) was the sister of Karl August Varnhagen von Ense, and therefore the sister-in-law of the famous Rahel Varnhagen, Lewald's idol. This gave Lewald a tenuous family connection to Rahel. Rosa Maria's poems were published after her death by Lewald's uncle. Sometimes Lewald refers to him as David "Assur," his name before he changed it.

10. Heinrich Simon (1805–1860), Lewald's first cousin, played a major role as leader of the liberal faction in the 1848–1849 Frankfurt Parliament and was appointed member of the Imperial Regency. After the dissolution of the Parliament, he fled to Switzerland and was sentenced to life imprisonment in absentia. He died in exile. Simon was also the object of Lewald's unrequited love for eleven years.

11. The problem caused by this law for young Jewish couples is a dominant theme in Lewald's 1849 historical novel *Prinz Louis Ferdinand,* the heroine of which is Rahel Varnhagen.

12. Karl Wilhelm Freiherr von Schrötter (1748–1819), chief justice of the East Prussian Supreme Court and from 1803 on, chancellor of Prussia.

13. See note 4.

14. Prussian Jews had been granted complete civil rights under the reforms of Stein and Hardenberg in 1812 with the pragmatic purpose of using Jewish wealth in the fight against Napoleon. The language of the emancipation edict was vague and the rights were gradually restricted or changed in the wake of Napoleon's defeat. By 1823,

Jews were no longer permitted civil-service posts. The civil rights then had to be regained, step by step, frequently in accord with the wealth of the plaintiff. Jews did not achieve complete civil equality until 1871 in a united Germany.

15. Frederick William II, nephew of Frederick the Great, ruled from 1786–1797.

16. Lewald's remoteness from her Jewish roots is shown here by her reference to "Jewish churches" rather than "synagogues," although she had used the proper word when referring to the activities of her maternal grandparents.

17. The Battle of Eilau was fought on February 7 and 8, 1807, by the combined forces of Prussia and Russia against Napoleon. The battle was bloody but indecisive. The Battle of Friedland, fought by Napoleon against the Russians on June 14 of the same year, resulted in a decisive victory for the French, who then occupied Königsberg and the surrounding area.

18. Ludwig Adolf Peter Count Wittgenstein was a Russian general despite his Germanic name.

19. Hans Davide Ludwig Count Yorck von Wartenburg (1759–1830). On October 3, 1807, Yorck's victory at the Battle of Wartenburg opened a passage for the Silesian and Northern armies to cross the Elbe.

20. Napoleon Francis Joseph, Duke of Reichstadt (1811–1832). Napoleon's son by Marie Louise.

21. Frederick Fröbel (1782–1852), German educator influenced by Rosseau and Pestalozzi, founded the first kindergarten in 1837. He pioneered the concept that children's games and toys should be educational, e.g., using cubes, spheres, and cylinders, and be used to teach as well as amuse.

22. Succoth, a harvest festival, when Jews build and eat in a "succah," or booth made of boughs and decorated with fruits and vegetables.

23. There would never have been only one candle burning. The Chanukah menorah is an eight-branched candlelabra. A ninth extra candle is the "shammas," or sexton, and is used to light the other eight candles—first one, then two, etc., for the eight days of the festival until all nine candles are burning on the last day. Chanukah actually has nothing to do with Christmas. It commemorates the victory of Judah Maccabee and his followers over the Syrians in 165 B.C. and the rededi-

cation of the Temple at Jerusalem. A very minor Jewish holiday, its proximity to Christmas has caused it to become the Jewish response to the Christian holiday, often much to the distress of Orthodox Jews.

24. Miss Japha makes a very common mistake. The capsule, or "mezuzah," does not contain the Ten Commandments but a piece of parchment or paper with passages from Deuteronomy 6:4–9 and 11:13–21. This begins with the Shema, the prayer that is the ultimate declaration of Jewish faith: "Hear, O Israel!: the Lord our God, the Lord is One!"

25. This wearing of the tzitzit, a fringed garment with a blue border, to remind the wearer of the "commandments of the Lord" is directed to Numbers 16:38–40. The modern version no longer has a blue border, and the fringes are now on the prayer shawl or tallilt. The "kittel" is a *sargentes* in Hebrew.

26. Johannes Müller (1801–1858) was one of the most significant medical, biological, anatomical, and physiological researchers of his era and the founder of modern physiology.

27. Juliane von Krüdner (1764–1824) was a mystically oriented Baltic writer. She wrote many travel books, influenced Czar Alexander I, and finally became a famous preacher after her conversion to Pietism.

28. Bilea's Comet appeared in 1815. It is no longer visible, because it broke into two pieces in 1846.

29. Lewald is very advanced here in her theory of the beneficial effect of fairy tales on the psychological development of young children, an idea that forms the nucleus of Bruno Bettelheim's important study *The Uses of Enchantment* (New York: Knopf, 1975).

30. Johann Christoph Friederich von Schiller (1759–1805). He and Goethe are the two most important writers of German classicism.

31. Rudolf Zacharias Becker (1752–1818), an educator who wrote simplified history books for use in schools.

32. These books included a geography book by Cannabich; a history book containing mostly dates and facts by Galetti; a history of Prussia by Heinel; the Bible stories of Kohlrausch; Campe's *Discovery of America*; a reader, which was an anthology of Betty Gleim's writings (travel memoirs, didactic essays, and essays about the German language, as well as translations of English literature), and the comedies of Countess Felicité de Genlis.

33. Eventually Eduard *von* Simson (1810–1899). He was the Königsberg representative to the Frankfurt Parliament in 1848 and was elected vice-president and then president of this body in the same year. Later he became president of the Prussian House of Representatives and from 1879 to 1891, was chief justice of the German Supreme Court. He led the parliamentary delegation to Berlin in 1849, which offered the imperial crown to Frederick William IV. The latter's refusal of this honor delayed German unity until 1871. Simson was obviously an exemplary role model!

34. Karl Witte (1800–1883) matriculated at the University of Leipzig at the age of 10, was awarded his doctorate in philosophy at the age of 14, and another doctorate in law at the age of 16. He was also a renowned Dante scholar.

35. "The Goose-Girl," in which the talking head of the horse Fallada plays an important and prophetic role, seems to be a particular favorite of intelligent and creative girls. Fallada also receives special mention in Eudora Welty's mini-autobiography, *One Writer's Beginnings* (Cambridge, Mass.: Harvard University Press,f 1984).

36. The battle of Kunersdorf (in Brandenburg), August 12, 1759, was a decisive setback for the Prussians in the Seven Years War (fought in America as the French and Indian War).

37. "Jean Paul" was the pseudonym of Johann Paul Friedrich Richter (1763–1825). *Levana* (1807) is a treatise that advances the idea that education should have the aim of raising the human soul above the limitations of the spirit of its age.

38. Lewald uses the words *der Herr*, which means "the master" but can also mean the Lord. A more casual terminology would have referred to David Markus as "Herr Markus."

39. *Er* (he) and *Sie* (she) are third-person *singular* form no longer employed for "you." *Sie*, the third-person *plural* form, is still universally used in German for the formal "you." To use *Du* for servants is the more modern practice.

40. Gustav Friedrich Dinter (1760–1831) advanced the use of the Socratic method for classroom instruction. *His School Teacher's Bible* (1826–1830) was a collection of Bible stories for school use.

41. August von Kotzebue (1761–1819), reactionary dramatist and journalist, was frequently in the Czar's service. The University of Jena was the extremist center of the liberal student movement, organized into "Burschenschaften" (University Student Associations). On March 23,

1819, a Jena student, Karl Sand, assassinated Kotzebue in Mannheim as an enemy of liberalism and a traitor to Prussia. Sand was executed on May 20, 1820. Frederick William III was so alarmed by this event that he formulated the Karlsbad Decrees, which fettered political and press freedom in Germany until well after his death in 1840.

42. Raphael Bock (1779–1837), received degrees in law, philosophy, and languages. He converted to Catholicism and entered a monastic order, but left to marry. Excommunicated, he became a librarian in Königsberg. He wrote romantic poetry and religious texts. Known as the "letzte Domherr" (the last canon), he was the model for the canon in 1847 in Lewald's story "Der Domherr." (*Bunte Bilder II*. Berlin: Janke, 1862.)

43. Zacharias Werner (1768–1823) specialized in tragedies of fate and religious plays.

44. Ludwig Wilhelm Sachs (1787–1848) was a physician and professor of medicine at the University of Königsberg.

45. Jakob Böhme (1575–1624) was a shoemaker and philosopher who created a mystical cosmology.

46. Gaius Mucius Cordus Scaevola tried unsuccessfully to assassinate Lars Porsena, the Etruscan king. During his trial he so impressed the king with his integrity and bravery that Lars Porsena pardoned him. Later Scaevola was instrumental in the defeat of the Etruscans and the saving of Rome. Horatius Cocles defended a bridge across the Tiber, also assisting in the saving of his city. Thomas Babington, Lord Macaulay's 1842 poem "Horatius at the Bridge" was a standard declamation piece for English and American school children for decades. Aristogeiton and his friend Harmodius attempted to overthrow the tyranny of Hippias and Hipparchus in Athens in 514 A.D. Harmodius and Hipparchus were killed, but Hippias lived another four years.

47. Some of these Yiddish words have been introduced into standard German, especially in Berlin and the rest of Prussia, e.g., *meschugge* (crazy).

48. See note 1.

49. The Jewish persecutions in 1819 spread from Würzburg all over Germany, Austria, and Denmark. They were called the "Hep-hep" riots because this was the cry of those destroying and plundering Jewish homes and businesses and molesting Jews on the street. These riots made it very clear to the Jewish community that the reforms of 1812 no longer applied.

50. Adam Gottlieb Oehlenschläger (1779–1850) was a Danish-German writer strongly influenced by Goethe and Schiller. *Correggio* was written in 1808.

51. See note 48.

52. The Herrenhut Community was an association of Pietist Christians formed by religious refugees on the estate of Count Nikolaus Ludwig von Zinsendorf in his estate of Herrenhut in Saxony in 1722.

53. Friedrich Kolhrausch (1780–1867). Lewald is obviously referring to his 1825 *Stories and Teachings of the Old and New Testaments* (Geschichten und Lehren der Heiligen Schrift alten und neuen Testamente). See note 31.

54. This obsession of David Markus with Fanny's piano lessons is an unintentionally amusing leitmotif in her autobiography. She may leave her father's house, but not his rented pianos or the instructions he sees that she always has. The piano becomes her albatross.

55. Lewald refers to a conversation between one of the major protagonists of the 1853 novel, Friedrich Brand, and his carpenter father. The senior Brand has not had the educational advantages of his son, who is studying theology at the university, and reproaches the latter for not appreciating these advantages when he wants to drop out of school (I, 32–33).

56. Schiller's *Kabale und Liebe* (1784), probably better known to the English-speaking world in its 1849 operatic form as Guiseppe Verdi's *Luisa Miller*.

57. Another evidence of the assimilation of the Markus family. The paternoster is a New Testament prayer, of course, and would not be recited by any observing Jew.

58. The statue of Laokoon (the Trojan priest who warned the people of the peril of the Greek horse) and his two sons, who are being strangled by sea serpents sent by the gods to punish him for his interference, was the subject of a 1766 eponymous treatise by Gotthold Ephraim Lessing on aesthetics. It discusses the parameters of the visual and literary arts and their differences. Any educated German would have read the treatise and recognized Lewald's reference.

59. In her second series of emancipatory essays, *Für und wider die Frauen* (For and Against Women) (1870), Lewald advanced the idea of communal kitchens as more efficient not only for working women, but all families—even a housewife could thus spend more time with her

children. She states that in Italy she and her husband lived on take-out food and restaurant meals because they had no kitchen and their marriage never suffered (84–85). (In typical Lewald fashion, she refers to her own prowess in the kitchen at the same time!)

60. A discussion of the novels of Sir Walter Scott (1771–1832) is featured in Lewald's third novel, *Eine Lebensfrage* (A Vital Question) (1845), as her characters try to define the role of the novelist and the material he uses in respect to his society (I, 194–209).

61. The plot of *Die natürliche Tochter* (1803) concerns the illegitimate daughter of a duke who is forced into a marriage with a commoner by her half-brother to save her country from a revolution.

62. The head of this family, Ludwig August Kähler (1775–1855), was a prominent Protestant theologian, minister, and professor of theology at the University of Königsberg.

63. Friedrich Jacobs (1764–1847). He wrote other stories besides *Rosaliens Nachlaß* (1812), which Lewald also read.

64. Some of these entries, selected by Lewald herself, were finally published in 1900, eleven years after her death, under the title of *Gefühltes und Gedachtes* (Thoughts and Feelings). Other Lewald diaries have never been published.

65. Immanuel Kant, *Anthropologie in pragmatischer Hinricht abgefaßt* (1798).

66. This prayer is still used by Orthodox Jews. As late as 1940, a Conservative prayer book contains as part of the morning prayer for men the words "Blessed are thou, O Lord our God, King of the Universe, who has not made me a woman." The woman's prayer ends, "who has made me according to thy will." (*Sephath Emeth*: Order of Prayers for the Whole Year. New York. Hebrew Publishing Co., n.d.) In more recent prayer books (Reform), the supplicant thanks God for "having created me in His image." The original purpose of the prayer was not necessarily sexist, but showed the gratitude of the men for having the time for prayer and study of the Torah, a time denied women because of their preoccupation with household duties and children.

67. In my English translation the passage reads:

> The lot of women is lamentable.
> Men rule at home and in the battlefield.
> Able are they to cope with life abroad.
> They bask in property; victory crowns them!
> An honorable death is prepared for them.

What narrow bounds encompass Woman's fate!
Just to obey a harsh husband
Is duty and comfort enough; how wretched then
She is when cruel fate drives her so far away!
Ipigenie auf Tauris, Act I, Scene 1.

68. See note 41. The Deutsche Burschenschaft (German Student Association) was an organization founded during the Wars of Liberation in 1815 and advocated German unity and the political rights of the bourgeoisie. One wing, of which Karl Sand was a member, became very radical after 1817.

69. Karl Theodor Körner (1791–1813). (*Leyer Und Schwerdt*) (Lyre and Sword) (1814) is a collection of patriotic lyrics. *Zriny* (1812) is a tragedy.

70. The unhappy saga of Moritz Lewald's brief life (he died of cholera in Tiflis at the age of 31) is a recurring theme in the autobiography. He is the only one of Lewald's siblings about whom we learn much, although she was probably closest to the older brother Otto.

71. It is still a mystery to us as it was to her—why David Markus terminated the relationship between Fanny and Leopold. According to a conversation with Margarita Pazi, there is evidence in unpublished family correspondence suggesting that Leopold's family objected to his marriage to a Jewish woman.

72. The five "July" Ordinances, establishing strict press censorship, dissolving the Chamber of Deputies and changing the electoral system to ensure a conservative majority.

73. See note 2.

74. Johann Jacoby (1805–1877)was a Königsberg physician and a leading Jewish liberal and was very involved with the events of the period before 1848, the "Vormärz" (Pre-March 1848). In 1841, his pamphlet *An East Prussian Answers Four Questions* had a tremendous impact on the political views of the "Vormärz"(pre-1848 period). He was a member of the Prussian National Assembly and the Frankfurt Parliament. He and Lewald remained lifetime close friends, but disagreed sharply after 1871 when Lewald became more conservative and a defender of Bismarck while Jacoby remained adamantly liberal.

75. Except for these early poems, Lewald never published anything but prose. There was a privately published and unperformed translation of a five-act play by the Italian Paolo Ferrari.

76. "Thence, thence!" ("Dahin, dahin!") is the refrain of Mignon's song from Goethe's *Wilhelm Meister* at the beginning of Book III, Chapter 1. Mignon is singing of her longing for her native land, Italy.

77. Frederick William, Elector of Brandenburg (1620–1688), great-grandfather of Frederick the Great. This reference is to his statue on Unter den Linden, which still stands there.

78. Karl Friedrich Schinkel (1781–1841), architect and painter, was one of the main proponents of classical architecture in Germany and designed a large number of buildings in Berlin. The museum here is the "Old Museum," finished in 1828.

79. Rahel Levin Varnhagen von Ense (1771–1833) was an idol of Lewald's, a Berlin-Jewish hostess of a brilliant salon and friends with all the leading intellectuals of her day. She is the heroine of Lewald's novel *Prinz Louis Ferdinand* (1849). Rahel's letters were published after her death by her husband, August Varnhagen von Ense, who was also a writer and diplomat. See also note 8.

80. See note 50.

81. On May 27, 1832, a gathering of 25,000 met at Hambach Castle and demanded a republic and German unity. It resolved to adopt armed revolt as well as peaceful means to ensure freedom of the press and the right of assembly. In June Metternich answered the demands by having the German Confederation adopt six extremely restrictive articles forbidding German rulers to do anything that would reduce their sovereignty, limiting the financial powers of state parliaments, and disallowing the states to prejudice any laws of the Federal Diet—laws that were considered an infringement of states' rights. Other measures followed promptly in July.

82. Johann Georg August Wirth (1789–1848) was a politician and writer and was one of the initiators of the Festival. He was subsequently arrested. Philipp Jakob Siebenpfeiffer (1789–1845), political writer, was equally involved in the Hambach Festival.

83. Arminius, chief of the Cheruscan (Germanic) tribe (16 B.C.–21 A.D.), was the first German leader to win a decisive battle over the Romans. He defeated the legions of General Varus in the Teutoberg Forest in 9 A.D.

84. August Heinrich H. Hoffmann von Fallersleben (1798–1874), poet and nationalist, is best known for his authorship of the German national anthem, "Deutschland über Alles." It should be mentioned that he was not advocating Germany's conquest of the world, but the concept of a

united Germany over the selfish interests of the individual German states.

85. Victor Hugo, Honoré de Balzac, and George Sand are familiar names. The less familiar are Alphonse de Lamartine (1790–1869), a politician and early Romantic writer; Jean-Marie-Mely Janin (1777–1827), a journalist and dramatist, who wrote historical plays; Eugène Sue (1804–1857), author of *The Secrets of Paris* and *The Wandering Jew;* Jean-Baptiste Alphonse Karr (1808–1890), novelist; Emile Souvestre (1808–1890), journalist and novelist, whose theory of the "social novel" influenced Victor Hugo and Emile Zola.

86.*Han d'Islande* (1823), a horror novel by Victor Hugo in which a monster from Iceland wreaks vengeance in the mountains of Scandinavia for the death of his child. Quasimodo is the protagonist of Hugo's *The Hunchback of Notre Dame* (1831). *Lucrezia Borgia* (1832) is a drama by Hugo. *La Historie des Treize* is a trilogy by Honoré de Balzac (1799–1850), detailing the mores of nineteenth century French society; *La Tour de Nesle* is a drama by Alexander Dumas père (1803–1870) about Marguerite de Bourgogne and her sister, who are said to have murdered their lovers in that tower after one night of love; *Le Salamander* is the eponymous name of the ship on which strange events take place in a novel by Eugène Sue (see note 86).

87. Bettina Brentano von Arnim (1785–1859) was part of a family of famous writers. She was the granddaughter of the novelist Sophie de la Roche, sister of the poet Clemens Brentano and wife of the poet Achim von Arnim. Earlier she was recognized mainly for her relationship with Goethe (her mother had been a close friend of his) and the publication of her correspondence with him, *Goethes Briefwechsel mit einem Kinde* in 1835. She is now esteemed in her own right as a writer.

88. All these were associated with the Young Germany movement like Heine and Börne: Karl Gutzkow (1811–1878), writer and politician; Heinrich Laube (1806–1894), dramatist, writer and eventually director of the Vienna Burgtheater; Theodor Mundt (1809–1861) university professor and husband of Luise Mühlbach, a famous woman novelist; Gustav Kühne (1806–1888) writer and later publisher of August Lewald's periodical *Europa;* Ludolf Wienbarg (1802–1872), teacher and journalist. Some of these writers were to become close friends or acquaintances of Lewald in later years.

89. Ludwig Tieck (1773–1853) was one of the leading figures of German Romanticism. With his daughter, Dorothea (1799–1841), and his fellow Romantic, August Wilhelm Schegel (1767–1845), he translated the plays of Shakespeare into German.

90. Novalis (pseudonym of Friedrich von Hardenberg) (1772–1801) was a leading Romantic poet and novelist. Wilhelm Weiblinger (1804–1830) was a writer first inspired by the great poet Friederich Hölderlin (1770–1843), a poet neither Romantic nor Classical. Weiblinger later became an anti-Romantic. Henrik Steffens (1773–1845) was a Norwegian nature philosopher and minerologist who was acquainted with many of the leading figures of his day and wrote about them in his memoirs. Anastasius Grün (pseudonym of Anton Alexander Graf von Auersperg) (1806–1876) was a writer of political poetry. Joseph Christian Freiherr von Zedlitz (1790–1862) was a late Romantic writer who wrote patriotic literature.

91. See note 6.

92. See note 37.

93. This regency, the Reichsregentschaft, was the provisional executive and administrative arm, set up by the Frankfurt Parliament under the leadership of Archduke John of Austria in June 1848. After the dissolution of the Parliament in June 1849, Simon was forced to flee to Switzerland. By January 1851, after a series of failed attempts at uniting the German states, the old Germanic Confederation was reestablished.

94. See note 1.

95. An editorial decision to delete lengthy didactic sections preclude insertion of this chapter in the present volume.

96. See note 80. Rahel's husband published *Rahel, Ein Buch des Andenkens für ihre Freunde* (Rahel: A Book of Remembrance for her Friends) and *Galerie von Bildnissen aus Rahels Umgang und Briefwechsel* (Gallery of Portraits of Rahel's Acquaintances and her Correspondence).

97. Mr. Motherby had been Lewald's teacher in Mr. Ulrich's school for German, French, and English language instruction (See Book I). Motherby also gave her private lessons in French. When she had to leave school, because it closed, he wrote in her autograph book the following advice, originally in French: "The great task of our life, the goal of all education, all education of ourselves, which begins when our teachers leave us, when the hand of the one who kept watch over our childhood no longer guides us, is to strive to free our spirit from error and our heart from selfishness."

Lewald recalls this aphorism several times in her autobiography.

98. Ludwig Crelinger had first come to Königsberg as defense counsel for Ebel and his co-defenant Heinrich Diestel in the "Mucker" trial. (See note 2.) Crelinger had married beneath him and was not

accepted by Königsberg society. He was befriended by the Lewalds and finally moved into an apartment in their house. He was well acquainted with many figures in the theater, because a good friend was Ludwig Devrient, a famous actor. Crelinger's sister-in-law Auguste Crelinger was one of the most famous actresses of her day. He also knew Sophie Schröder and her daughter, Wilhelmine Schröder-Devrient, two other famous actresses whose performances Lewald had admired in Königsberg and Berlin.

99. Carl von Holtei (1798–1880) was a close friend of Crelinger and an actor, director, and writer of light musical pieces for the stage.

100. After Napoleon won the battles of Jena, Auerstadt, and Eylau in 1806, the royal residence was moved to Memel in East Prussia.

101. Luise von Mecklenburg (1776–1810) was Frederick William III's first wife. She inspired widespread devotion among the Prussian people and is a character in several of Lewald's novels, including *Prinz Louis Ferdinand* and *Die Familie Darner* (1887). Princess Liegnitz (1800–1873) was Frederick William III's considerably younger second wife; he married her in 1824.

102. Nicholas I (1796–1855) was married to Charlotte, the eldest daughter of Frederick William III.

103. See note 98. The memoir is in Lewald's *Zwölf Bilder aus dem Leben* (Berlin: Janke, 1888: 35–64). Schröder–Devrient (1804–1860) was also an enthusiastic liberal supporter of the 1848 revolution.

104. Lewald uses actresses as major characters in a number of her novels, most notably Sophie Harcourt in *Eine Lebensfrage* and Hulda in *Die Erlöserin* (1873). The latter was published in an English translation by Mrs. A. L. Wister in five separate editions from 1874 to 1889 by Lippincott as *Hulda the Redeemer*.

105. Clara Stich and her sister Bertha were the daughters of Auguste Crelinger (see note 97) and members of the Königsberg Royal Theatre troupe.

106. Heinrich's love was Countess Ida von Hahn-Hahn, a famous writer of extremely romantic novels. Lewald gained a belated revenge by savagely and hilariously parodying these novels, which she found a poor imitation of those of George Sand, in her own novel, *Diogena* (1851), published under the pseudonym "Iduna Countess H.H." (See Hanna Lewis, "The Women's Novel Parodied: Fanny Lewald's *Diogena*." *Continental, Latin-American, and Francophone Women Writers*, Lanham, Md.: University Press of America, 1987: 107–118.)

107. Count August von Platen (1796–1835) was a prominent lyric poet.

108. Karl Friedrich Zelter (1788–1832), a friend of Goethe's, was a composer and conductor, as well as a pioneer in music education.

109. Eduard Gans (1798–1839) was a prominent legal scholar. Anna Milder-Hauptmann (1785–1838) was the Austrian soprano, for whom Beethoven originally wrote the role of *Fidelio*. Henriette Sontag (1806–1854) was also a famous soprano. Georg Wilhelm Friedrich Hegel (1770–1831) was the world-famous philosopher who formulated a system of the historical sequence of philosophic ideas that has influenced almost every major modern historical, political, or philosophic thinker. Alexander von Humboldt (1769–1859) was a world traveler and renowned geographer. Various geographic locations and the Humboldt Current are named for him, as is an important foundation that provides stipends for foreign scholars to study in Germany. Wilhelm von Humboldt (1767–1835) was a diplomat and scholar, who founded the University of Berlin. (The original university, presently in East Berlin is now named for him.) Both brothers were "Renaissance" men, humanists and active in a number of different fields.

110. The most famous of those were the salons of Rahel Varnhagen von Ense, Henriette Herz, and Dorothea Veit Schlegel. Lewald herself had a well-regarded salon after her marriage.

111. Ottilie is one of the heroines in Goethe's *Die Wahlverwandtschaften.*

112. Lewald's future husband, classical and art historian Adolf Stahr (1805–1876).

113. Ernst Wagner (1829–1888) was a pathologist, histologist, and clinician. Edward George Earle Lytton Bulwer-Lytton (1803–1873), English novelist and playwright, whose works Lewald had read and admired.

114. "Ein modernes Märchen" was republished under the title "Tante Renate," in *Bunte Bilder* (1862), a collection of Lewald's early short stories.

115. Johann Karl August Musäus (1735–1787) collected and published *Volksmärchen der Deutschen* (German Folk Tales).

116. Jacques Callot (1592–1635) was a French graphic artist whose series of etchings, "Capricci," depicted Florentine street life. Another anti-war series was entitled "Miséres de la guerre." Although Lewald hyphnenated the two names, the Hoffmann reference is undoubtedly to E.T.A. Hoffmann.

117. "Der Stellvertreter." *Bunte Bilder* I. Berlin: O. Janke, 1862.

118. *Clementine.* Leipzig: Brockhaus, 1843: 23–25.

119. The figure of the mechanical doll in E. T. A. Hoffmann's "Die Automate" (1814) is better known through Jacques Offenbach's opera *Les Contes d'Hoffmann* (1880) and the ballet *Coppelia.*

120. Orthodox Jewish funerals are conducted in the same manner now, and some of the rituals are still even observed by Reform Jews.

121. The quotation is from the 1828 novel *Pelham,* or the *Adventures of a Gentleman,* by Edward Bulwer-Lytton.

122. Karoline von Wolzogen (1763–1847) was the sister-in-law and biographer of Friedrich von Schiller. *Agnes von Lilien,* her autobiographical novel, appeared in 1798.

123. *Archiv für vaterländische Interessen oder Preußische Provinzialblätter,* ed. O. W. L. Richter. Königsberg, 1843: 421–433.

124. Friedrich Schleiermacher (1768–1834) was a theologian whose ideas strongly influenced early German Romanticism and the religious philosophy of the nineteenth and twentieth centuries.

125. Anna Dorothea Therbusch (1721–1782) was one of the most famous woman painters of the eighteenth century and was especially renowned for her portraits.

126. Anton Graff (1736–1813) was a Swiss national who became court painter in Dresden. Among his portraits were ones of Frederick the Great and Lessing.

127. Willibald Alexis (1798–1871) was a journalist and novelist, but also dabbled in real estate and owned a bookstore. Henriette Jeanette Paalzow (1788–1847) was a popular writer of historical novels about the aristocracy.

128. Felix Mendelssohn's sister, Fanny Mendelssohn Hensel (1805–1847), was a prolific composer in her own right. Not permitted by her father and her brother to publish her works, she allowed Felix to use them in his works without formal acknowledgment. She and Felix were extremely close, and he survived her death by only a few months. Both she and Felix were grandchildren of famous Jewish philosopher and friend of Frederick the Great's, Moses Mendelssohn (1729–1786), who was the model for hero of Lessing's drama *Nathan der Weise* (Nathan the Wise). Abraham Mendelssohn, father of Felix and Fanny and son of Moses, was once quoted as saying that all his life he was known only as the son of his father and the father of his son.

129. The upper chamber of the German parliament.

130. Friedrich von Raumer (1781–1873) a historian, wrote an excellent history of the Hohenstaufens. Dr. Schönlein was Lewald's neurologist. Christian Friedrich Tieck (1776–1851) was a sculpter and brother of Ludwig Tieck. See note 90.

131. Joseph Joachim (1831–1907) was a composer, conductor, and world-famous violinist. His close friend, Johannes Brahms, wrote many violin pieces for him, including the well-known violin concerto.

132. George Sand had been Liszt's mistress.

133. Henriette Solmar had a small salon. After the death of Rahel, she was a very close friend of the widower Varnhagen von Ense.

134. David Veit (1771–1814) was a leading Jewish intellectual and a friend of Rahel Varnhagen von Ense. David Friedländer (1750–1834) was a Jewish merchant and writer, friend of Moses Mendelssohn, and early fighter for the emancipation of the Jews. He was the first Jewish city councilman of Berlin.

135. Prince Louis Ferdinand (1772–1806), the great-nephew of Frederick the Great, was the close friend of Rahel Varnhagen von Ense and the eponymous hero of Lewald's only historical novel (see note 100). Rahel's widower placed the prince's correspondence with his mistress, actress Pauline Wiesel (1779–1848), whom Rahel had befriended, at Lewald's disposal when she was writing the novel. (See Hanna Lewis, "The Outsiders.")

136. Lewald uses the masculine form here.

137. Heinrich Laube (1806–1884), writer and an important member of the Young German group, was a playwright, novelist, journalist, critic, and member of the Frankfurt Parliament. For more than 30 years, he was an important theatrical director in Vienna.

138. The Catholic social movement, led by Adolf Kolping and Bishop Emanuel von Ketteler, began a "social ministry" aimed toward young journeymen, artisans, and craftsmen. Ketteler also promoted trade unionism.

139. Karoline von Woltmann (1782–1847) was a writer of short stories, dramas and folklore, as well as a translator. She wrote under the pseudonym Luise Berg.

140. David Friedrich Strauß was a theologian and philosopher. His *Life of Jesus* was an interpretation of the Gospels as myths. Ludwig Feuerbach (1804–1872) was a founder of the philosophy of materialism. He published a series of lectures about the nature of religion.

141. Fanny did eventually get married, as did most of her sisters, Elisabeth married a well-regarded landscape painter, Louis Gurlitt, whom Fanny met on her first visit to Rome. This marriage was of some advantage to Lewald, since it not only gave her better access to the artist circles in Rome and Berlin—an access she used to advantage in her artist novels, *Helmar, Benvenuto,* and *Stella*—but led her to meet Friedrich Hebbel, who was a friend of Gurlitt but whose work Fanny did not like very much.

142. *The History of Sir Charles Grandison* (1754), an epistolary novel by Samuel Richardson.

143. Lewald expresses similar sentiments in *Diogena*. See Hanna Lewis, "George Sand and Fanny Lewald," *George Sand Studies.* Vol III, nos. 1 & 2, 1986/1987: 38–45.

144. Andreas Schlüter (1660–1714) was a noted Prussian architect and sculptor, responsible for many famous buildings and statues in Berlin, including the equestrian statue of Frederick William, the Great Elector of Brandenburg (1640–1688).

145. Theodor Mundt (1809–1861) was a writer, teacher, and journalist, and later, the librarian at the University of Berlin. Clara Mundt (1814–1873) wrote many novels, some concerned with the emancipation of women, under the pseudonym of Luise Mühlbach. See note 89.

146. Therese von Bacheracht (1804–1852) wrote travel books and novels. She divorced Bacheracht in 1849 to marry her cousin Heinrich von Lützow and accompanied him to Java, where she met an untimely death. Between her marriages she was the mistress of Karl Gutzkow (1811–1878), young German writer and radical politician. Both became close friends of Lewald, but Fanny had a falling out with him over his treatment of Therese.

147. Theodor Mügge (1806–1861) also wrote travel books and historical novels. He was especially known as a folklorist.

148. The Sonderbund was a league of the seven Catholic cantons of Switzerland formed in 1845 to protect Catholic interests in the Swiss Confederation. In 1847 a war resulted because of the efforts of the Liberals in the Dilt to force a dissolution of the Sonderbund. The forces of the Confederation quickly won the war, dissolved the Sonderbund, and strengthened the federal government.

149. Berthold Auerbach (1812–1882) was a liberal politician and writer who was prominent in his efforts for the emancipation of the Jews. He remained a lifelong friend of Lewald.

150. Countess Elise von Ahlefeld (1788–1855) was the widow of Adolf von Lützow, a Prussian officer who led a group of volunteers, known as the "Black Troop" or the "Black Fusiliers," against Napoleon's troops. Although they were unsuccessful, their wild and reckless exploits are memorialized in a very famous German folk song.

Karl Immermann (1796–1840) began as a Romantic writer, later became a Young German. He wrote novels, stories, and dramas and was director of the theater in Düsseldorf.

151. Friedrich de la Motte Fouqué (1777–1843) wrote novels and stories about the Middle Ages. *The Magic Ring*, a novel, was published in 1813.

Selected Bibliography

Primary Sources

This is only a partial listing of Lewald's works—those that are particularly relevant to her autobiography.

Editions of the Autobiography

Lewald, Fanny. *Meine Lebensgeschichte*. Berlin: Janke, 1860–1861.
———*Meine Lebensgeschichte*. Revised. Berlin: Janke, 1871.
———*Meine Lebensgeschichte*. Ed. and intro. Gisela Brinker-Gabler. Fischer: Frankfurt a.M., 1980 (an abridged version).
———*Meine Lebensgeschichte*. Ed. Ulrike Helmer with essay by Regula Venske. Ulrike Helmer Verlag: Frankfurt a.M., 1988.

Other Works

Lewald, Fanny. "Andeutungen über die Lage der weiblichen Dienst-boten." (Remarks about the Situation of Women Servants). *Archiv für vaterländische Interessen oder Preußische Provinzialblätter*. Königsberg: Neue Folge, 1843: 421–433.
———*Bunte Bilder* (Brightly Colored Pictures). Berlin: Janke, 1862.
———*Clementine*. Leipzig: Brockhaus, 1843.
———*Der dritte Stand* (The Third Estate). Berlin: Reimarus, 1845.
———*Diogena*. Leipzig: Brockhaus, 1847.
———*Eine Lebensfrage* (A Vital Question). Leipzig: Brockhaus, 1845.
———*Erinnerungen aus dem Jahre 1848* (Recollections of 1848). Abridged and ed. Dietrich Schaefer. Frankfurt/Insel, 1969.
———*Für und wider die Frauen* (For and against Women). Berlin: Janke, 1870.

331

———— *Gefühltes und Gedachtes* (Emotions and Thoughts). Ed. Ludwig Geiger. Dresden u. Leipzig: Minden, 1900.

———— *Jenny*. Leipzig: Brockhaus, 1843.

———— *Liebesbriefe eines Gefangenen* (A Prisoner's Love Letters). Braunschweig: Vieweg, 1850.

———— *Osterbriefe für die Frauen* (Easter Letters for Women). Berlin: Janke, 1863.

———— *Politische Schriften für und wider die Frauen*. Ed. and intro. Ulrike Helmer. Frankfurt a. M.: Ulrike Helmer Verlag, 1989. (Contains *Osterbriefe* and *Für und wider die Frauen*.)

———— *Prinz Louis Ferdinand*. Breslau: Max u.Co., 1847.

———— *Wandlungen* (Changes). Braunschweig: Vieweg, 1853.

Other English Translations of Lewald Books

———— *Hulda or the Deliverer* (Die Erlöserin). Tr. Mrs. A. L. Wister. Philadelphia: Lippincott, 1874, 1875, 1881, 1896, 1897.

———— *Italian Sketchbook* (Italienisches Bilderbuch). London: Simms, 1852.

———— *The Italians at Home* (Italienisches Bilderbuch). Tr. Countess D'Avigdor. London: Newby, 1848.

———— *The Lake-House* (Der Seehof).

———— *The Mask of Beauty* (Das Mädchen von Hela). Tr. Mary M. Pleasants. New York: Robert Bonner's Sons, 1894.

———— *Prince Louis Ferdinand*. Tr. Linda Rogols-Siegel. Lewiston/ Queenston: Edwin Mellen, 1988.

———— *Stella*. Tr. Beatrice Marshall. New York: Seaside Library, 1882; Leipzig: B. Tauchnitz, 1884; New York: G. Munro, 1885.

———— *Stories and Novels*: "The Aristocratic World" ("Vornehme Welt") and "The Maid of Oyas" ("Das Mädchen von Oyas"). (A bilingual edition of *Novellen, Humoresken, und Skizzen* no. 2, published in two small paperback volumes at $.20 and $.25 respectively so that the readers could teach themselves German!). Chicago: Louis Schick, 1885.

Secondary Literature

Bäumer, Konstanze. "Reisen als Moment der Erinnerung: Fanny Lewalds (1811–1889) 'Lehr und Wanderjahre'." Out of Line/Ausgefallen: *The Paradox of Marginality in the Writings of Nineteenth-Century German Women*. Ed. Ruth-Ellen Boetcher Joeres and Marianne Burkhard. Amsterdam: Rodopir, 1989: 137–157.

Beaton, Kenneth Bruce. "Fontanes *Irrungen, Wirrungen* und Fanny Lewald." *Jahrbuch der Raabe-Gesellschaft* (1984): 208–224.

Bitter Healing: German Women Writers, 1700-1830. Eds. Jeannine Blackwell and Susanne Zantop. Omaha: University of Nebraska Press, 1990.

Brinker-Gabler, Gisela. "Fanny Lewald." *Frauen*. Ed. Hans Jürgen Schultz. Stuttgart: Kreuz, 1981: 72–87.

Frauenemanzipation im deutschen Vormärz. Ed. Renate Möhrmann. Stuttgart: Reclam, 1978.

Frederiksen, Elke, and Archibald, Tamara. "Der Blick in die Ferne: Zur Reiseliteratur von Frauen." *Frauen-Literatur-Geschichte. Schreibende Frauen vom Mittelalter bis zur Gegenwart*. Eds. Hiltrud Gnüg and Renate Möhrmann. Stuttgart: Metzler, 1985: 104–122.

Frenzel, Karl. *Erinnerungen und Strömungen*. Leipzig: Wilhelm Friedrich, 1890.

German Women in the Eighteenth and Nineteenth Centuries: A Social and Literary History. Eds. Ruth-Ellen B. Joeres and Mary Jo Maynes. Bloomington: Indiana University Press, 1986.

German Women in the Nineteenth Century. A Social History. Ed. John Fout. New York/London: Holmes and Meier, 1984.

Goodman, Katherine. *Dis/Closures. Women's Autobiography in Germany between 1790 and 1914*. New York, Berne, Frankfurt a.M.: Lang, 1986.

Großherzog Carl Alexander und Fanny Lewald-Stahr in ihren Briefen 1848-1889. Ed. and intro. Rudolf Göhler. Berlin: Mittler, 1932.

Jacobi-Dittrich, Juliane. "Growing up Female in the Nineteenth Century," *German Women in the Nineteenth Century*. New York: Holmes & Meier, 1984: 197–217.

Joeres, Ruth-Ellen Boetcher. "1848 from a Distance. German Women Writers on the Revolution." *Modern Language Notes* 97 (1982): 590–614.

——— "German Women in Text and Context of the Eighteenth and Nineteenth Centuries: A Review Essay of Feminist Criticism." 232–263.

——— "Self-Conscious Histories: Biographies of German Women in the Nineteenth Century." *German Women in the Nineteenth Century*.

Ed. John Fout. New York/London: Holmes and Meier, 1984: 172–196.

Lewis, Hanna B. "Fanny Lewald and George Sand." *George Sand Studies*. Vol. VIII, nos. 1 & 2, 1986/1987: 38–45.

———— "Fanny Lewald and the Revolutions of 1848." *Horizonte*. Tübingen: Max Niemeyer Verlag, 1990: 79–91.

———— "Fanny Lewald and the Emancipation of Women." *Continental, Latin-American and Francophone Women Writers* III. Lanham, Md.: University Press of America, forthcoming.

———— "The Misfits: Jews, Soldiers, Women and Princes in Fanny Lewald's *Prinz Louis Ferdinand*." *Crossings/Kreuzungen*. Columbia, S.C.: Camden House, 1989: 195–207.

———— "The Women's Novel Parodied: Fanny Lewald's *Diogena*." *Continental, Latin-American and Francophone Women Writers*. I. Lanham, Md.: University Press of America, 1987: 107–118.

Maurer, Doris. "Nähe nicht—lebe!" *Die Zeit* (32) 11 August 1989: 19.

Literatur von Frauen. 19. und 20. Jahrhundert. Ed. Gisela Brinker-Gabler. München: C.H. Beck, 1988.

Möhrmann, Renate. *Die andere Frau. Emanzipationsansätze deutscher Schriftstellerinnen im Vorfeld der Achtundvierziger Revolution*. Stuttgart: Metzler, 1976.

———— "The Reading Habits of Women in the 'Vormärz'." *German Women in the Nineteenth Century*: 104–117.

———— "Women's Work as Portrayed in Women's Literature." *German Women in the Eighteenth and Nineteenth Centuries*. Ed. Ruth-Ellen B. Joeres and Mary Jo Maynes. Bloomington: Indiana University Press, 1986. 61–77.

Pazi, Margarita. "Fanny Lewald—das Echo der Revolution von 1848 in ihren Schriften." *Juden im Vormärz und in der Revolution von 1848*. Ed. Walter Grab and Julius H. Schoeps. Stuttgart/Bonn: Burg, 1983: 233–271.

Prutz, Robert. *Schriften zur Literatur und Politik*. Ed. Bernd Hüppau. Tübingen: Niemeyer, 1973.

Rheinberg, Brigitte van. *Fanny Lewald: Geschichte einer Emanzipation*. Frankfurt/New York: Campus, 1990.

Schlüpmann, Grete. *Fanny Lewalds Stellung zu sozialen Frage*. Diss. Münster, 1920.

Secci, Lia. "German Women Writers and the Revolution of 1848." *Ger-*

man *Women in the Nineteenth Century.* Ed. John Fout. New York/London: Holmes and Meier, 1984: 151–171.

Segebrecht, Ruth. *Fanny Lewald und ihre Auffassung von Liebe und Ehe.* Diss. München, 1922.

Steinhauer, Marieluise. *Fanny Lewald, die deutsche George Sand.* Diss. Berlin, 1937.

Venske, Regula. *Alltag und Emanzipation. Eine Untersuchung über die Romanautorin Fanny Lewald.* M.A. thesis, Hamburg, 1981.

——— *Ach Fanny!* Berlin: Elefanten Press, 1988.

——— "Discipline and Daydreaming in the Works of a Nineteenth Century Woman Author: Fanny Lewald." *German Women in the Eighteenth and Nineteenth Centuries.* Ed. Ruth-Ellen B. Joeres and Mary Jo Maynes. Bloomington: Indiana University Press, 1986: 175–192.

——— "'Ich hätte ein Mann sein müssen oder einen großen Mannes Weib.' Widersprüche im Emanzipationsverständnis der Fanny Lewald." *Frauen in der Geschichte* IV. Düsseldorf, 1983. 368–396.

Ward, Margaret, "'Ehe' und 'Entsagung': Fanny Lewald's Early Novels and Goethe's Literary Paternity." *Women in German Yearbook* 2. Lanham, Md.: University Press of America, 1986: 57–77.

Weber, Marta. *Fanny Lewald.* Diss. Zürich, 1921.

Women Writers of Germany, Austria, and Switzerland: An Annotated Biobibliographical Guide. Ed. Elke Frederiksen. Westport, Conn.: 1989.

Index